Profit-Making Speculation in Foreign Exchange Markets

The Political Economy of Global Interdependence
Thomas D. Willett, Series Editor

Profit-Making Speculation in Foreign Exchange Markets

Patchara Surajaras
and Richard J. Sweeney

Westview Press
BOULDER • SAN FRANCISCO • OXFORD

The Political Economy of Global Interdependence

Copyright © 1992 by Westview Press, Inc.

Published in 1992 in the United States of America by Westview Press, Inc., 5500 Central Avenue, Boulder, Colorado 80301-2847, and in the United Kingdom by Westview Press, Inc., 36 Lonsdale Road, Summertown, Oxford OX2 7EW

Library of Congress Cataloging-in-Publication Data
Patchara Surajaras.
   Profit-making speculation in foreign exchange markets /
Patchara Surajaras and Richard J. Sweeney
      p. cm. — (Political economy of global interdependence)
   Includes index.
   ISBN 0-8133-8076-6
   1. Foreign exchange futures. I. Sweeney, Richard J. (Richard
James), 1944–   . II. Title. III. Series.
HG3853.P38   1992
332.4′5—dc20   90-24417
                                                                      CIP

Printed and bound in the United States of America

The paper used in this publication meets the requirements
of the American National Standard for Permanence of Paper
for Printed Library Materials Z39.48-1984.

10   9   8   7   6   5   4   3   2   1

To our parents,

Paitoon and Panee Surajaras
and Johnny and Peggy Sweeney

Contents

Preface

The Efficient Markets Hypothesis (EMH) has been the dominant paradigm in financial economics since the mid–1960s. It has proved to be a powerful intellectual tool for understanding and investigating financial markets. One of its key insights is that "You can't beat the market." It has long been thought that inability to beat the market means that technical analysis is essentially worthless; the majority of financial economists treats technical analysis with unreserved scorn. Nevertheless, we have found that computer simulations of technical analysis using real data from foreign exchange markets produce substantial risk–adjusted measured profits. Evidently, the case against technical analysis is not so clear as many believe. By the same token, the case that foreign exchange markets are fully efficient is also not clear. And most disturbingly, it is a puzzle to explain how we can find these profits in a world where financial markets in general are supposed to be efficient.

Some readers will be interested in this book for what it says about the practical use of technical analysis, and others will be interested for what it says about how financial markets in general behave and how foreign exchange markets in particular behave. We try to give both readers a fair deal.

In this book, we make very careful attempts to produce measures of risk–adjusted profits. Further, we use techniques that can be used in practice, ones that assume no more knowledge than is actually available and that assume trades that could actually be made at attainable transactions costs. We believe that these techniques would have generated measured profits over the period we examine. But we urge two caveats. First, the fact that these techniques worked in the past is no guarantee that they will work in the future. Second, as with any computer simulation in financial markets, you cannot know how accurate the analysis is until you try it in real time, on real currencies, with real money.

The profits that we find are of some substantial interest in their own right. For academic financial economists, the profits may be more important as a challenge to the EMH. Of course, it is well known that any test of the EMH is a test of joint hypotheses. Here the crucial hypothesis is that risk premia in assets' rates of return are constant over the sample, or more weakly that risk premia are on average the same on days the speculator is "in" the currency as on total days. There is very little evidence one way or the other on whether time–varying risk premia can explain the measured profits that we document. There can be little doubt, however, that technical analysis is a useful tool for finding measured profits. Our own view is that financial markets are pretty efficient but that at some level there are some profits to be made by some speculators. Looked at this way, the profits we find may be telling us about the level at which markets are efficient rather than answering a yes/no question about whether markets are efficient.

The authors thank Marc Bremer, Peter Frost, Doug Joines, Tom Kerr, Myung Soo Kim, Dennis Logue, Ed Lee, Mohand Merzkani, Arthur Warga, Clas Wihlborg, and Tom Willett for many conversations and letters on the behavior of exchange rates, technical analysis, the measurement of risk–adjusted profits, market efficiency, and many other issues related to this book. Their help has greatly improved this book. In addition, the authors thank Clas Wihlborg and Tom Willett for extremely helpful comments on chapters of this book. The computer work in this book was done at the Claremont Graduate School; we thank the staff for their help. Much of the intellectual work in this book was done at Claremont McKenna College and the Claremont Graduate School; we are grateful for the stimulating and receptive environment we found there. The staff of Georgetown University's School of Business Administration was very helpful to us in finishing this book; we thank in particular William Moncrief, Director of Computing, and Frank Lau.

Patchara Surajaras
Richard J. Sweeney

PART 1

Introduction

1

Introduction

Since the mid-1960s, the vast majority of academic financial economists has held the view that financial markets are efficient. One commonly cited implication of efficiency is that speculators using simple, mechanical buy-and-sell rules cannot make consistent risk-adjusted profits. Academic financial economists have been almost uniformly of the view that such technical analysis cannot beat financial markets. This book shows that in the spot foreign exchange markets, however, carefully chosen rules produce substantial and consistent measured profits over time, profits that are both economically and statistically significant. Furthermore, these profits remain even after some careful adjustments for risk. For example, over a 2000-day test period, an equally weighted portfolio of 15 major currencies, using four different technical trading approaches, averaged risk-adjusted profits of 3.4 percent per year with a t-statistic of 3.34.

Much of the financial advice given to private decisionmakers is based on the premise that financial markets are efficient, including advice about how to manage overseas investments and deal with foreign-exchange risk exposure. Furthermore, much advice to government policymakers also assumes financial market efficiency, including advice on exchange-rate policy. The results in this book call into question, then, a major premise in very influential private and public policy views.

1A. Overview

This is a research book, but one with substantial practical implications for private and official policy makers. The core of this book is its original research on the profitability of computer trading strategies in foreign exchange markets. We think the approach and results will be of great interest to profession researchers in the area. We think the approach and results will also interest investors, asset managers, international traders, and government and central bank officials. In writing this book, there has been no way to avoid

3

some complicated analytical issues. On the other hand, we have tried to make the book readable and intuitive.

The first step in investigating speculative profits in the foreign exchanges is to find a measure and statistical test of risk-adjusted profits. The book uses a generalization of the measure and test in Sweeney (1986a); previous studies of exchange-market efficiency found mixed evidence but had no test of significance (Dooley and Shafer 1976, 1983; Logue, Sweeney and Willett 1978; Cornell and Dietrich 1978). This book is the first full-length study of speculation in foreign exchange markets, or indeed any financial markets, that is based on a statistical test of risk-adjusted profits. Finding significant profits in one period is not enough, however, to show consistent profits or to question seriously market efficiency. Typically, authors search over a large number of rules, so it is highly likely that there will be some rule that gives profits. The strategy in this book is to look for rules and currencies that produce substantial and statistically significant risk-adjusted profits in an exploratory period, with profits measured net of transactions costs. The key question is whether these same rules and currencies yield risk-adjusted profits, net of transactions costs, in following periods. The answer is yes. Evidently, the profits are not simply statistical flukes.

The book focuses on the period from the adoption of the current regime of managed floating exchange rates up through mid- 1986. Daily data are used from the Board of Governors of the Federal Reserve System for 15 major currencies. Much of the effort is on testing for the stability of speculative profits over time and also testing for which technical approaches to speculation seem to work best. The evidence is that there is enough stability in profits to comfort speculators, and far too much to be consistent with the view that the foreign exchange markets are efficient. The book discusses how the measured profits may be consistent with efficiency if exchange rates contain time-varying systematic risk premia. Further research, however, casts doubt on this explanation (Sweeney 1990a).

The book's implications are unsettling. The pervasive view of financial market efficiency may not be tenable for the foreign exchanges, a major set of markets that are active, high volume, followed by many traders with billions of dollars of liquid assets and open 24 hours a day around the world. The consistent risk-adjusted profits found in foreign exchange markets have to be damaging to the conventional wisdom that in general markets are efficient.

Part of the book is devoted to an evaluation of just how damaging our findings are. In particular, any test of efficiency is also a joint test of other hypotheses, as is well known. In the case of this book, the key assumption is that systematic risk premia are constant over time, or at least do not move with the same periodicity with which the rules have the investor in and out of the foreign assets. If the risk premia are higher than average on days the investor is in the foreign currency, and lower than average on days he is out, the measured profits may simply represent payment for bearing higher-than-average risk. We argue that conventional performance measures all assume that risk premia are constant over the period evaluated. Hence these measures cannot tell whether measured profits arise from time-varying risk premia. Even if one suspects that time-varying risk premia explain measured profits, it is currently very difficult to formulate and use performance measures based on this view. In effect, those who evaluate performance are stuck with conventional measures. Because conventional measures of performance can never detect any difference between measured profits and true economic profits, money managers who are judged by such measures of performance have every incentive to use technical analysis to add to their measured profits.

On the level of public policy, inefficiency in the foreign exchange markets is particularly disturbing in a world where international interdependence seems to be growing and financial market integration is very high. Many economists have opposed government intervention in exchange markets because of their general view that these markets are at least tolerably efficient; the book's results severely damage this rationale. Nevertheless, presenting evidence that the foreign exchanges show signs of inefficiency is not at all the same thing as saying that various proposals for government intervention or exchange-rate management make sense. On the contrary, as discussed in the concluding chapter, government policy may well contribute to the signs of inefficiency documented here. Furthermore, many proposals for intervention are aimed at curing problems that seem to have little to do with the speculative profits documented in this book.

1B. Outline of the Book

Following this introductory chapter, the rest of the book falls into Parts 2 through 5. In Part 2, Chapters 2, 3, and 4 discuss some necessary preliminaries, such as data and the statistical tests used. In Part 3, Chapters 5, 6, 7, 8, and 9, we discuss the results of our statistical work on alternative approaches to profit-making speculation in spot foreign exchange markets. In the single chapter in Part 4, we explore in some detail various issues about the stability of speculative profits. Finally, in Part 5, Chapters 11 and 12, we present some implications and conclusions drawn from the work in earlier chapters; we focus particularly on issues for private and official policymakers.

Part 2 --Chapters 2 through 4

In Chapter 2, we review academic work on market efficiency, with particular focus on technical analysis on the one hand and on spot foreign exchange markets on the other. Academics have been very skeptical over the past two decades or more about the possibility of detecting patterns in asset prices that can be used to make speculative profits after adjustment for transactions costs. Much academic empirical work supports this skepticism; a major weakness of this past work has been the lack of a statistical test of profits. In the spot foreign exchange markets, there has long been evidence suggesting profit opportunities to technical analysis (Dooley and Shafer 1976; Logue, Sweeney and Willett 1978; Cornell and Dietrich 1978). Sweeney (1986a) suggests a statistical test of filter rule profits and applies it to spot foreign exchange markets; both he and Dooley and Shafer (1983) find evidence of continuance of the profitability noted in earlier studies.

In Chapter 3 we discuss in some detail the statistical test used in later chapters. The test is a generalization of the method developed in Sweeney (1986a). By assuming that the systematic risk premia in the expected rate of return on each asset are constant over the time period studied, the test gives a measure of risk-adjusted profit that has an expectation of zero under the null hypothesis that there are no patterns in asset prices that can be profitably exploited after transactions costs. This approach is particularly attractive in that the risk adjustment requires no identification of risk factors, no estimation of premia on these factors, and no estimation of asset returns' betas on movements in these factors. This is in contrast to capital asset pricing models or arbitrage pricing models where all of these factors, premia and betas must be found and estimated, necessarily introducing measurement error and leading to very wide confidence bounds and perhaps little likelihood of detecting profits even if they are there. In the test used here, the confidence bounds are tight enough that the null hypothesis is very often rejected for currency portfolios.

A potential weakness in the test is the assumption of risk premia that are constant over time. If the risk premia are time-varying, the test may but need not lead to spurious profits, that is, profits that are measured but are not true economic profits. Intuitively, the technical rules may have the investor in the currencies when systematic risk is extra high and out of them when risk is below average, so that measured profits are due to bearing extra risk. In the same way, however, if the investor's portfolio shifts roughly keep systematic risk constant, time-varying risk premia cannot explain measured profits. In other words, to explain away measured profits, we require not only time-varying risk premia but also that the investor be in the currency on high-risk days and out on low-risk days.

In Chapter 4 we discuss the technical approaches used in later chapters. Since the mid-1960s, economists investigating technical approaches to financial market speculation have focused mainly on so-called filter rules (Alexander 1961, 1964; Fama and Blume 1966). In addition to the Alexander filter rule, this book uses the single moving average and double moving average rules that are very popular among practicing technicians. We also use a "mixed" rule, where some currencies in a portfolio are managed under say an Alexander rule while others are under a single or double moving average rule. As this book shows, these other simple approaches seem to give better speculative results than the Alexander filter rule. In particular, moving average rules, especially single moving averages, tend to yield substantially better results. Some of the negative view among economists with regard to technical analysis may be due, then, to using the inferior approach of filter rules.

Furthermore, past investigations of technical analysis have often failed to select speculative strategies that are designed to give the maximum risk-adjusted profits, instead mixing together very promising speculations with those that look like losers (for example, Fama and Blume 1966). The approach used in this book aims at picking winners over time and rejecting losers (as in Sweeney 1981, 1986a, 1987a, 1987b, 1988).

This chapter also covers the approach used in later chapters for selecting which rules to use. Through most of the book, we search for "best" rules over 900 observations, and then test these best rules on 1,000 later observations. This approach ensures that any predictive power of the rules we find over the 1,000-observation test period is not spurious. Using a sample of 900 observations to select best rules was decided on arbitrarily before any empirical work was done, as was the decision to test these best rules on 1,000 observations.

Part 3--Chapters 5 through 9

Perhaps the single most important message of post-World War II financial economics is the importance of diversification. In Part 3, Chapters 5 through 8 we discuss the results of four different approaches to using technical analysis in exchange markets to form diversified portfolios of currencies, and in Chapter 9 we compare the performances of the four approaches.

In Chapter 5 we apply the Alexander filter, the single moving average and double moving average rules to each of the 15 major currencies studied. The results are very promising. Think of this approach as each currency having a mutual fund devoted solely to it. When the speculator is in the foreign currency, his or her funds are deposited in Euro accounts for that currency, and when the speculator is out of the currency, the funds are deposited in Eurodollar accounts. It is clear, though, that speculation on currencies requires a portfolio approach of some type. Chapter 5 we simply combine the individual funds that speculate on one currency apiece into an equally weighted portfolio. Each of the three technical rules tried leads to portfolios that make economically and statistically significant profits in the first 1,000-observation test period and in the overall 2,000-observation test period, and the profits are substantial though not statistically significant in the second 1,000-observation test period. For example, the single moving average rule gives profits (with t-statistics) of 3.47 percent (2.19), 3.09 percent (1.67), and 3.28 percent (2.69) per year in the first, second and overall test periods. A mixed strategy, with some currencies following say an Alexander filter rule and others a single moving average rule, depending on which rule worked best in the prior selection period, also gives substantial profits.

In Chapter 6 we try another approach to combining the individual currencies, a variably weighted portfolio approach in which the individual mutual funds of Chapter 5 can in effect borrow from and lend to each other. To be concrete, suppose the investor uses a single moving average rule for each currency, and suppose the rule for the DM gives a sell signal today. If no other currency gives a buy signal today, all the funds realized from closing the DM position go into a common pool. If, on the other hand, two currencies give buy signals today, all the proceeds from selling the DMs plus whatever is in the common pool are divided equally to take positions in the currencies with buy signals.

This variably weighted approach has two advantages if technical analysis really works. First, instead of letting funds lie idle as often happens under the 15-separate-mutual-funds view in the equally weighted portfolio approach, the funds are kept more fully invested in foreign currencies. If the technical rules really work, the more active are the funds, the larger the profit. For example, under the equally-weighted portfolio approach, Sweeney (1986a) found funds were idle roughly 50 percent of the time, while under the variably weighted portfolio approach they are idle perhaps only 12 percent of the time. Second, sometimes the buy signals will meet with a lack of funds and so no currencies will be purchased, because all funds are currently tied up. This reduces transactions costs.

The results in Chapter 6 seem to verify these advantages. The single moving average rule give variably-weighted portfolio profits (with t-statistics) of 6.57 percent (2.45), 5.97 percent (2.19), and 6.27 percent (3.28) per year for the first, second and overall test periods.

In Chapter 7 we apply the technical trading rules to indexes (or baskets) of currencies rather than individual currencies, for example, an equally weighted index. When the index movements give a sell signal, the entire equally weighted basket is sold. And when the index gives a buy signal, each currency is bought, with one-fifteenth of all funds available put into each currency. The intuition behind using an index is to diversify away some of the noise in individual currencies' movements and thus get clearer signals. The cost is that the investor no longer tailors his/her decisions for each currency and may, for example, be buying the index when say the DM is giving a strong sell signal. Are the gains worth the costs? Clearly, this is an empirical question. The answer seems to be that the equally weighted index approach works about as well as Chapter 5's equally weighted portfolio approach based on individual currencies, but not as well as the variably weighted portfolio approach of Chapter 6.

In Chapter 7 we also consider indexes using weights based on mean-variance portfolio theory. These indexes work well in the first test period. They fail in the second, because the indexes contain only two currencies. This lack of diversification is always a serious threat when using the mean-variance approach with no short sales allowed.

Another way to combine currencies for diversification is the portfolio upgrade approach, considered in Chapter 8. The investor first computes relative strength indexes, defined as the current price of the currency relative to its average value over the past six months, the currency with the largest index being ranked number one, the currency with the second largest being ranked number two, and so on. Buy a portfolio of, say, the six top ranked currencies. When any currency's rank falls below, say, number eight, sell that currency and use the proceeds to buy the currencies that are currently the top six, spreading the proceeds equally over the top six. The optimum number of currencies to hold is an empirical matter, as is the rank at which to sell a currency.

The portfolio upgrade approach is the only one of the four portfolio approaches considered that does not use the Alexander filter, single moving average or double moving average rules. Note, though, that the relative strength index is related to the single moving average approach.

The portfolio upgrade approach works very well in the first test period, giving profits per year (with a t-statistic) of 5.78 percent (2.21), but not very well in the second test period, giving profits of 0.95 percent (0.35), with profits for the overall period of 3.36 percent (1.78).

In Chapter 9 we compare the performances of the different technical approaches to generating buy and sell signals, and the four different approaches to combining currencies in portfolios. Overall, the variably weighted portfolio approach appears to outperform the other approaches, and by an economically and statistically significant amount. The single moving average rule appears more profitable than the other technical rules, and is significantly more profitable than the Alexander rule.

Part 4--Chapter 10

In Part 4 we examine two issues that arise in Part 3. First, the filter sizes and moving average lengths were all chosen for the test periods on the basis of experimentation over 900 preceding days of data, and were then used on 1,000-observation test periods. These two lengths were chosen arbitrarily before any empirical work was done. There is no reason to believe that 900 observations is the optimal length of the period for searching for rules, or that 1,000 observations is the best period to stick with rules once found. In Chapter 10 we explore the evidence on optimal lengths of both types of periods. One result is that using a portfolio of lengths of search periods seems to be better than picking a particular length. It also seems clear that mechanically changing rules every year is not as profitable as sticking with ones over longer periods.

Second, the discussion in Chapter 10 sheds light on the issue of whether the performance of the technical rules decays over time. The results from Chapters 5 through 9 reported above show positive profits for the second 1,000-observation test period, but profits that are lower than in the first test period and generally statistically insignificant at the 95 percent confidence level. This apparent decay is only an artifact, however, of the way in which the test periods were set up. Earlier chapters divide the final 2,000 observations into two 1,000-observation test periods. In Chapter 10 we use the final 1,500 observations divided into two 750-observation test periods. In Chapter 10, the second test period often gives substantially larger profits, and significant ones, compared to the first 750-observation test period. Average profits from the 1,500-observation test period are generally not as large as from the 2,000-observation test period, however. This leaves it somewhat open as to what level of average profits one might want to forecast for the future.

Part 5--Chapters 11 and 12

In Part 5, Chapters 11 and 12, we discuss some implications and conclusions from the book. Chapter 11 deals with the implications for financial decisionmakers, beginning with a summary of the results of Chapters 5–10. In Chapter 12 we discuss the implications for public policymakers.

It is clear that careful technical analysis leads to substantial, consistent and by-and-large statistically significant measured profits over time. These results raise two important issues. First, are these measured profits true economic profits? Second, what are the policy implications of these results for both private and public policymakers?

As discussed in Chapter 11, these measured profits may simply be payments for bearing risk, and hence not economic profits at all. In this interpretation, days when a successful trading rule has the investor in the currency are particularly high risk, with the higher than average returns on those days merely compensation for risk. In other words, the measured profits might be explained away as due to time-varying risk premia. Further, these risk premia must be due to systematic risk, or the risk could be diversified away while the profits remain. At this stage of research, there is little evidence one way or the other about this issue, but what little evidence there is from spot foreign exchange markets (Sweeney 1990a) provides no support for the view that the profits from technical analysis can be explained by time-varying systematic risk premia. Other relevant evidence is from forward foreign exchange markets, but it does not give much support to the view that there are time-varying systematic risk premia. For example, Hodrick and Srivastava (1984), Sweeney and Lee (1990) and Sweeney (1990d), using different asset pricing models, reject the hypothesis that time-varying risk premia can explain profits to forward exchange speculation. In the one study on spot foreign exchange markets, Sweeney (1990a) asks whether time-varying betas in a market model are of the right size and sign to explain measured profits from technical speculation and finds no evidence that this is so.

The results in this book are from computer experiments on data, not from actual trades. There is always the possibility that for some reason the trades the computer calls for could not be made at the prices used. In particular, there may be some bias such that the investor would have to buy on average at a higher price and to sell at a lower price than in the data. There are arguments that can be made pro and con on this issue (Sweeney 1988); indeed, it may be that the reported results understate the profits that could be made. Our view is that the only way to know for sure is to try these approaches in real time, on real currencies, with real money.

To the extent that this book's results cannot be explained as due to time-varying risk premia (or biases in the data), they present problems and opportunities for both private and public decisionmakers. It is clear that many money managers, for example, mutual fund managers who hold assets denominated in a variety of currencies, have to deal with the possibilities of making or losing money due to inefficiencies in the foreign exchanges. The same is true of firms that are not at all primarily money managers but have assets and liabilities denominated in a variety of foreign currencies. Further, from the viewpoint of public policymakers, inefficiencies increase the scope for active intervention, capital controls, trade policies and monetary policies to improve or worsen economic performance.

Much current advice to private decisionmakers, for example, chief financial officers of multinational corporations, is based on the assumption of financial market efficiency, including the efficiency of the foreign exchange markets. The book's results cast serious doubt on the foundations of these policies. Some recommendations, however, depend explicitly or implicitly on inefficiencies in the foreign exchanges. Here the issue is whether the supposed inefficiencies are consistent with or imply the inefficiencies we seem to find. Those advocating policies that are inconsistent with efficiency ought to explain how these policies are consistent with this book's results.

The implications are equally serious for financial firms, for example, mutual funds. Current practices in adjusting measured performance for risk have no scope for accommodating time-varying risk premia that move on a day-by-day basis as they would have to in order to explain this book's results. Instead, performance is often judged by an ex post security market line, where say a fund's beta and rate of return for a period are compared to a line based on the market's return and an average risk-free rate over the same period. There is no room in this construct for either a time-varying beta for the fund or a time-varying risk premium on the market.

For practical purposes, then, the private decisionmaker might well act on the assumption that technical analysis actually can produce economic profits—there is little evidence against this hypothesis, and current performance measures treat all measured profits from this source as true profits. A decisionmaker not currently trying to exploit technical profit opportunities might well be reluctant to try them, however. There are superiors to convince of the wisdom of adopting the new strategy, there is corporate inertia to overcome, and there is always some risk of loss. Corporate structures that punish losses severely and give small rewards to gains are in effect asking for extreme conservatism in the face of opportunities.

The public policymaker is in a somewhat different situation, as discussed in Chapter 12. While there is no evidence that the measured profits are not true profits, the public policymaker is often judged on different criteria from the private policymaker and hence there is not the prima facie case that the public policymaker ought to act on these profits. The public policymaker may then be even more reluctant to act than the most conservative private decisionmaker.

Nevertheless, the existence of these profits is a major blow to the anti-intervention side in arguments over exchange-rate policy. Many times a key part of the anti-intervention case is an assertion that financial markets are efficient, including exchange markets, and hence exchange markets should be left alone. Indeed, problems in exchange markets are often laid at the doors of public policymakers who run "bad" policies. An example is when a currency has had large ongoing depreciation that is, however, argued to arise from overly expansionary monetary policy.

In the face of this book's results, the anti-intervention side must rethink its arguments. The general argument from market efficiency is damaged for exchange markets. It is still possible to blame policy makers for poor exchange-rate behavior, but now a fully satisfactory argument would have to show how undesirable policy links up to the measured profits. For example, can the measured profits be shown to be due to intervention policy, as some assert? How do the profits in day-to-day speculation relate to macroeconomic policy in general and to monetary policy in particular?

The results in this book are not a blank check for policymakers to adopt just any scheme of exchange–market intervention or exchange-rate management. On their face, many proposed policies have nothing to do with the problems implicit in the inefficiencies detected here, and many proposed policies would seem likely to make the inefficiencies worse.

We are left, then, with a large and difficult research agenda, one that is of great importance to both private and public decisionmakers. With the growing importance of international economic relations, the issues will only grow more pressing.

PART 2

Tests and Data

2

Previous Studies of Technical Analysis

The past three decades have seen many studies of market efficiency. A substantial number of these studies has focused on technical analysis. Section 2A discusses various concepts of market efficiency as well as the basic ideas behind technical analysis. We place much of our emphasis on equity markets because the bulk of the literature concerns these intensively studied markets. Several tests used in the literature are discussed—particularly random walk and runs tests—and their pros and cons. We argue that technical analysis is perhaps a better way to test for market efficiency. Section 2B is a review of the literature on tests of market efficiency in spot exchange markets, focusing particularly on technical analysis in these markets. Section 2C is a summary.

2A. Financial Market Efficiency, Random Walk Theory, and Technical Analysis

Concepts of Financial Market Efficiency

The generally accepted definition of market efficiency is that prices should "fully reflect" all available information at all times. As an empirical matter, however, this definition is too broad. How much information should be incorporated into prices to enable them to "fully reflect" information, and how can this be empirically measured? Fama (1970) categorizes tests of market efficiency into three classes. First are "weak form" tests, where the only available information is the past prices of securities. Second are "semi-strong form" tests that consider the adjustment of prices to all publicly available information. Finally, "strong form" tests consider all information, whether or not available to the public, including insider information.

If prices do not fully reflect all available information, then it may be possible for a trader to exploit the information to earn excess profits. Keane (1986)

classifies these market inefficiencies into three categories. "Class I inefficiency" is the complicated inefficiency that is perceptible only to some skilled
analysts with technical know-how; this is the sort of edge that a huge research
staff is supposed to give some money managers. Once information on the
inefficiency is published, however, the market will respond so rapidly that
it is virtually impossible for general investors to exploit this information.
"Class II inefficiency" is defined as general inefficiency that some rules of
thumb are capable of detecting. It requires almost no analytical skill and can
be performed even by nonspecialists. This includes some simple technical
analyses, the "weekend" effect, the "small firm" effect, and the "January"
effect.[1] Finally, "class III inefficiency" happens when there are lags in the price
reaction to the inefficiencies in class I such that class I techniques can be
effectively exploited by nonspecialists. The Value Line phenomenon, where
the buy and sell recommendations put out by the Value Line service seem
to offer some hope of profits to the service's subscribers, is perhaps the best
example of this class of inefficiency. (See, for example, Bjerning, Lakonishok, and Vermaelen 1981.)

Technical Analysis and Market Efficiency

Technical analysis can be thought of as seeking to exploit "weak form
market inefficiency," according to Fama's (1970) categorization, or to exploit
a "class II market inefficiency," under Keane's (1986) concepts. Under weak-
form market efficiency, past prices are not informative in the prediction of
future price movements. Technical analysis, however, attempts to make
profits by inferring the direction of future price movements from past and
present prices. According to technical theory, all the relevant information
and factors affecting the demand and supply of assets are incorporated in
prices—price is the ultimate indicator of the market's status. As Edwards
and Magee (1958, p. 5) state:

> Of course, the statistics which the fundamentalists study play a part
> in the supply-demand equation—that is freely admitted. But there are
> many other factors affecting it. The market price reflects not only the
> differing value opinions of many orthodox security appraisers but also
> all the hopes and fears and guesses and moods, rational and irrational, of
> hundreds of potential buyers and sellers, as well as their needs and their
> resources—in total, factors which defy analysis and for which no statis-
> tics are obtainable, but which are nevertheless all synthesized, weighed
> and finally expressed in the one precise figure at which a buyer and seller
> get together and make a deal (through their agents, their respective
> brokers). This is the only figure that counts.

Technical school advocates' arguments generally cut across the academic's definitions. Technicians argue that inefficiencies in both the weak-form or strong-form sense are captured by technical analysis. In addition, class III inefficiencies, in the view of technical analysts, frequently exist and can be detected by technical methods. That is, the information reflected in prices includes not only all the underlying publicly available information, but insider information as well. According to Chestnut (1965, p. 12), the argument is that once the insider exercises his/her information, it will be captured by the price:

...We do not need to know why one stock is stronger than another in order to act profitably upon the knowledge of the fact. The market itself is continually weighing and recording the effects of all the bullish information and all the bearish information about every stock. No one in possession of inside information can profit from it unless he buys or sells the stock. The moment he does, his buy or sell orders have their effect upon the price. That effect is revealed in the market action of the stock.

Because insider information, once exploited, is embedded in price, it is noticeable to the chartists. Inside information is not as easily detected by fundamental analysts, however, who spend a vast amount of time and resources to analyze the many (though still limited number of) factors underlying their forecasts of future prices. Technical analysts believe that prices also embody other types of information that are not explicitly considered by the chartists and offer the chance to outperform the fundamental analysts. The forward exchange market studies by Goodman (1980, 1981) provide at least modest support for this view. By evaluating the accuracy of a number of econometric and technical foreign exchange rate forecasting services in terms of speculative return when the investor blindly follows these services, Goodman reaches the conclusion that technical services substantially outperform econometric services. The performance of the poorest technical forecaster was far better than the average performance of the econometric forecaster. And although following econometric forecasting services yields a marginal profit in excess of buy-and-hold, following technical forecasting services yields returns that are between three and four times the return on buy-and-hold. The results are essentially the same when other measures, such as long and short returns on selective hedgings, are used. While Goodman's evidence is that technicians outperform fundamental analysts in foreign exchange markets, it is not clear that he has measured profits correctly, so we cannot say at this point that either group of analysts can make consistent, risk-adjusted profits over time. Chapter 3 takes up the issue of how to measure risk-adjusted profits.

Random Walk Theory and Serial Correlation Tests

Technical analysts believe that price is the ultimate result of the market equilibrium that incorporates a vast amount of information, whether or not the information is numerically measurable. Further, they argue that price will show trend patterns that will tend to continue until something happens to change the equilibrium between supply and demand. These patterns, according to the technical school advocates, can be exploited for profit. Market efficiency advocates, however, provide a counterargument that even though there seems to be a pattern in price levels, these patterns are generated simply by the accumulation of random price changes. No profit opportunities, therefore, can be exploited through these patterns. This counterargument is shown in simulations by Roberts (1959), who generates counterfeit price patterns from the accumulation of a series of random numbers. These price patterns resemble the stock price patterns beloved of technical analysts. At the least, these simulations provide a case where technical analysis would not work as it should. Chartists can always object, however, that these simulation results do not prove that technical analysis will never work. The problem is, do the actual prices behave in a way similar to the simulated prices?

According to random walk theory, the answer is yes. This theory is probably the most critical indictment of technical analysis. In this view, any patterns in price offer speculative profits opportunities. Speculators will rush in to exploit these opportunities and in the process will destroy the patterns. The theory argues that successful activities of the chartists and other speculators will help produce independence of successive stock price changes. Therefore, these changes in prices should be close to random, with any deviations from randomness explained by transactions costs that make it unprofitable to exploit the small remaining patterns in the prices.[2] If the price sequences thus follow something close to a random walk, the serial correlation of return sequences should be very close to zero. This implies the possibility of direct statistical tests based on serial correlation tests, spectral analysis, or runs tests. For the stock market, these tests tend to uphold the efficient market model.[3]

Statistical tests of the random walk model, particularly serial correlation tests, are subject to several criticisms. It can be argued that zero serial correlation is neither necessary nor sufficient for market efficiency. The random walk hypothesis is a stronger assumption than is needed to attain market efficiency. As Fama (1970, p. 395) states, "market efficiency does not require a random walk." These statistical tests based on random walk are actually tests of joint hypotheses of market efficiency (i.e., information on past prices is efficiently processed in today's price) and an equilibrium expected return generating process where the expected return is constant over time. In the case where the equilibrium expected return varies considerably over time, market efficiency requires that the actual return fluctuates randomly around the time-varying expected return. Therefore, in an efficient market, serial correlation in the actual return can be observed if the expected return is generated from a process that does not have a constant expected return. For example, suppose that the expected return generating process is conformed to a k-factor linear model, as in the world of the Arbitrage Pricing Theory. If the factor risk premia or the assets' betas on the risk factors that explain expected returns on the assets are serially correlated, then the return itself will be serially correlated. Still, the market is efficient by assumption.

The implicit assumption underlying the serial correlation tests is that the mean of the distribution of the returns on an asset is constant over time. If these returns are drawn from a distribution that is nonstationary in the mean, however, significantly nonzero serial correlation can be observed even though the market is efficient. In terms of a nonstationary mean, as shown in Sweeney (1982a), a shift in the mean rate of return may easily generate significantly positive serial correlation. For example, suppose that over the first half of a sample the expected rate of return is y%, and over the second half it is y% + z%, where z is not zero. Then, there will generally be positive first–order serial correlation in the data, with the correlation more likely to be significant the larger z is. Suppose that z > 0. What the correlation is saying is that once we are in the second half of the period a large return is likely to be followed by another large return simply because both are in the range where the expected return is y% + z% > y%. There is no profit opportunity to be exploited from this phenomenon, however, because by assumption the expected return is the equilibrium risk-adjusted return in both halves of the period.

Further, if the variance of the distribution is not constant (that is, is heteroscedastic) but the test assumes the variance is constant (assumes it is homoscedastic), the test will understate the actual chance of rejecting the null hypothesis of zero serial correlation when the null is true.[4] Therefore, the observed significant serial correlations when variances are heteroscedastic are subject to type I error.

Zero serial correlation is not sufficient to conclude market efficiency, however. It is true that serial correlations for all lags of price changes should vanish if price changes are identically distributed and follow a fair game model. Zero serial correlations, however, do not necessarily imply a fair game, because a fair game also requires many other types of nonlinear independence.

For these reasons, it may be more desirable to consider direct tests of the profitability of trading rules used by technical analysts, which are sometimes called "filter tests." The essence of a filter test is that if the market processes information efficiently, then it is impossible for an individual to earn consistent, abnormal profits from speculation based on past price behavior.

Tests Involving Technical Trading Rules

As mentioned above, technical analysis uses past prices' patterns to seek profit opportunities. These patterns include both linear and nonlinear relationships among past prices. The study of past price movements can be traced back to the period when trading in securities began. The first widely popular technical system, however, the antecedent of numerous systems, is the Dow theory.[5] In its simplest form, Dow theory is used to forecast the future movements of the entire market. A "buy" signal is triggered if today's industrial and transportation closing prices are higher than each average's most recent peak and most recent trough by x percent and y percent, respectively. In the more complex forms of the theory, volume and price movements may be incorporated into the system. The Dow theory has been modified and extended to many derivatives and variations; some of them have evolved into other well-known technical systems such as line charting, head-and-shoulders bar charting, the Alexander filter, exponential prediction, and the moving average system.[6]

The first major evidence on trading rules, from the standpoint of academic research, is Alexander's (1961, 1964). The trading rule mainly used in his study is often called the Alexander filter rule. The rule says that if the price of a security moves up x percent above its previous local low, buy and hold the security until it moves down x percent from a subsequent local high, at which time sell and go short in that security. Remain in the short position until the price rises x percent above the previous local low, at which time cover the short position and go long in the security. Alexander's (1961) results indicate that profits from filter rules are substantially greater than those of a simple buy-and-hold strategy. He regards these results as evidence invalidating the independence assumption of the random walk hypothesis.

Alexander's method was criticized by Mandelbrot (1963) on the ground that Alexander assumes that transactions can always be made at exactly x percent above the previous low and x percent below the previous high.[7] This introduces positive bias to the profits, because the speculator will likely have to buy at a price higher than the upward trigger price and sell at a price lower than what would trigger a sell. Alexander (1964) corrects this bias in a later study. The profits from filter rules drop dramatically after this adjustment; but some rules still show superiority in comparison to a buy-and-hold strategy. Fama and Blume (1966) offer a careful, thorough investigation of the profits to filter analysis, one designed to minimize problems with Alexander's studies. They also find that some filters yield superior returns in comparison to buy-and-hold strategies. They argue, however, that profitable rules are generally those with small filter sizes that generate frequent transactions. These profits will disappear when transactions costs are taken into account.

This is true, they argue, even for a floor trader whose transactions costs are very small. Their results, therefore, favor market efficiency.

Sweeney (1988) extends Fama and Blume's (1966) study for the more recent nonoverlapping period of 1970 to 1982. Only stocks that look promising in Fama and Blume's study are selected. The results turn out to be the contrary of Fama and Blume's. The one half of 1 percent filter rule is significantly profitable for floor traders even when transaction costs of one twentieth of one percent are taken into account. As opposed to previous tests, Sweeney uses a statistical test of profitability, the X-statistic, discussed in some detail in Chapter 3. The average profits from these individual asset speculations, as shown by the X-statistic of the equally weighted portfolio of these speculations adjusted for cross correlations, are highly significant even when transactions costs as high as three twentieths of 1 percent per round trip are deducted. Further, when Sweeney (1990c) applies the one half of 1 percent filter to individual stocks in portfolios of fifty stocks, where the stocks are changed every year based on the preceding year's performance, he finds average profits of over 14 percent per year from 1971 to 1982 with a t-statistic above 14, even after taking account of transactions costs that money managers can obtain. He explains his different results from Fama and Blume's by arguing that they look both at stocks with good potential for profits and those with little potential, while he focuses only on stocks with profit potential.

Most of the technical rules are "one security and cash" rules; i.e., only one asset is speculated in at a time with the speculative funds being held either in an interest-earning asset (as in Sweeney 1988, 1990c) or simply in cash when not invested in a speculative position. Portfolio results in most studies of technical analysis are simply aggregates of results for individual securities. One rule mentioned in the literature that speculates on a portfolio-of-assets basis, however, is "portfolio upgrading," discussed by Levy (1967a). Brealey (1983, p. 14) gives a summary of the approach of this rule:

> Each month measure the [relative] strength of the stock price by calculating the ratio of the current price to the average price over the previous six months. Start by investing equal amounts in the twenty stocks with the highest relative strength. Then continue to hold each of these stocks as long as they remain in the top 160 stocks in terms of relative strength. If any stock drops below this position, sell it and reinvest the proceeds in the current top twenty.

This quote assumes for illustration that 20 stocks are invested in out of the top 160 stocks; clearly it is up to the analyst to choose these two numbers, based on a trade-off between the benefits of diversification and the costs of analyzing many stocks and of holding some stocks that are not particularly good performers. Because relative strength is used for decisionmaking in this rule, it is sometimes called the relative strength index rule. Levy (1967a) selects only the stocks used in the construction of Standard and Poor's Industry Index that are also listed in both the New York Stock Exchange and the 1965 edition of Moody's Handbook of Widely Held Common Stocks. Based on his study, Levy finds that the best rules are those that hold 10 percent and 5 percent of the total stocks analyzed, with the maximum allowable total numbers of 160 and 140, respectively. His results show that some trading rules yield returns that are substantially above those of buy-and-hold.

Jensen and Benington (1970, p.470) argue that Levy's work is subject to "selection bias" in the sense that the significant results he finds are essentially the fruits of trying 68 variations of these rules in his Ph.D. dissertation on an ex post basis. Therefore, it is not surprising that the best-performing rule searched out from a set of data will certainly work when it is then applied to the very same set of data:

> ... given enough computer time, we are sure that we can find a mechanical trading rule which "works" on a table of random numbers—provided of course that we are allowed to test the rule on the same table of numbers which we used to discover the rule.

To further illustrate their point, Jensen and Benington (1970) collect 29 sets of 200 stocks each from the Center for Research in Stock Prices (CRSP) daily tape and use the two best rules suggested by Levy on these sets. It turns out that the average return on 29 upgraded portfolios of these 29 sets of stocks is about 1.4 percent higher than the average buy-and-hold return. After adjusting for transaction costs, however, upgraded portfolios show absolutely no superiority in comparison to buy-and-hold.

It can be argued, however, that Jensen and Benington's method, too, is biased in the sense of not giving the rule a fair chance. The two best rules selected from Levy's results are based on a sample of two hundred stocks selected by Levy's criteria described above. Therefore, there is no guarantee that these rules will work for the 29 sets of 200 stocks randomly selected from the CRSP tape. It may well be that any technical approach has to be tailored to the assets considered. There may be no technical approach that works for all assets, and there may be some assets for which no technical approach works, even if well-chosen technical approaches can be made to generate consistent risk-adjusted profits over time for many assets.

It is of course virtually impossible to find a universal rule that will work for all sets of stocks. A good approach, then, may be to find the rules that work best in one period for a particular stock or set of stocks and then apply these rules to the same assets but for later time periods. The success of these best rules in subsequent time periods should be a good indication of the validity of the trading rules.

2B. Technical Analysis and Spot Exchange Market Efficiency

The concept of efficiency used in the finance literature is often extended to the study of foreign exchange markets. The tests of efficiency in foreign exchange markets, therefore, follow those of equity markets quite closely. Many studies have conducted serial correlation tests for foreign exchange markets. In most cases, significant departures from randomness are found. Poole (1967) analyzes the percentage change (as measured by the difference of the log of the rate) in daily exchange rates for nine currencies during the floating exchange rate period following World War I. He finds significant first order serial correlations in all of the nine currencies studied. In addition, he also observes variability in the variances of these return series. Because these nonstationary variances show no relevant shifting patterns over time, however, Poole considers his results as evidence confirming the presence of nonrandom behavior.

Most previous studies have focused on the behavior of the foreign exchange market during the current float. Burt, Kaen and Boothe (1977) find significant serial correlation during the period April 1, 1973 to April 27, 1975 for the Deutsche mark, British pound, and Canadian dollar. They regard these correlations as spurious, however, because no economically meaningful pattern in these correlations is detected. Runs tests support their conclusion except for the Canadian dollar. The observed number of runs for the Canadian dollar is more than three standard deviations away from the expected value. They blame this inefficiency on central bank intervention and the institutional nature of the Canadian dollar market. Their runs test results are consistent with those of a study by Sweeney (1985) in which he finds that the significant autocorrelation is not stable throughout the floating period of 1973 to 1980 for ten currencies he studied. The exception is the Canadian dollar, which exhibited consistent, significant first order autocorrelations.

Taya (1980) tests for evidence of random walk behavior in the foreign exchange market, using various schemes. The realized probabilities of small and large changes in currency prices are compared to the expected probabilities in the transition matrix if the changes in exchange rates follow a Markov chain. The results indicate that successive exchange rate changes are not independent, and there is a strong tendency for large changes to be followed by successive large changes. Parametric results show that the successive large changes will follow the initial large changes for 15 to 26 trading days, which may be evidence of a noninstantaneous exchange rate adjustment process that is not consistent with efficient market hypothesis. In addition, Taya finds that the larger the current exchange rate change, the larger the variability of future exchange rates. Therefore, past and present exchange rates may be useful in assessing or predicting the variability of future exchange rates.

As discussed above, statistical tests based on random walk theory are not adequate to draw any decisive conclusions. There are examples in the exchange rate literature where random walk and filter rule tests give very different results. Cummins, Logue, Sweeney, and Willett (1976) show that the Canadian dollar displays marked serial correlation but filter rules over their sample seem to make no profits. Logue and Sweeney (1977) show that the French franc displays no serial correlation but seems to give substantial filter rule profits in the period they examine. It is useful, then, that many studies of foreign exchange market efficiency also adopt a trading rule approach in addition to serial correlation tests.

Cornell and Dietrich (1978) analyze the efficiency of spot exchange markets for five currencies (British pound, Canadian dollar, Netherlands guilder, Deutsche mark, and Japanese yen) for the period March 1973 to September 1975. Only four of their estimated serial correlation coefficients are significant. All of these are very small and show no obvious pattern. The only case where the Box-Pierce Q-statistic is significant is for the German mark, though only at a marginal level. Runs tests also support the random walk hypothesis. They find significantly high profits, however, for trading rule speculation in the Deutsche mark, Netherlands guilder, and Swiss franc. These profits remain significant even when adjusted for interest-rate differentials and risk, as measured through an application of the CAPM. Although Cornell and Dietrich conclude that there is evidence of market inefficiency, they tend to believe that these high excess profits are returns on the risks due to unexpected government intervention that cannot be captured by the CAPM.

Sweeney (1986a) criticizes Cornell and Dietrich's analysis on two grounds. First, they do not comprehensively compare filter returns to those of a buy-and-hold strategy. Even though the British pound and Japanese yen show annual profits of less than 4 percent, they provide substantial profits in excess of a simple buy-and-hold strategy. On the other hand, the annual profit of 10.2 percent for the Swiss franc is not considerably superior to buy-and-hold, which provides a 8.3 percent annual return. Second, their implementation of the CAPM cannot explain filter rule profits in excess of buy-and-hold strategies. The estimated CAPM betas can explain both the return on filter rule and the return on buy-and-hold, but not the difference between the two. Even worse, any significant excess profit from filter rules over buy-and-hold implies the rejection of the CAPM.

In their early study, Dooley and Schafer (1976) observe that sample autocorrelations from each subperiod show little apparent stability over time. They argue that although sample autocorrelations are significant, the patterns have changed too rapidly to permit profitable speculation. Trading rule tests, however, show that substantial profits can be made using filter sizes of 1, 3, and 5 percent. They argue that it is not apparent that the optimum size of the filter can be determined ex ante, and in fact the profits seem to have declined or even become negative in later subperiods. Their later study (Dooley and Shafer 1983), however, shows the contrary to be true. Following rules with filter sizes of 1, 3, and 5 percent still earns substantial profits. Similar results on filter rules are found in Logue, Sweeney, and Willett (1978). These authors, however, draw quite different conclusions. The latter tend to believe that the foreign exchange market is less than perfectly efficient, while the former address their evidence to other joint hypotheses such as a difference in equilibrium rates of return.

A more recent study of trading rules and spot exchange market efficiency is that of Sweeney (1986a), where the results show grave signs of inefficiency. The tests are conducted on ten currencies: the Belgian franc, Canadian dollar, Deutsche mark, French franc, Italian lire, Japanese yen, Swiss franc, Swedish krona, Spanish peseta, and British pound. Alexander filter rules with filter sizes of 0.5, 1, 2, 3, 4, 5, and 10 percent are arbitrarily tried. There are eight cases out of 70 in which filter rules significantly beat buy-and-hold on a consistent basis for both subperiods studied. When the three best ex post rules found in subperiod 1 are used to speculate in subperiod 2 on an ex ante basis, the averages of speculative returns under these three best rules beat buy-and-hold significantly for eight of these currencies; exceptions are the Deutsche mark and Japanese yen. The average returns on speculations in these currencies, unadjusted for the cross-correlation between the X-statistics of these currency speculations, show that all the filter rules of 4 percent or less yield significant profits. (The X–statistic is discussed in Chapter 3.)

2C. Summary

Technical analysis may be used as an alternative, perhaps better, way to test for market efficiency as compared to random walk type tests. Technical analysis exploits information embedded in past and present prices for the inference of future price movements. Unlike serial correlation tests, or any of the other direct statistical tests in the literature, technical methods include the possibilities of both linear and nonlinear relationships and are not limited to direct time-dependent relationships. Serial correlation tests have been proven to be deficient in the sense that they are neither necessary nor sufficient conditions for market efficiency. Past studies have shown cases where significant serial correlation is present but trading rules cannot earn profits, and there are counter cases where substantial profits can be exploited by trading rules although serial correlation is very small and trivial.

Results from past studies using technical trading rules to test for stock market efficiency tend to uphold the efficient market hypothesis. Most studies argue that although some filter rules yield returns that are slightly higher than buy-and-hold, these higher returns are due to transaction costs. Nevertheless, in the more recent literature, there are cases where filter rules beat buy-and-hold significantly even when the transaction costs involved have been deducted.

The evidence confirming efficiency in the foreign exchange market is far less apparent. Filter rules tend to beat buy-and-hold in most of the studies, even when the effect of transactions costs is accounted for. Different conclusions have been drawn in different studies, however. Market efficiency advocates focus on the issues of risk or other joint hypotheses such as the differences in the equilibrium return generating process; others are more inclined to believe the evidence of inefficiency. In any case, the evidence shows that foreign exchange markets seem far less obviously efficient than security markets. It is worthwhile, then, making a systematic and extensive investigation of foreign exchange market efficiency.

Notes

1. The "weekend effect" arises from the observation that the rates of return between Friday closing prices and Monday opening prices tend to be smaller than average and in fact negative. The "small firm effect" states that risk-adjusted returns from small firms' shares tend to be greater than those of large firms. The "January effect" refers to the evidence that excess returns earned by small firms occur entirely in January. For further discussion of these effects, see Rogalski (1984), Reinganum (1981), Keim (1983), Tinic and West (1984), Cross (1973), and French (1980).

2. In this view, there may well be speculative profit opportunities for the most talented speculators. These speculators will wipe out the patterns in prices that offer the opportunities, and thus the speculators who look only at price data will be out of luck.

3. See Kendall (1953), Cootner (1962), and Fama (1965) for serial correlation tests; Granger and Morgenstern (1963) and Godfrey, Granger, and Morgenstern (1964) for spectral analysis; and Fama (1965) again for runs tests.

4. How likely is it that yesterday's large positive change will be followed by a large positive change today if in fact there is no relationship? This obviously depends on the variance of the distribution generating rates of return. If the variance is quite large on days when we observe such a relationship, we may not be impressed. But if we think only in terms of the smaller average variance, we might be mistakenly impressed and believe there is something going on when there is not.

5. The theory is named after Charles H. Dow, one of the founders of Dow Jones and Company. For discussion and later variations of Dow theory, see Bishop (1960).

6. For discussions of these Dow descendants and other trading rules, see Latane and Tuttle (1970), Wilder (1978), and Bookstaber (1985, Section III).

7. This issue is discussed in more detail in Section 4A of this book.

3

Statistical Tests of Risk-Adjusted Profits from Trading Rules: The X–Test

Tests of market efficiency using technical trading rules generally compare the returns obtained from the trading rules to the returns from a simple buy-and-hold strategy. Most of the tests in the literature are informal, simple comparisons of the returns from the two strategies and involve no statistical tests of hypotheses. To obtain a clear-cut result from comparing the returns from the trading rule and from buy-and-hold, however, requires an appropriate statistical test. The literature has provided few statistical tests to evaluate trading rules relative to buy-and-hold strategies. Moreover, some of these tests have important limitations and deficiencies. The most useful, but still simple, test is probably the X-test discussed below. The X-test can be extended in a variety of ways to cover single-asset speculation or simultaneous speculation on several assets or a portfolio of assets. It gives a measure of risk-adjusted profits from speculation. Further, these are real risk-adjusted profits. Later chapters report X-statistics of from 3 percent per year to over 5 percent per year; these are impressive in a world where estimates of real rates of return on riskless assets are essentially zero and of the real return on the market are on the order of 8 percent to 10 percent.

This chapter discusses statistical tests of trading rule effects, with special emphasis on deriving the X-test and discussing the relationships among the various forms of X-tests. Section 3A briefly discusses statistical tests in the literature other than the X-test. It analyzes the limitations and deficiencies of these tests.

Section 3B discusses the X-statistic for the special case of one asset. The purpose is to give a simple and relatively intuitive introduction to the test as well as to its strengths and weaknesses. Later sections then give a more general presentation of the tests used in later chapters. Section 3C derives the X-statistic for the case of portfolio speculation where the buy-and-hold benchmark portfolio involves no rebalancing; the benchmark portfolio's weights evolve stochastically over time according to the difference between the return on a particular asset versus the overall return on the portfolio. The other X-statistics are derived from this X-statistic in the sections that follow. Section 3D discusses the X-test when the benchmark buy-and-hold portfolio uses rebalancing to keep a constant weight for each asset. Section 3E then shows how the X-test for speculation on a single asset relates to the more general development in section 3C.

Section 3F analyzes the statistical assumptions underlying the X-tests. The section also reports on some tests of whether the data used in later chapters conform to these assumptions. Section 3G discusses the possibility and some limitations of using nonparametric tests as an alternative to the X-test. Finally, Section 3H offers some concluding remarks.

3A. Previous Tests of Profits from Technical Analysis

One of the problems in the early studies using technical analysis is the lack of an explicit test statistic with confidence bounds to test the statistical significance of trading-rule profits. Praetz (1976) makes some methodological comments on tests of filter effects. He specifically considers the case where the investor takes a short position when a "sell" signal is triggered, with this short position equal to the long position that the speculator is closing. Using a power series expansion and neglecting moments of order higher than two, he shows that the expected return on the filter rule when short sales are allowed is approximately a(1 - 2f) with a variance of v/N, where a and v are the population mean and variance of the rates of return, N is the number of trading days analyzed, and f is the fraction of N when the investor is short in the asset or does not have a long position. The expected return on buy-and-hold is simply a. The expected return on the filter rule suggests that direct comparison between the filter rule return and the return on buy-and-hold leads to a bias—in favor of buy-and-hold if a > 0 and in favor of the filter rule if a < 0. This bias is equal to 2af.[1] Praetz (1976) did not, however, provide any rigorous statistical test to go along with this discussion of the bias inherent in usual filter rule tests such as those of Fama and Blume (1966).

Cornell and Dietrich (1978) apply Praetz's (1976) concept to test filter returns in the foreign exchange market. They argue that Praetz' test amounts to dividing the difference between the daily return provided by the trading rule and the daily return from buy-and-hold by the standard deviation of the mean daily return. However, Praetz (1976) does not offer any rigorous statistical test. Even worse, the test Cornell and Dietrich propose involves a direct comparison between the filter rule return and that of buy-and-hold and hence fails to adjust for the bias strongly emphasized by Praetz (1976).

Praetz (1979) offers a statistical test for the filter effect. He suggests the test statistic,

$$\text{phi} = \ln\{2/[1 + (1 + RS + 2af)/(1 - RS)]\},$$

where RS is the rate of return when the filter is in a short position. The term 2af is included to adjust for the bias discussed previously. Clearly, the computation of this statistic generally requires knowledge of the population rate of return on buy-and-hold, a. The only exception, where the term 2af vanishes, is when a = 0. In most cases, however, a is not known. Because the algebraic expression of the statistic involves a in a nonlinear fashion, there is no guarantee that the use of the sample rate of return as a substitute for a will cause the statistic to converge to its expected value, unless it is known beforehand that this sample rate of return is exactly equal to its population value.

One way to avoid this problem in the Praetz test is to construct a statistic that uses information on the sample mean rate of return, which is not necessarily equal to the population mean for a finite sample, such that the test is independent of knowledge of the population mean return. This is essentially the approach used in the X-statistics proposed by Sweeney (1981). In his later papers, the concept of the X-test is extended to test multiple-asset speculation (see Sweeney 1986a, 1986b, 1987b, 1990c). Unlike Praetz's (1979) test for combinations of securities, the X-test does not require constant weights for each security in the *buy-and-hold* portfolio and, therefore, can be used to test the performance of a typical mutual fund's portfolio that has variable weights. The form of the X-statistic used to test portfolio performance may look different from that of the one used for single asset filter rule testing. They are closely related, however.

The statistical test based on the X-statistics is sometimes called the X-test. The next three sections show that the X-statistic is the average return from a trading rule in excess of the return on a comparable buy-and-hold strategy. The X–test is a parametric t-test of the null hypothesis that the X-statistic is not different from zero. Equivalently, the average return on a trading rule is not significantly different from that of buy-and-hold if the null hypothesis holds. Alternatively, under certain assumptions discussed below about the constancy of risk premia in the assets' returns, the X-statistic is the risk-adjusted profit rate from using the rule for speculation.

3B. Speculating on a Single Asset

Foreign exchange market speculation makes most sense when done over a portfolio of currencies. This is not surprising, given Markowitz's classic work on the benefits of diversification. Nevertheless, it is worthwhile to start the discussion of tests of portfolio performance by looking at a single asset. Later sections present more general discussions.

For convenience, think of speculation from the point of view of a U.S. resident, though the reader can easily make the changes necessary for the resident of any country. Let R_t be the excess rate of return on the asset. Because this book concentrates on foreign exchange, suppose R_t is the excess rate of return on the DM in a Euro–DM deposit, or is the rate of appreciation of the DM plus the Euro-DM interest rate less the Euro-dollar interest rate, or is the excess of what the speculator gets for putting funds in a Euro-DM account rather than a Euro-dollar account; the excess rate of return from putting funds in a Euro-dollar account is then always zero. The average excess return from simply putting funds in the Euro-DM account and leaving them there is the average return on buy-and-hold, or is

$$R_{BH} = (1/T) \sum_{t=1}^{T} R_t,$$

where T is the total number of days in the period.

The speculator using technical analysis will be "in" the DM some days, other days "out" of the DM; assume that on days in the speculator puts all funds in the Euro-DM account, on days out all in the Euro-dollar account. To be concrete, suppose the speculator is using a filter rule to make buy and sell decisions. The average excess return on days "in" the speculation is

$$R_F = (1/T_{in}) \sum_{t \in I}^{Tin} R_t,$$

where T_{in} is the number of days "in," the subscript "F" denotes "filter," and I is the set of days the filter has the investor in the DM.

The intuition behind the X-test is to compare these two average (excess) rates of return, R_{BH} and R_F. If the technical analysis has no information, the speculator is just as likely to be out of the DM as in the DM on days when the DM goes up more than average—the expected value of the difference between the two averages is zero.

This argument, however, requires a conditionally constant mean for R_t, and in current asset-pricing theories the value of this mean depends on the asset's riskiness. In the Sharpe-Lintner CAPM (Capital Asset Pricing Model), the Black (1972) CAPM, the Merton (1973) intertemporal CAPM, the Ross (1976) APM (Arbitrage Pricing Model), or the Breeden (1979) consumption-based asset pricing model, the expected excess return on asset j equals the product of asset j's beta on each risk factor k ($B_{j,k}$) in the economy times the risk premium on factor k (PR_k), summed across all of the K risk factors—call the sum of these products asset j's risk premium pr_j ($= \sum_{k=1}^{K} B_{j,k} PR_k$). (Different theories have different implications for which factors are priced, that is, have nonzero risk premia. For example, the Sharpe-Lintner CAPM implies only the market factor is priced, though there may be other nonpriced risk factors; in APMs many factors may be priced.)

Suppose all of these risk premia pr_j are conditionally constant over time (conditionally constant betas and factor risk premia are sufficient but not necessary). Then all of these theories predict constant expected values for all $R_{j,t}$ with $ER_{j,t} = pr_j$. (These risk premia may of course change over time, a complication discussed below.) The prediction that $ER_j = pr_j$ is the content of the EMH in these theories.

The technician using past price movements to take positions views these movements as containing information helpful in beating the market. The EMH counterview is that there is no helpful information in past prices *or* in the positions that the technician takes based on these past prices. In the EMH view, knowing that a stock's price rose 4 percent yesterday is of no help in predicting whether being in the stock tomorrow will beat the market, and knowing that the investor has bought in is also no help. In particular for the tests below, suppose that looking back but *before* we examine the sequence of prices, we know the sequence of in and out positions taken by the investor who used only prices known at the time the positions were taken. These positions should have no information useful in guessing whether the investor beat the market in this period.

An operational test requires some assumptions about the timepath of expected returns under the EMH. Assume for the time being that the risk premium on the asset, pr_j, is conditionally constant and that from the EMH, $ER_j = pr_j$. Thus, there is no serial correlation in any asset's returns and no lead/lag correlation across assets' returns, with only contemporaneous cross correlations. The speculator, however, views the expected returns as sometimes higher, sometimes lower than the risk premium and hopes to make risk-adjusted profits by being in the currency on days when the expected return exceeds the risk premium, out when the expected return is less than the premium.

There are two useful and logically equivalent ways of looking at the issue of whether the technical strategy conveys information helpful in beating the market; both approaches involve a comparison of returns to the technical strategy with those on buy-and-hold. First, form the statistic

$$x = R_F - R_{BH} = (1/T_{in})\sum{}^{Tin}_{t \in I} R_t - (1/T)\sum{}^{T}_{t=1} R_{t,}$$

where $Ex = 0$ from the assumptions of constant risk premia and the EMH. Second, think of the overall excess return on the technical strategy as a weighted average of the return on days in and on days out, or

$$R_F = (1 - f) R_i - f R_{o,}$$

where f is the percentage of days out (and hence $(1 - f)$ the percentage of days in), R_i the average excess rate of return to the strategy on days in ($= R_F$ above), and R_o is the average excess rate of return to the strategy on days out, with

$$R_o = 0,$$

because the excess rate of return to putting funds in a Euro-dollar account is always zero (the Euro-dollar rate is taken as the risk-free rate). Comparing R_F directly to R_{BH} would give a bias, because $ER_F = (1 - f) ER$ and $R_{BH} = ER$. Thus, adjust R_{BH} by multiplying it by $(1 - f)$ and form the statistic

$$X = R_F - (1 - f) R_{BH},$$

where $EX = 0$.

Both x and X have an expected value of zero under the null hypothesis that pr_j is constant and $ER_j = pr_j$ in every time period. One reason for using X is that it measures the average amount by which the technical strategy beats buy-and-hold on a per day basis; x measures this superiority on a per-day-in basis.

A key issue is whether any measured profits from a positive x or X are statistically significant. The standard deviations of the two statistics are

$$\sigma_x = \sigma_R [f/(1 - f)]^{1/2}/T^{1/2}$$

and

$$\sigma_X = \sigma_R [f(1 - f)]^{1/2}/T^{1/2},$$

where $\sigma_R{}^2$ is the variance of the excess rate of return on the asset and the formulas rely on no serial correlation and only contemporaneous cross correlations. Because $X = (1 - f) x$, it is easy to show that the ratios x/σ_x and X/σ_X are equal, and hence the two tests are identical.

Both the x and the X tests are conditional on the value f, the fraction of days out of the asset. f is, of course, endogenous and stochastic and will differ over samples. The tests treat f as a constant, but this is legitimate because under the null, the in and out decisions that determine the overall f have no predictive power regarding whether future rates of return are higher or lower than their expected value. Indeed, consider an ex post experiment. Looking back, suppose that R_{BH} was 10 percent and f was 0.5. Conditional on this information, what is the expected value of x or X? Under the EMH (and with the assumption of conditionally constant risk premia), the prediction would have to be zero for both; we would expect the speculator to have been in the market about half of the days that it was higher than R_{BH} and out the other half and similarly for days when the market was below R_{BH}.

It is clear that the tests require constant means and constant finite variances for the returns distributions. The results, however, may not be too sensitive to deviations from these assumptions.

Consider a case where $ER_j = pr_j$ under the EMH but pr_j is not conditionally constant over time. At one extreme, suppose the speculator has a consistent tendency to get in the DM on days when its risk premium pr_{DM} is high and out when it is low. The X–statistic will tend to show measured profits, but these are simply a reward for bearing risk. At the other extreme, suppose the risk premium varies but the speculator's moves show no consistent relationship to these changes, with the average risk premium the same on days in as days out. In this case, a positive X would be measuring genuine economic profits (see below and Sweeney 1988). This is a general point, applicable to all of the X-tests discussed here. Time-varying risk premia do not invalidate the test; rather, if one suspects that measured profits are due to time-varying premia, one should test for whether this is so.

If X is heteroscedastic due to movements in σ_R^2, the estimated standard errors will be biased, as will be t-tests of the significance of X. This suggests using care in interpreting the significance of X rather than simply being unwilling to consider the results. Similarly, if the reader believes that the variance of R is not finite, standard advice is to use a higher-than-usual confidence level. (Note that there is much evidence that rates of returns on assets do have finite second moments, even if the rates are heteroscedastic.)

Risk–Adjusted Profits

The X–statistic gives a measure of risk–adjusted profits, as noted above. This subsection gives precise content to this idea. Suppose that the excess rate of return is equal to three components, the sum of the risk premium pr_t, a serially uncorrelated error e_t, and an error s_t that has an unconditional mean of zero, may be serially uncorrelated and is known in advance of t to the technician but is unobservable by the average market participant. Then $R_t = pr_t + e_t + s_t$. The unconditional expectation of R_t is $ER_t = pr_t$. The expectation of R_t conditional on I_u, the information set of the average uninformed market participant, is $E(R_t \mid I_u) = pr_t$. The expectation conditional on I_i, the information set of the informed technician, is $E(R_t \mid I_i) = pr_t + s_t$; thus, the technician can take advantage of knowledge of s_t to choose to be in on days with expected returns higher than pr_t and out on days with returns less than pr_t.

Consider the version of the x–statistic that looks at profits per day in,

$$x = R_F - R_{BH} = (1/T_{in}) \sum\nolimits^{Tin}_{t \in I} R_t - (1/T) \sum\nolimits^{T}_{t=1} R_t.$$

Then,

$$x = pr_{in} + s_{in} + e_{in} - (pr_{tot} + s_{tot} + e_{tot}),$$

where the "in" and "tot" subscripts indicate sample averages over days in and for the total period. The unconditional expectation of x is $Ex = pr_{in} - pr_{tot}$. Under the assumption that the risk premium is constant, $pr_{in} = pr_{tot}$ and $Ex = 0$.

The expectation of x conditional on I_i is $E(x \mid I_i) = pr_{in} + s_{in} - (pr_{tot} + s_{tot})$; with pr constant, $E(x \mid I_i, pr_t = pr) = s_{in} - s_{tot}$. The risk premium drops out of the expectation of profits when pr is constant; it is easy to show that this is so for all versions of the X–statistic used in the book. This is the sense in which the X–statistic is risk adjusted.

Presumably, the speculator buys in only if the average s over the projected period before a sell is positive and sufficiently large to justify transactions costs and risks and sells out when the coming average s is negative enough that the risk and transactions costs make it look desirable. This implies that for any sequence of in and out positions, s_{in} is necessarily greater than s_{tot}. Thus, for the speculator who genuinely has better information, the conditional expected x is always positive.

True risk–adjusted expected profits per day in are, in the case of a constant risk premium, simply $pr + s_{in} - pr = s_{in}$. Thus, the value $E(x \mid I_i, pr_t = pr) = s_{in} - s_{tot}$ is a biased estimate of expected risk–adjusted profits whenever s_{tot} is nonzero. Over a long enough period, s_{tot} should be close to zero, but even for a period as long as the four year subperiods typically considered here, there may be bias of unknown direction and magnitude; note, however, that the sign of risk-adjusted expected profits is always positive as long as the speculator takes a series of buy and sell moves.[2]

Real Risk–Adjusted Profits

Suppose the adjustment to make any rate of return a real rate of return is simply to subtract the rate of inflation over the period of the return. Because the excess return R_t is net of the risk–free rate, the excess return is both a real and nominal rate. All of the X–statistics are then real risk-adjusted profits.

Portfolios of Currencies

Rates of return on currencies are very noisy, though less so on average than those for equities markets. This suggests forming portfolios of currencies to get more precise tests. One straightforward way to do this is to form an equally weighted average across the X's of, say, N different currencies. Because the expected value of each X is zero, so is the expected value of the average. With N currencies, the variance of the distribution of the average is 1/N times the average variance of the individual X's, plus an adjustment for the covariances of the X's. These covariances can be quite low; Sweeney (1988) reports that in experiments on portfolios of 50 stocks on the New York and American Stock Exchanges, the average correlation of the X's was 0.015, while for the 14 stocks he studies the average was 0.08. For the 15 major currencies studied in this book, the covariances are often substantial, however.

It is not at all clear that this equally weighted portfolio is the optimum approach. It comes to using a buy-and-hold benchmark portfolio where there is rebalancing every day to keep weights equal to 1/N in the benchmark portfolio. The following sections provide a more general discussion that provides for a wide range of possible benchmark portfolios.

Like most parametric tests, the X-test assumes that the X-statistic comes from a normal distribution. Hence, the test relies on the central limit theorem, which assures the normality of a large sample of X-statistics as long as the sample returns are drawn from parent populations that are independently and identically distributed (i.i.d.) with finite second moments. The i.i.d. assumption can be broken down into subsets of assumptions; some of these are required for the convergence of the X-statistic to its expected value of zero, and others are required for normality of the test statistic as assumed for hypothesis testing. For the X-statistic to converge to an expected value of zero, the return's distribution must have a conditionally constant mean (equal to the asset's constant risk premium), implying no serial correlation in the return on each asset, and in a portfolio, no lead–lag correlations across assets. For hypothesis testing, the return's distribution must have a conditionally constant variance, and this constant variance must be finite so that the central limit theorem can be applied. (If changes in the assets' covariance matrix are known or estimated, the test can easily be revised to use this knowledge.) Section 3E provides tests and discussions of these assumptions.

3C. The X–Test for Portfolio Performance, Using a No–Rebalancing Buy–and–Hold Benchmark

Like most other tests of trading rules' performance, the X-test involves a comparison between returns from the trading rule strategy and a buy-and-hold benchmark portfolio. This section deals with the case where the benchmark portfolio follows a buy-and-hold scheme with no rebalancing. That is, after assets are bought to form this buy-and-hold benchmark portfolio in the initial period, they will be held as is no matter how asset prices and hence portfolio weights change in the subsequent periods. In terms of investing in equities, this benchmark assumes that a certain number of shares of each asset are bought at the start and this number is held constant no matter how share prices change (any dividend distribution for a stock or interest payment for a bond or deposit being reinvested in the asset so that dividends or interest payments have the same effects as price appreciation on weights).

Consider a mutual fund fully investing its funds across N assets with the weight of w_{jt} for asset j at time t. (In the case this book studies, there are 16 assets composed of Euro-deposits in the 15 nondollar currencies plus Euro-dollar deposits.) The average return on this mutual fund's portfolio is

$$R_F = (1/T)\sum_{t=1}^{T}\sum_{j=1}^{N} w_{jt} R_{jt} \tag{3.1}$$

where R_{jt} is the excess rate of return on asset j at time t. (We use the same notation R_F here and in Section 3B because that section's discussion is a special case of (3.1), with one risky and one risk-free asset and all funds in either one or the other asset.) To evaluate the fund's performance, the observer constructs a buy-and-hold benchmark portfolio that has weight w'_{j1} for asset j in the initial period 1. This benchmark portfolio is strictly held through period T without any buying, selling, or other adjustment (save for the possible dividend or interest payment reinvestment noted above). As prices of assets evolve through time w'_{j1} will no longer hold, even though the number of shares held of each asset does not change. Denote the evolving weight of asset j in the buy-and-hold benchmark at time t as w'_{jt}; then the excess rate of return on the buy-and-hold benchmark due to asset j will be $w'_{jt} R_{jt}$ at time t, the excess rate of return on the benchmark will be $R_{BH,t} = \sum_{j=1}^{N} w'_{jt} R_{jt}$ at time t, and the average return on the buy-and-hold portfolio from the start of the period at time 1 to the end at time T is

$$R_{BH} = (1/T)\sum_{t=1}^{T}\sum_{j=1}^{N} w'_{jt} R_{jt}. \tag{3.2}$$

Let w_j and w'_j be the time averages of w_{jt} and w'_{jt}; then form the statistic

$$X = R_F - R_{BH} + (1/T)\sum_{t=1}^{T}\sum_{j=1}^{N} (w'_j - w_j) R_{jt}, \tag{3.3}$$

where the last set of terms is an adjustment factor necessary to make EX equal to zero, just as an adjustment factor had to be used in Section 3B (the X-statistic of that section is the same as the one in (3.3) if there is only one risky asset; see Section 3E below). Rewrite (3.3) as

$$X = (1/T)\sum_{t=1}^{T}\sum_{j=1}^{N} (w_{jt} - w_j)R_{jt} - (1/T)\sum_{t=1}^{T}\sum_{j=1}^{N} (w'_{jt} - w'_j)R_{jt},$$

or

$$X = (1/T)\sum_{t=1}^{T} \sum_{j=1}^{N} u_{jt} R_{jt} - (1/T)\sum_{t=1}^{T} \sum_{j=1}^{N} u'_{jt} R_{jt'} \qquad (3.4)$$

where $u_{jt} = w_{jt} - w_j$ and $u'_{jt} = w'_{jt} - w'_j$. Because each of the sums of w_{jt}, w_j, w'_{jt}, and w'_j across assets is unity by weight definition, it is obvious that the sum of u_{jt} and the sum of u'_{jt} across j must equal zero for all t. In addition, as u_{jt} and u'_{jt} are in the form of deviations from their means, their sum across t must also equal zero for all j. Assuming that there are no serial or lead-lag cross correlations in R_{jt}, as is implied by conditionally constant risk premia in conjunction with the EMH implication that the expected return on each asset equals its risk premium, the expected value of X is

$$E(X) = (1/T)\sum_{t=1}^{T} \sum_{j=1}^{N} u_{jt} E(R_j) - (1/T)\sum_{t=1}^{T} \sum_{j=1}^{N} u'_{jt} E(R_j)$$

$$= (1/T)\sum_{j=1}^{N} E(R_j) \sum_{t=1}^{T} u_{jt} - (1/T) \sum_{j=1}^{N} E(R_j) \sum_{t=1}^{T} u'_{jt}$$

$$= 0.$$

To gain an intuitive insight into the X-statistic, note that if the weights w_{jt} are always set equal to the benchmark weights w'_{jt}, then X is identically zero. Further, if all w_{jt} are constant over time, then again X is identically zero. Nonzero X's arise from the investor varying weights in order to take advantage of periods when s/he expects extra high or low returns relative to average. Under the null, such attempts are only randomly successful.

The variance of X is given by

$$\sigma^2_X = E[(1/T) \sum_{t=1}^{T} \sum_{j=1}^{N} (u_{jt} - u'_{jt})(R_j - E(R_j))]^2 \qquad (3.5)$$

$$= (1/T^2) \sum_{t=1}^{T} [\sum_{j=1}^{N} (u_{jt} - u'_{jt})^2 \sigma^2_{Rj}$$

$$+ \sum_{j=1}^{N} \sum_{h=1}^{N} (u_{jt} - u'_{jt})(u_{ht} - u'_{ht}) Cov(R_j, R_h)],$$

or

$$\sigma^2_X = Var(P_t)/T^2 = Var(P)/T, \qquad (3.6)$$

where P_t is the rate of return on a portfolio with weight $(u_{jt} - u'_{jt})$ for asset, $Var(P_t)$ its variance, and $Var(P)$ the time average of $Var(P_t)$. If asset returns follow a multivariate normal distribution, then X, which is a linear combination of returns, will also be normally distributed with mean zero and variance σ_X^2. A normal distribution, however, is a strong assumption and is not necessary for the validity of the X-test. The only necessary assumption for the statistical test using the X-statistic is that the assets' returns have constant, finite second moments such that an asymptotic normal sampling distribution is assured by the central limit theorem. Hence, given the existence of the population variances of returns, the ratio between the X-statistic and its associated standard deviation has an asymptotic standardized normal distribution. For a finite sample, a standard t-test can be used to test if X is indeed significantly nonzero.

If the covariance matrix of returns is not constant over time, then the variance of X would have to be reformulated to take account of the time-varying matrix. In the tests below, the covariance matrix is assumed constant. The reader may then want to take the reported t-statistics as simply an indication rather than a test. Note that heteroscedasticity may bias the standard error of X up or down, depending on whether terms such as $(u_{jt} - u'_{jt})^2$ and $(u_{jt} - u'_{jt})$ $(u_{ht} - u'_{ht})$ are larger or smaller on average when variances and covariances of the assets' returns are above or below average.[3]

It is clear that the X-statistics and X-tests in this section are all conditional on the w_{jt}'s and w'_{jt}'s, or equivalently on the u_{jt}'s and u'_{jt}'s, which are endogenous and generally stochastic. It is legitimate to take these as given for the test, however, because they are formed only on the basis of prior information and under the null hypothesis such information cannot be used to beat the market; this is the equivalent of taking the f as given in Section 3.B. With conditionally constant risk premia and under the EMH, no pattern of u's or w's should make the expectation of X nonzero. In particular, even if given the average rate of return to buy-and-hold on all assets and the patterns of u's or w's, the expected value of X would still be zero since the investor uses at each step only prior information that has no value in beating the market.

This section discussed the time-varying w'_{jt} as arising from a no-rebalancing buy-and-hold strategy, but the proofs made no use of this rationale. In fact, the test is perfectly general for any set of w"s no matter how they arise. For example, one might compare an active strategy actually followed (the w'_{jt}'s) with a proposed alternative (the w_{jt}'s).

The implications of the X-statistic when the no-rebalancing buy-and-hold benchmark is used are quite complex and not readily obvious at this point. The intuition will become more evident, however, as we move to the less complicated cases in the sections that follow.

3D. The X–Test for Portfolio Performance, Using a Rebalancing Buy–and–Hold Benchmark

As an alternative to the previous case, w'_{jt} in the benchmark portfolio may be held constant at all times through rebalancing. For instance, if the price of asset i increases while the prices of the other assets remain constant, asset i will now have more weight in the benchmark portfolio than before and the weights of other assets will decrease (because the sum of the weights is unity).

To return to the original weight structure, sell a portion of asset i. Use the funds obtained from this sale to purchase the other assets to preserve their original weights. Let w'_j denote the time-constant weight of asset j in the benchmark portfolio. Then the average return on the buy-and-hold benchmark portfolio is

$$R'_{BH} = (1/T) \sum_{t=1}^{T} \sum_{j=1}^{N} w'_j R_{jt}. \qquad (3.7)$$

R'_{BH} differs from R_{BH} by using time-constant rather than time-varying weights.

Because w'_{jt} is kept constant through rebalancing, it is always equal to its time-averaged weight, w'_j. Thus, (3.3) becomes

$$X = R_F - R'_{BH} + \sum_{j=1}^{N} (w'_j - w_j) R_j. \qquad (3.8)$$

It follows from (3.7), however, that $\sum_{j=1}^{N} w'_j R_{jt}$ is equal to R'_{BH}. Therefore, (3.8) collapses to

$$\begin{aligned} X' &= R_F - (1/T)\sum_{t=1}^{T} \sum_{j=1}^{N} w_j R_{jt} \qquad (3.9) \\ &= R_F - R''_{BH} \\ &= (1/T) \sum_{t=1}^{T} \sum_{j=1}^{N} (w_{jt} - w_j) R_{jt} \\ &= (1/T) \sum_{t=1}^{T} \sum_{j=1}^{N} u_{jt} R_{jt}. \end{aligned}$$

where $R''_{BH} = (1/T) \sum_{t=1}^{T} \sum_{j=1}^{N} w_j R_{jt}$, and X' is used for the constant-weight, buy-and-hold benchmark portfolio and X for the variable-weight benchmark (with all of them generically referred to as X-statistics).

R''_{BH} may be interpreted as the average return of a rebalancing buy-and-hold benchmark portfolio with weights equal to the time-average weights of the mutual fund's portfolio. It is obvious from (3.9) that in this case the X-statistic is simply the difference between the average return on the mutual fund's portfolio and the comparable average return on buy-and-hold.

The transition from (3.8) to (3.9) implies that no matter what constant-weight value of w_j is used initially, the algebraic process will transform the expression such that an w_j equal to the average weight of asset j in the mutual fund's portfolio will be used eventually. Therefore, an obvious choice of weights to form the buy-and-hold benchmark in this case is the average weight of the mutual fund's portfolio.

The X-statistics may be interpreted in terms of arbitrage. Rewrite (3.9) as

$$X' = (1/T) \sum_{t=1}^{T} \sum_{j=1}^{N} (w_{jt} - w_j) R_{jt}. \qquad (3.10)$$

Because $\sum^N_{j=1} w_{jt} = \sum^N_{j=1} w_j = 1$ for all t, it is obvious that X' is the average return on an arbitrage portfolio. The zero expected value of X' therefore means that the EMH implies there should be, on average, no profit earned from arbitrage. With this implication, the results in (3.3) for the case with no rebalancing of the buy-and-hold benchmark's weight become more apparent. Recall from above that we can rewrite (3.3) as

$$X = (1/T) \sum^T_{t=1} \sum^N_{j=1} u_{jt} R_{jt} - (1/T) \sum^T_{t=1} \sum^N_{j=1} u'_{jt} R_{jt}' \qquad (3.11)$$

where $u_{jt} = w_{jt} - w_j$ and $u'_{jt} = w'_{jt} - w'_j$. Hence, in the case with no rebalancing of the weights of assets in the buy-and-hold benchmark, the X-statistic consists of average returns of *two* arbitrage portfolios. The first arbitrage portfolio is exactly the same as that in the case with rebalancing in (3.10). The second arbitrage portfolio, however, appears because we let the weights of the assets in the buy-and-hold benchmark evolve as prices change. The zero-profit arbitrage condition requires that the profits from this arbitrage portfolio, too, should vanish. The difference between X and X' is only a sample phenomenon under the null hypothesis of constant risk premia and the EMH. Because both X-statistics have zero expected value, the difference between these statistics should asymptotically vanish as the sample size increases. Results reported below show that empirically the difference between X and X' is small; tests using both statistics yield quite similar results. Moreover, the ranks of their time-series match exactly, which indicates that the differences between the two statistics are a matter of degree rather than order.

From (3.5), the variance of X' is

$$\sigma^2_{X'} = E[(1/T) \sum^T_{t=1} \sum^N_{j=1} u_{jt}(R_j - E(R_j))]^2 \qquad (3.12)$$
$$=(1/T^2) \sum^T_{t=1} [\sum^N_{j=1} (u_{jt})^2 Var(R_j) + \sum^N_{j=1} \sum^N_{\substack{j=1 \\ j \neq h}} u_{jt} u_{ht} cov(R_j, R_h)],$$

or

$$\sigma^2_{X'} = (1/T^2) \sum^T_{t=1} Var(P'_t) = Var(P')/T \qquad (3.13)$$

where P'_t is a portfolio with a weight of u_{jt} for asset j and Var(P') is the time average of Var(P'_t).

The X-tests for the mutual fund's portfolio performance can be used to test the significance of trading rule profits when the speculator takes positions in more than one currency. The results reported below use both cases of buy-and hold benchmark portfolios.

Estimated Standard Errors

It is unclear how much weight to put on the covariance terms in finding the standard error of measured rates of profit. For example, in (3.12) these terms are of the form

$$u_{jt}u_{ht}\,\mathrm{cov}(R_j,\,R_h),$$

where the standard error formulas take the u's as given. Patterns of u's that show positive cross correlation lead to a higher standard error in (3.12), because the covariances of assets' rates of return (the cov's) are mostly positive. Empirically, the u's do show positive cross correlation on average for foreign exchange trading rule experiments; this is to be expected in a world of managed floating where, for example, currencies of members of the European Monetary System floated within bands relative to each other from 1981 on.[4]

The intuition of the X-statistics is that with conditionally constant expected rates of returns on all assets, no patterns of weights (w_{jt}'s) or weight-deviations (u_{jt}'s) can lead to a nonzero expected value of X. The tests take the u_{jt}'s as given, since their value cannot affect EX.

There may well be a difference, however, in the pattern of u's expected under the null hypothesis, of conditionally constant risk premia and the EMH, and the pattern of u's actually observed. To the extent that positive cross correlations of the u's are due to inefficiencies (positive cross correlations of divergences between expected returns and conditionally constant risk premia) and are higher than would be expected under efficiency (no divergences of expected returns from risk premia and hence no cross correlations of speculative positions from cross correlations of such divergences), the standard error is artificially high and the X-test is biased in favor of the null hypothesis. In this way, it makes sense to view the estimate from the standard error formulas developed above as an upper bound. A truncated version that ignores the covariance terms may serve as a lower bound; indeed, to the extent that the u's would get completely out of sync under efficiency, the contribution of the covariance terms to the standard error is negative.[5] Sweeney (1990a,b) reports evidence that a substantial amount of the positive correlation in positions in both currencies and equities are explicable in terms of correlations in divergences between expected rates of return and assets' risk premia.

For these reasons, it is unclear exactly how best to report standard errors and t-statistics. In Sweeney (1988), the t-statistics for results for U.S. equities are relatively insensitive to whether the covariance terms are included or not. For foreign exchange markets, the difference can be substantial. Most of the tables in later chapters show results only of the more stringent tests that use standard errors that include the effects of positive cross correlations in the u's. Chapter 10 reports some results that give a feel for the difference between the two measures of standard errors.

Treating the u's as Constant

Some readers are bothered by treating the u's as constant in the X-statistics and X-test, since clearly the u's depend on the path of prices that are stochastic. The appropriate interpretation is to think of the us as predetermined.

To see this, consider a time series of X'-statistics, from the rebalancing, constant-weight benchmark portfolio case. Let

$$X'_t = \sum_{j=1}^N (w_{jt} - w_j) R_{jt} = \sum_{j=1}^N u_{jt} R_{jt},$$

where $X' = (1/T) \sum_{t=1}^T X'_t$. As of time t, the u_{jt}'s are predetermined and in this book depend only on prices (and, in principle, other information) from time t-1 and before. Under the null hypothesis of conditionally constant risk premia and the EMH, so that the expected return on each asset equals its risk premium,

$$E_t X'_t = \sum_{j=1}^N u_{jt} ER_j,$$

where the notation E_t means the expectation is taken as of time t. In general, $E_t X'_t$ is nonzero, because the ER_j are not constant across all j (though they are assumed constant across all t). From the fact that the weights u_{jt} sum to zero over the period from t = 1 to T, however, the time average of $E_t X'_t$ must equal zero.

The variance of X' around $E_t X'_t$ is the var(P'_t) described above. With the u's taken as predetermined, the correlation of P'_t with P'_{t+h} is zero under the null hypothesis for any non-zero h, and the formula above for the variance of X' clearly holds. Note that mutatis mutandis the same argument can be made for the case where the returns' covariance matrix is not conditionally constant.

One might object that all w_{js} are unknown until the end of period T and hence the discussion of $E_t X'_t$ is illegitimate. Suppose, however, that a large range of vectors of [w_j] is considered. Call one of these vectors [w^*_j]. The X'-statistic based on [w^*_j] is $(1/T) \sum_{t=1}^T \sum_{j=1}^N (w_{jt} - w^*_{jt}) R_{jt}$, whose expectation in general is non-zero, unless [w_j] = [w^*_j]. But with a wide enough set of vectors considered, the actual [w_j] is among the set, and the above arguments stand.

3E. The X-Test for Single-Asset Speculation

Section 3 B introduced the X-statistic by giving a relatively intuitive discussion of the special case of speculation in just a single currency. The following two sections looked at cases of multi-asset speculation with two possible types of buy-and-hold benchmark portfolios. This section shows how the results for single-asset speculation in Section 3B relate to the more general cases discussed in Sections 3C and 3D.

In the case of single asset speculation, the asset subscript j is dropped because there is only one risky asset under consideration. It is clear that the weight of the single asset in the buy-and-hold portfolio, w', is equal to one because there is only one asset in the portfolio at all times. For the speculator's portfolio, however, the weight of the single asset, w_t, in the portfolio is equal to one in the periods when the investor is in the market and zero if the investor is out of the market. Because the average weight of trading–rule speculation, w, is equal to $\Sigma^T_{t=1} w_t/T$, it is obvious that w is simply the fraction of days the investor is in the market. Letting f be the fraction of days the fund is out of the market, then w = 1 - f. Therefore, the X-statistic in (3.8) collapses to

$$X'' = R_F - R_{BH} + [1 - (1 - f)] R_{BH} \qquad (3.14)$$
$$= R_F - (1 - f) R_{BH}.$$

The term (1 - f) is the adjustment factor reflecting the fact the investor is in the market only (1 - f) of the time. This adjustment corrects for the bias that occurs because filter rules tend to outperform buy-and-hold in a long-term falling market and tend to be beaten by buy-and-hold in a long-term rising market. It is apparent from (3.14) that X" can be significantly positive (which indicates that the filter rule can beat buy-and-hold) even if the average return per day (not per day in) on the filter rule is actually less than that of buy-and-hold (see Sweeney 1986a). This adjustment is consistent with Praetz's observation discussed above.

Because there is only one risky asset, it follows from (3.12) that the variance of X" is

$$\sigma^2_{X''} = (1/T) [(1/T) \Sigma^T_{t=1} (w_t - w)^2 \sigma_R^2] \qquad (3.15)$$
$$= (1/T) [\Sigma^T_{t=1} w_t^2 - w^2] \sigma^2_{R'}$$

which uses the fact that because w_t takes values of either 0 or 1 we have $w_t = w_t^2$. Thus, we can rewrite (3.15) as

$$\sigma^2_{X''} = (1/T) [w - w^2] \sigma_R^2 \qquad (3.16)$$
$$= (1/T) [(1 - f) - (1 - f)^2] \sigma^2_R$$
$$= (1/T) f(1 - f)\sigma^2_{R'}.$$

This is the form shown in Sweeney (1986a, 1988).

3F. The Normality Assumption,
the Stationarity of the Returns Distributions,
and the X-Statistics

The X-test, like most of the standard parametric tests, makes use of the normality assumption. In the least restrictive case, where the normality assumption may not hold for the rates of return on the assets, the test requires the existence of the second moments of the returns' distribution such that an asymptotically normal sampling distribution is assured by the central limit theorem. Past studies examining the distribution of the daily rates of return for stocks and exchange rates show that the assumption of normality can be decisively rejected. Mandelbrot (1963), for instance, notes that the empirical distributions of stock price changes have extraordinarily long tails and are peaked relative to samples that were drawn from a normal distribution (see Mandelbrot 1963; Fama 1963; Mandelbrot and Taylor 1967). He suggests using the non-normal stable Paretian distribution as an alternative, which resulted in a substantial number of later studies of the distribution of price changes. The non-Gaussian Paretian stable distribution received considerable support from these studies, as in the case of differences in stock prices by Fama (1965) and Teichmoeller (1971) or in the case of the changes in other speculative prices such as U.S. government treasury bills by Roll (1970) and commodity futures by Dusak (1973). Since the mid-1970s, however, the bulk of the evidence has favored formulations retaining normal distributions, for example subordinated stochastic processes or diffusion plus jump processes, as opposed to Paretian stable distributions.

In the case of the foreign exchange rate, studies have focused on the distribution of either the changes in the level of exchange rates or on percentage changes in exchange rates.[6] In all cases, departures from normality were discovered, generally more so for the pre-floating period. The distribution apparently has a longer tail with a higher degree of leptokurtosis than is expected from the normal distribution. Different conclusions include those of Rogalski and Vinso (1978), where they offer the Student t-distribution with approximately 3.9 degrees of freedom as an alternative to the symmetric Paretian stable distribution. Theoretically, however, this t-distribution has an even lower coefficient of kurtosis than the normal distribution; the moment coefficient of kurtosis is undefined. As a result, it has a lower peakedness than normal and fails to explain the high peakedness in sample distributions of the exchange rate that other studies observe.

To examine the conformity of the data used in this study to the normality assumption, Figure 1 shows the histograms of the data on the percentage rates of change (or rates of return) on the 15 currencies used in this study. The data consist of 2,000 observations for each currency. The figure shows both the sampling histogrammatic frequency and the hypothetical normal frequency with mean and variance equal to the observed mean and variance of the sample returns. In all cases, the sample distributions exhibit excessive peakedness and fatter tails than would be expected from normal distributions.

Kolmogorov-Smirnov tests give some useful information on the sample returns of the 15 exchange rates studied.[7] Theoretical distributions among the class of symmetric Paretian stable distributions, with the value of the characteristic exponent (alpha) ranging from 1.0 to 1.9 with step increment of 0.1, were obtained from Fama and Roll (1968). These theoretical distributions are based on a standardized variable of the form

$$u = (x - d) / c$$

where d is the location parameter and c is the scaling parameter. Because the true value of d is unknown in all cases other than the normal, the sample average with the extreme 25 percent of each tail truncated is used, as Monte Carlo results (Fama and Roll 1968) indicate that this is the best estimate of the location parameter. The scaling parameter is estimated from

$$c = (x(0.72) - x(0.28)) / 2 (0.827)$$

where $x(f)$ is the $f(N+1)$st order statistic used to estimate the f fractile of the data distribution of size N. This estimator has an asymptotic normal distribution with an asymptotic bias of less than 0.4 percent. In the case of normal distribution (alpha = 2.0), where the exact distribution function is known, the cumulative normal distribution function is used to enhance the power of the Kolmogorov-Smirnov test.

Table 1 shows the empirical results. In all cases, the assumption of a normal distribution can be rejected at the 99 percent confidence level. In 12 of the 15 cases, the assumption of a symmetric Paretian stable distribution with alpha equal to 1.5 cannot be rejected. The results suggest that these distributions come from the class of symmetric Paretian stable distribution with alpha ranging between 1.4 and 1.6. Exceptions are the Australian dollar, Japanese yen, and Spanish peseta, where all classes of the symmetric Paretian stable distribution, including the normal distribution, are rejected.[8] Results reported below make it very probable that these three exceptions arise because these currencies have significantly skewed distributions.

Like other tests of market efficiency, the X-tests described above are tests of the joint hypotheses of market efficiency and the stationarity of the sampling distribution. Table 2 presents the results of the tests on some central tendency parameters. Mann-Whitney U-tests for stationarity in both location and dispersion were performed. All currencies have relatively stable location parameters, and the tests indicate significant volatility in variances in all cases. The third column in Table 2 shows the skewness statistics. These skewness statistics are computed as

Skewness = $\{[(\text{Number of observations below mean})/T] - 0.5\}\ 2\ T^{1/2}$,

where T is the total number of observations. For large samples this statistic is normally distributed with zero mean and unit variance (see Roll 1970). The results indicate that the Australian dollar, Japanese yen, and Spanish peseta have significantly skewed distributions. This matches with the above results that the sample distributions of returns on these three currencies do not seem to belong to any of the symmetric Paretian stable distributions. One possibility is that they are drawn from asymmetric stable distributions. Testing this hypothesis, however, would require the theoretical development of the parameters of distributions that are not yet available.

In all cases, the distributions of all currencies are highly leptokurtic as indicated by the level of kurtosis in column 4 of Table 2. Kurtosis is computed from

$$\text{Kurtosis} = (1/T)\ \Sigma^T_{t=1}\ [(R_t - R)/s]^4 - 3,$$

where R is the sample mean and s and T are the standard deviation and total number of observations. This kurtosis statistic has an expected value of zero if the samples are drawn from a population that is normally distributed. The variance of the kurtosis of a sample drawn from a normal population is $24/T = 0.012$, and thus the standard deviation is 0.10954. The currency with the smallest kurtosis is the Japanese yen with a kurtosis value of 2.509, which is more than 20 standard deviations away from zero. For the other currencies, the kurtoses are even higher.

The nonstationarity in dispersion raises the issue of whether the samples are really drawn from a symmetric Paretian stable distribution. Because the U-test for stationarity in dispersion is a distribution-free test, the nonstationary results should be valid even if the true population distribution has infinite variance.[9] If the true parent population is stable, however, then there should be no shift in the scaling parameter. The problem then is whether the resulting leptokurtic sampling distribution is the product of shifts in a normal distribution or shifts in another type of stable distribution.

Beyond the non-normal Paretian stable hypothesis, there is a number of alternative views to explain the empirical phenomenon of highly leptokurtic distributions; here we discuss two that are prominent in the stock-market literature. The first alternative is that the observed exchange rates are in fact drawn from normal distributions; these normal distributions, however, have nonstationary variances. The variability in parameters of these distributions distort the empirical results when tests that assume stationary parameters are used.

Another alternative posits that the exchange rates contain discrete jumps. This may be due to government intervention, market overreactions, or some other reasons. Assuming that these discrete jumps occur uniformly around the mean such that they have no ex ante effect on the sample mean, the estimated variance still tends to be biased upward. Therefore, tests for normality that use estimated variances to generate hypothetical normal distributions will create a smaller degree of peakedness in the hypothetical normal distribution than otherwise, which makes the sampling frequency apparently too peaked in comparison and, thus, leads to the rejection of the null hypothesis. If the mean frequency of these jumps is constant, then this can be modeled through a combination of Poisson and diffusion processes (Adler and Dumas 1983).

Both alternative hypotheses lack good, rigorous empirical support so far for exchange rates. We examine the problem more closely below. Note at the outset, however, that the following analysis is not intended as a rigorous test of either of the two alternative views, but rather to give some insight into the problems with our data.

Consider calendar monthly averages of the daily returns data. If the actual population distributions of these currencies are stable distributions other than the normal, then, by the property of stability under addition, these monthly averages should also belong to non-normal stable distributions. As shown in Table 3, however, the normality assumption cannot be rejected at the 95 percent confidence level for these monthly averages. Leptokurtosis still persists but drops dramatically and in some cases turns out to be statistically indistinguishable from zero. Thus, the evidence for Paretian stable distributions is not as conclusive as the results in Table 1 might indicate. The data might as well come from normal distributions that suffer from some sort of nonstationarity—perhaps one of the external distortions mentioned above.

Suppose that the data are actually drawn from nonstationary normal distributions. If this is so, which of the two alternative views discussed above is more likely to be correct? It should be noted that the two alternatives are by no means mutually exclusive. For instance, if there is government intervention or market overreaction in some periods that creates discrete jumps in the exchange rates, then the variance of returns in those periods should be different from that in other periods, and this will create a shift in the parameters of the distribution. In such a case, both views should be considered valid. However, the shifts in parameters will happen on an irregular basis if they are caused by discrete jumps. That is, given that the occurrences of these discrete jumps do not happen on a regular basis (e.g., every month), there should be no pattern in the nonstationarity of parameters in such cases.

Table 3 shows another interesting result. Mann-Whitney U-tests for stability in dispersion indicate that the problem of nonstationary variances seems to disappear when monthly averages of daily data are used. (The exceptions are the Australian dollar and Japanese yen, two of the three currencies that show significant skewness in daily data. The high degrees of skewnesses of these two currencies vanish, however, when monthly averages are used.) These results on stationarity of dispersion with monthly averages would not necessarily be expected if nonstationarity in variances exists in a systematic fashion. For example, if months with high variances alternate with months with low variances, the averaging should not reduce measured nonstationarity of variances. However, there is evidence of day-of-the-week effects both in means and variances for U.S. equities and for currencies. Nonstationary variances in daily data that are due to these effects should disappear in monthly averages. In order for the first view to account both for fat tails in daily exchange rate variation and for apparent stationarity of dispersion in monthly averages, the shifts in variances would have to occur essentially within calendar months.[10]

The alternative view, that there are discrete jumps in the exchange rate that distort the sampling distribution of the data, can also explain the disappearance in monthly averages of the skewness and nonstationary dispersion problems present in daily data; taking monthly averages reduces the effect of discrete jumps in the data and hence the problems of skewness and shifts in dispersion caused by these discrete jumps. It is not possible, then, to use the results from monthly averages to discriminate between the view that the nonstationarity in dispersion of daily data arises from time-varying variances and the view that there are discrete jumps.

Based on other preliminary results not shown here, skewness and nonstationarity in dispersion are also much reduced in daily data by eliminating the largest 1 percent (in absolute value) of outliers from the daily data. This indicates that the results in daily data may well be related to discrete jumps.

In addition, simulations generated 2,000 observations of a series of random numbers from a standardized normal distribution. Then 20 observations (i.e., 1 percent of the total normal observations) of outliers with random sizes ranging from three to nine standard deviations away from mean were randomly mixed into this series of standardized normal random numbers. The resulting samples had similar properties to the return data used in this study. The Kolmogorov-Smirnov test rejects the null hypothesis of a normal distribution at the 95 percent level, and the sample distribution tends to have a high degree of peakedness and kurtosis in comparison to the normal distribution. This illustrates the effects that discrete jumps can have on the sample distribution.

If the argument is correct that the leptokurtosis and nonstationarity of dispersion in the daily exchange rates are due to discrete jumps in exchange rates, then the estimated variances of returns on these currencies will tend to be overstated by these jumps. This, however, does not pose much of a problem because the worst thing that can happen is we may fail to reject the null hypothesis of zero trading rule profits when it is false. Therefore, the test is not biased in favor of trading rules.

If the non-Gaussian stable distribution hypothesis is true, however, the bias will be reversed. That is, the estimated variances will understate the true (infinite) variances and the test is biased in favor of trading rules. It can be argued that under a non-Gaussian Paretian stable distribution, however, the X-statistic is also likely to be substantially smaller than in the case of a normal distribution. The arguments presented below are for speculation using an Alexander filter rule. They are, however, applicable to all trading rules.

Alexander (1961) assumes the investor can buy (sell) at exactly the price that triggers a y percent buy (sell) signal. Fama and Blume (1966) point out that the investor will likely have to buy (sell) at a higher (lower) price because prices vary in discrete moves over time. This problem will certainly arise in this study where transactions are made at noon prices and the investor will almost always have to buy (sell) at prices higher (lower) than y percent above the previous low (high). The issue is, At how much higher a price? For an investor using an Alexander filter rule, the difference between the minimum price that triggers a y percent buy signal and the price at which he can actually buy depends on the kind of distribution the samples are drawn from. When the distribution is non-normal Paretian stable, the oscillations of price movements tend to be higher due to the fat tails of the distribution than if the distribution were, say, rectangular or normal. Thus, by the time the investor can act on a buy signal that the filter triggers, the realized price may have already gone up substantially more from the y percent above the previous low than it would have if drawn from a distribution with finite variance. Therefore, it is more likely that the investor has to buy and sell when the prices are substantially higher and lower than with distributions with finite variances, which implies lower returns than otherwise. Thus, for a given filter size, the underestimated variance is likely to be associated with a lower X-statistic. Although it is not necessarily so that the two effects will cancel out, the problem of type I errors posed by the Paretian stable distribution is probably not as severe as one might expect by simply looking at the issue of the variance.

3G. An Alternative Nonparametric Test

Although we are more inclined to believe that the data used in this study are drawn from a normal population with either intra-month variations in variance or some distorting discrete jumps rather than other classes of stable distributions, the test results reported above are not clear-cut enough to rule out completely the Paretian stable hypothesis. Given the current knowledge regarding non-Gaussian stable Paretian distributions, however, the modification of the parametric X-tests to account for this problem is not possible. The exact probability distribution functions of most of these distributions are unknown and, at best, only an approximation of these distributions, based on some transformed variables, can be obtained. Standard advice in this situation is to use higher-than-usual confidence levels in interpreting results of parametric tests that assume distributions with finite variances. One might alternatively use nonparametric distribution-free tests to alleviate the problem. While there are corresponding nonparametric tests that can be used as alternatives to the parametric t-tests, use of these tests may be limited both because of the nature of the tests and the nature of the speculation.

Perhaps the best feasible nonparametric test is Wilcoxon's matched-pair signed-rank test. The asymptotic efficiency of this test as compared to the parametric t-test is approximately 95 percent.[11] To make the test comparable to the X-test, the time-series of the trading rule return is compared to the time-series of the comparable return on buy-and-hold. In the case of the X-test for single-asset speculation, the return on buy-and-hold is simply the asset return, R_t, times $(1 - f)$. Thus, in the periods when the investor is in the market the test compares the return to speculation, R_t, to the buy-and-hold return $(1 - f) R_t$, giving a difference of $f R_t$. On days when the investor is out of the market, the test involves comparison of the time series of $(1 - f)R_t$ for buy-and-hold and the constant series of 0 for the trading rule, giving the difference $- (1 - f) R_t$. On days out, then, the test makes comparisons between a sampling variated series and an absolutely truncated series. However, unlike the parametric t-test, the Wilcoxon signed-rank test does not effectively use the parametric score of the periods "in" the market to adjust for the parametric score of the periods "out" of the market. Such "adjustment" is only done through changes in rankings of the series. Because of this, the Wilcoxon matched–pair signed-rank test may incorrectly imply that the two series are different when the fraction of days out of the market is too high or too low. A simple example is given below.

For simplicity, assume that the return on assets follows a random walk with a positive drift parameter high enough that for every realization $R_t >$ 0 for all t, such that the difference between these two series will be negative $(= -(1 - f)R_t)$ when the investor is out of the market and positive $(= fR_t)$ when the investor is in the market. Suppose that, for the particular realization, the rule has the investor out of the market most of the time and also does not result in a profit superior to that of buy-and-hold. The signed-rank of the difference between these two series will only show a few counts of positive rank and numerous counts of negative rank. Because Wilcoxon's test considers only the minimum between the sum of positive and negative ranks, it will turn out that the sum of the positive ranks will be used. This sum, however, is likely to be substantially smaller than the expected value of sum rank, which leads to the rejection of the null hypothesis when it is true. One can also show that the same type I error can occur when the rule has the investor in the market most of the time and did not make a profit any better than that of buy-and-hold. Hence, for the test to work properly, the value of f must not be "too" high or low.

Another shortcoming of the signed-rank tests is that they assume symmetry in the distribution of the difference between the two series.[12] In other words, if a signed-rank test is performed on the matched-pair W and V, it requires that the distribution of W - V must be symmetric. In terms of the application of the Wilcoxon signed-rank test to the X-test, the distribution of the X-statistic must be symmetric. The previous section showed that the distributions of returns on some exchange rates are significantly skewed. Although the test does not require symmetry in the distribution of the return, it is quite obvious that the skewness in the return distribution can produce significant skewness in the distribution of the X-statistic.

The X-statistic is equal to fR_t in the period when the investor is in the market and equal to $-(1-f)R_t$ when s/he is out of the market. Hence, the X-statistic is highly related to the return and will be likely to have a skewed distribution if the distribution of the return is skewed. Given high skewness in the return distribution, whether or not the distribution of the X-statistic is skewed depends mainly on f and the nature of the trading rule. Suppose that the distribution of returns is positively skewed and the rule is profitable by putting the investor in the market when the return is high. Then, the periods when the investor is in the market are likely to contain most of the observation points that lie on the positively skewed side of the distribution. Therefore, whether or not the distribution of the X-statistic will be positively skewed depends upon the value of f. If f is small, then the skewness in the return is partially offset by the fact that the observations that lie on the positively skewed side of the distribution are weighted by a small f, and the other observation points are weighted by a larger value of (1 - f). However, if f is large, then the skewness of the X-statistic will be amplified by weighting the positively skewed observations more. In the same way, when the return distribution is negatively skewed, the value of f has to be sufficiently large to maintain symmetry in the distribution of the X-statistic.

As argued above, for the Wilcoxon signed-rank test to work properly, without type I error, the value of f should be neither too high nor low. On the other hand, if the distribution of the return is skewed, then f has to be sufficiently high or low, depending upon the skewness, to produce symmetry in the distribution of the X-statistic. Therefore, the test may be unavoidably deficient if the return distribution is skewed.

The application of the Wilcoxon signed-rank test to the case of single currency speculation may be limited, then, if either the value of f is not around 0.5, or the returns distribution is not symmetric, or both. In the case of multicurrency speculation, however, the problems are considerably less severe. Because multicurrency speculation generally involves positions in several currencies at the same time, it is likely that the f's will tend to balance out. Further, the problem of skewness in the returns distributions is alleviated by the fact that more than one currency is held in any period of time. Even though the returns on some currencies are highly skewed, the returns on the portfolio may not be. For instance, the returns on holding the Australian dollar and the Japanese yen are both highly skewed. The returns on holding both currencies in the portfolio, however, may not be as skewed because part, if not all, of the negative skewness in the Australian dollar will be offset by the positive skewness in the Japanese yen through the portfolio formation process. For these reasons, this study implements the Wilcoxon signed-rank test only in the cases of portfolio speculations. The Wilcoxon signed-rank test is used to confirm the results of the parametric X-test.

3H. Conclusion

Various types of X-statistics are available to test the statistical significance of trading rule returns in excess of buy-and-hold. X-statistics can be used to test the speculative performance of both portfolios and single assets. The X-test does not require knowledge of population statistics such as the means and covariances of asset returns, though it requires estimates of the covariance matrix. These various versions of the X-statistic are closely and intuitively related to each other.

This book uses two X-tests for portfolio performance. The first method uses a buy-and-hold benchmark portfolio with no rebalancing for comparison. The absence of rebalancing means that the individual assets' benchmark weights tend to evolve over time. The second method uses a constant weight buy-and-hold portfolio, requiring rebalancing, as the benchmark. Although the two methods are equivalent in large samples under the null hypothesis of constant risk premia and the expected excess rate of return equal to the risk premium for each asset, the results may differ somewhat for a finite sample.

The X-test is a test of the joint hypotheses of market efficiency and stationarity of distributions. The test also relies either on the normality assumption or, more weakly, on the existence of the second moment of the distribution. Tests of the data used in this study show some evidence of non-normal stable distributions, in which the variances of these distributions are not defined. Nonparametric tests also provide evidence of stationarity in location parameters but nonstationarity in dispersion, with extremely high degrees of kurtosis. When these daily data are transformed into monthly averages, however, the distributions appear much more normal and the level of kurtoses drops dramatically. In addition, the problem of nonstationary variance in daily data seems to vanish when monthly averages are used. This is consistent with the view that variances are normal but vary within the month, perhaps through day-of-the-week effects. This is also consistent with the view that the data are drawn from parent populations that are normal and stationary with some discrete jumps in the data due to external factors such as government intervention or market overreactions. These discrete jumps produce outliers in the data that distort the distribution tests and seemingly pose the problem of nonstationary variances in the daily data.

One might use distribution-free tests as an alternative to the X-test when the distribution of returns is unknown. The Wilcoxon matched-paired signed-rank test can be used as a substitute for the parametric X-test. It can be shown, however, that the signed-rank test may be deficient under some reasonable circumstances. This is particularly true in the case of speculation in a single currency. In multi-currency speculation, because many currencies are likely to be held at the same time in the speculator's portfolio, the problems should be less severe and the test more robust. Hence, in the case of multi-currency speculation, the Wilcoxon signed-rank test is performed to confirm the results obtained from the X-test.

Notes

1. In the case where short sales are not allowed, this bias is equal to af.

2. The investor might in principle face a period where every s is positive, so she or he makes no sales until closing positions at the end of the period. In this case the x- (or X-)statistic would be zero even though there are risk-adjusted profits. This is, of course, a bias in favor of the null of no profits.

3. Sweeney (1990c) discusses in detail how to modify X-tests when the investigator knows that either the means or variances and covariances of the assets' returns distributions are time varying.

4. Buy and sell signals, and hence u's, show substantially greater correlation for exchange rates than for U.S. equities. Government intervention in exchange markets may explain a major part of this difference.

5. For example, suppose that there are 14 currencies, and that for every period seven have positive u's and seven have negative u's. Let u_{1t} be negative. Then, $u_{1t}u_{it}$

for all i not equal to 1 shows seven negative values and six positive values. If the covariances across currencies are roughly the same or there is no systematic pattern of u-products and covariances, then the net impact of the covariance terms on the standard error will be negative.

6. These studies include Giddy and Dufey (1975), Cornell and Dietrich (1978), Westerfield (1977), Logue, Sweeney, and Willett (1978), McFarland, Pettit, and Sung (1982), and Calderon-Rossell and Ben-Horim (1982).

7. The Kolmogorov-Smirnov test is used for convenience because the hypothetical probability table provided by Fama and Roll (1971) is presented in cumulative distribution form. Some studies also argue that the Kolmogorov-Smirnov test is more powerful than the Chi-square test of goodness of fit in the sense that it treats individual observations separately and hence uses the information more efficiently. This is correct if we are testing the data against some hypothetical distribution with a known density function. However, because the test implemented here uses the hypothetical frequency in the tabulated form, the test simply collapses to the Kolmogorov-Smirnov two-sample test. Therefore, it is not clear that the Kolmogorov-Smirnov test will be substantially superior to the Chi-square test.

8. These results are highly consistent with the work by Calderon-Rossell and Ben-Horim (1982), which is the most recent study that analyzes the distribution of the rate of return rather than changes in exchange rate.

9. The Mann-Whitney U-test for stationarity in dispersion used in this study is a test for the stability of the dispersion or scaling parameter of the distribution. Therefore, the fact that a non-Gaussian stable distribution has infinite variance does not invalidate the results.

10. Although this book does not take into account possible time variation in variances, Sweeney (1990c) shows in detail how the X-test can take these into account.

11. Mood (1954). It is not argued here, however, that the Wilcoxon signed-rank test is the best test in the sense that it has the highest power efficiency among classes of nonparametric tests for two related samples. A randomized test for matched pairs should be considered as the best in terms of power efficiency because it is as powerful as the parametric t-test. However, this test involves comparison of all the combinations of the observations and is not practical for a large sample. With only eight observations, for example, there are 256 combinations to be considered. The Wilcoxon signed-rank test, therefore, is considered the most attractive in terms of high power-efficiency and less computational time.

12. The assumption of symmetry in the distribution of the differences between the two series is required in spite of the fact that the Wilcoxon signed-rank test is a nonparametric test. The test is distribution-free in the sense that it does not rely on the distribution of the two series. However, the null distribution of the Wilcoxon statistic is determined by the assumption that the population distribution of the difference between the two series is symmetric such that the signs of the signed-rank series are mutually dependent and equally likely to be positive or negative. In an asymptotic sense, the test relies on the distribution of the sum of the signed ranks, which is assured to by asymptotically normal by the Liapounov Central Limit Theorem if the symmetry assumption is satisfied. For further discussion, see Pratt and Gibbons (1981, Chapter 3).

57

FIGURE 1

Observed Sampling Frequency Distributions of Returns on Exchange Rates, and the Associated Hypothetical Normal Distribution Curves

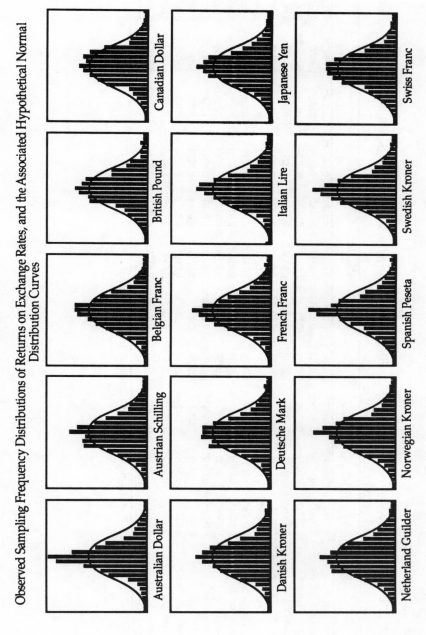

TABLE 1 Kolmogorov-Smirnov Test for the Distributions of Returns on Foreign Exchange Rates Based on Various Classes of Symmetric Paretian Stable Distributions.

CURRENCY	ALPHA										
	1.0	1.1	1.2	1.3	1.4	1.5	1.6	1.7	1.8	1.9	2.0
Australian Dollar	0.0380**	0.0380**	0.0380**	0.0380**	0.0380**	0.0385**	0.0394**	0.0464**	0.0528**	0.0587**	0.1641**
Austrian Schilling	0.0657**	0.0538**	0.0430*0	0.0333	0.0245	0.0169	0.0164	0.0174	0.0238	0.0297	0.0602
Belgian Franc	0.0594**	0.0474	0.0365	0.0264	0.0183	0.0191	0.0196	0.0234	0.0303	0.0367**	0.0640**
British Pound	0.0609**	0.0491	0.0384	0.0289	0.0203	0.0138	0.0192	0.024	0.0284	0.0324	0.0618
Canadian Dollar	0.0654	0.0534	0.0425	0.0324	0.0231	0.0153	0.0099	0.0118	0.0178	0.0232	0.0472
Danish Krone	0.0589**	0.0471	0.0364	0.0269	0.019	0.0191	0.0234	0.0307	0.0375	0.0437	0.0822
Deutche Mark	0.0629**	0.0511	0.0404	0.0309	0.0223	0.0174	0.0183	0.0228	0.0293	0.0357	0.0684
French Franc	0.0574**	0.0456	0.0349	0.0254	0.0168	0.0147	0.0194	0.0258	0.0318	0.0372	0.069
Italian Lire	0.0586**	0.0466	0.0357	0.0258	0.0191	0.0195	0.0198	0.0215	0.0259	0.0299	0.0754
Japanese Yen	0.0625**	0.0507**	0.0404**	0.0399**	0.0395**	0.0392**	0.0390**	0.0389**	0.0388**	0.0412**	0.0730**
Netherland Guilder	0.06	0.0482	0.0378	0.0284	0.0203	0.0211	0.0216	0.0224	0.0288	0.0347	0.0646
Norwegian Krone	0.0571	0.0451	0.0342	0.0243	0.016	0.0159	0.02	0.0274	0.0343	0.0407	0.0898
Spanish Peseta	0.0500**	0.0382**	0.0371**	0.0381**	0.0388**	0.0393**	0.0418**	0.0468**	0.0516**	0.0560**	0.0906**
Swedish Krona	0.0624**	0.0504**	0.0395**	0.0295	0.0203	0.0174	0.0173	0.0244	0.0313*	0.0377**	0.0914**
Swiss Franc	0.0642**	0.0523**	0.0415**	0.0318*	0.023	0.0187	0.0185	0.0222	0.029	0.0352*	0.0726**

NOTE: * significant at 95% confidence level, ** significant at 99% confidence level

TABLE 2 Tests of Stationarity of Various Moments of the
Distributions of Daily Rates of Return on Foreign Exchanges.

CURRENCY	MANN-WHITNEY TEST		SKEWNESS	KURTOSIS
	LOCATION	DISPERSION	STATISTICS	
Australian Dollar	-0.0153	-14.5466**	-3.3988**	85.7350
Austrian Schilling	-0.0004	-3.3779**	-0.7603	6.8860
Belgian Franc	-0.2695	-4.8042**	0.7155	5.0690
British Pound	-1.5138	-4.0484**	-0.6261	3.5830
Canadian Dollar	-0.2853	-3.3993**	-0.2236	3.1260
Danish Krone	-0.4220	-4.9896**	1.0286	18.2540
Deutche Mark	-0.0814	-4.9898**	0.5814	4.5160
French Franc	-0.1152	-6.4232**	-0.4472	6.7950
Italian Lire	-0.2020	-6.9496**	-0.8497	5.1390
Japanese Yen	-2.2970*	-4.9950**	3.3094**	2.5090
Netherland Guilder	-0.0766	-4.7102**	0.2236	6.0350
Norwegian Krone	-0.8093	-6.3698**	-0.8050	16.6720
Spanish Peseta	-0.3392	-11.5033**	-2.0572*	17.3890
Swedish Krona	-0.0570	-4.8633**	-1.1628	50.7000
Swiss Franc	-0.0264	-0.0186**	1.4311	19.8650

1. Total number of daily observations is 2000 trading days.

2. * and ** indicate that the estimated statistic is significant at 95 and 99 percent confidence levels respectively.

3. Under a normal distribution, the coefficient of kurtosis has an expecte value of zero and standard deviation, given the 2000 observations sample size, of 0.10954.

TABLE 3 Tests for Stationarity and Normal Distribution of the Monthly
Averaged Rates of Return on Foreign Currencies.

| CURRENCY | MANN-WHITNEY TEST | | SKEWNESS | | K-S Dmax |
	LOCATION	DISPERSION	STATISTICS	KURTOSIS	TEST FOR NORMALITY
Australian Dollar	-1.0534	-3.6149**	-0.5077	-2.2690	0.1161
Austrian Schilling	-0.0072	-0.1010	1.1169	2.6550	0.0697
Belgian Franc	-0.2958	-0.3391	0.7107	2.3560	0.0756
British Pound	-1.2194	-0.9164	0.5077	1.2990	0.0552
Canadian Dollar	-0.3030	-1.7028	0.1015	0.2960	0.0910
Danish Krone	-0.3247	-0.2237	0.7107	2.2290	0.0933
Deutche Mark	-0.0794	-0.1804	0.9138	1.7170	0.0731
French Franc	-0.1227	-0.4546	1.1169	1.5720	0.0629
Italian Lire	-0.2670	-0.4329	-0.1015	4.6280	0.0464
Japanese Yen	-1.2916	-2.2007**	1.3200	0.5070	0.1170
Netherland Guilder	-0.0938	-0.4185	1.3200	2.0130	0.0670
Norwegian Krone	-1.0246	-0.4401	0.7107	2.4040	0.0749
Spanish Peseta	-0.7720	-1.1978	0.1015	3.8820	0.0587
Swedish Krona	-0.0216	-0.1876	-0.3046	2.0110	0.1066
Swiss Franc	-0.0361	-1.3637	1.7261	2.3010	0.1045

1. Total number of monthly-averaged observations is 97 months.

2. * and ** indicate that the estimated statistic is significant at 95 and 99 percent confidence levels respectively.

3. Under a normal distribution, the coefficient of kurtosis has an expected value of zero and a standard deviation, given the 97 observations sample size, of 0.49741.

4

Selecting Trading Rules

As discussed in Chapter 2, most studies of technical analysis focus on speculation in one asset at a time. For the spot exchange market, none of the past studies has analyzed the case of simultaneous speculation in several currencies as part of a unified strategy, though some have formed equally weighted portfolios of single-currency speculations. The basic intuition of portfolio theory suggests the wisdom of speculating in many currencies at the same time. In Chapters 5 through 8 we analyze speculations using four different approaches to forming portfolios. In this chapter is much of the groundwork for the investigations in these later chapters. In particular, we discuss the trading rules investigated in coming chapters and how we select the parameters, such as the filter size in the Alexander rule, used in the speculations.

In Section 4A we explain the three types of technical trading rules used in this book—the Alexander filter rule, the double moving average rule, and the single moving average rule. The pros and cons of each are analyzed and the similarities among rules discussed. We make extensive use of these rules in Chapters 5, 6 and 7.

In Chapter 5 we report results of using these rules, with individually tailored parameter values, on each of the 15 currencies. Also reported are the results of aggregating these currencies into an equally weighted portfolio. In Chapter 6 we use the same individually tailored parameters but combine the results for the currencies into variably weighted portfolios. In Chapter 7 we do not aim at finding individualized parameters for each currency, but instead aggregate the currencies into four separate indexes; the same technical trading rules as in previous chapters are used on these indexes but with parameters tailored to the indexes rather than to individual currencies.

In Section 4B we describe how we choose the optimum parameters for the trading rules. For example, which filter size is best to use for the Swiss franc in the Alexander rule? Which lag lengths are best for the long and short moving averages for the British pound in the double moving average rule? In our approach, we divide our data into test periods and also earlier periods, called prior periods, that we explore to find the best or optimum parameter values to use in the later test periods. Choosing the optimum parameters on an ex ante basis from earlier, prior period data reduces the chance of finding spurious profits in the test period and hence gives a more convincing rejection of the market efficiency hypothesis if trading rules beat buy-and-hold.

In Section 4C we discuss the related issues of short sales, the interest rate differential, and the issue of whether risk can explain any measured profits. Transaction costs and their effects on the empirical results are the subject of Section 4D. Section 4E is a discussion of the data used in this study as well as the time period covered and here we detail how the time series were divided into prior periods and test periods, called subperiods, for the trading simulations; these periods were selected before any empirical work was done, and hence our results do not show any effects of data mining. Finally, Section 4F summarizes the models and procedures used in this book.

4A. Trading Rules

This book studies three popular types of trading rules: the Alexander filter rule, the single moving average rule, and the double moving average rule.

Alexander Filter Rule

This rule, proposed by Alexander (1961), has received the most attention in the academic literature on technical analysis. The form of this rule used here is: If the price goes up y percent above the previous local low, buy and hold until it moves down y percent below the previous local high, at which time sell until price again goes up y percent. (Note that this version does not involve short sales, as many other studies do; see Section 4C for a discussion.)

The intuition behind this rule is what Alexander called "the persistence of moves" phenomenon. According to his interpretation, past data suggest that even though price changes appear to be random over time, the price level itself tends to exhibit patterns. That is, if the market has moved up y percent, it is likely to move up further before it moves down. The value percent is called the filter size, because it acts to filter out price movements that are due to nonsystematic noise patterns. The optimum filter size should be large enough to filter the noise out of the series so that speculation is based mainly on the persistent patterns or trends. If the filter size is too small, incorrect signals may be triggered because the rule misinterprets movements due to noise as patterns. Too large a filter size, however, may not produce any signal or may produce signals when it is too late to make profits, particularly when the price movements are comparatively flat.

As discussed in Chapter 2, Alexander''s early approach was criticized (see Mandelbrot 1963) on the grounds that he assumed that, for example, if today's price rises more than y percent from the past local minimum, there will be at least one instant when the price has gone up exactly y percent. According to his approach, the asset should be bought at exactly this instant that, as a practical matter, may not exist. To avoid this problem, we use the actual recorded price both as the price at which buy or sell signals are triggered and the price at which trades are made. That is, if today's price moves up x percent or more from the previous low, then the currency is bought at exactly the recorded price. As this problem is also applicable to trading rules other than the Alexander filter, the same method of using the actual price for the transaction is also applied to the other rules throughout this book.

Single Moving Average Rule

A very popular trading rule among practitioners is the "single moving average trading rule." A moving average, as is well known in forecasting theory, smooths out the noise in a series. Further, any one element in the series will have a smaller effect on the moving average than on the level of the series itself. As a result, a moving average of prices will respond to changes in market conditions more slowly than the price series itself. In the view of those using moving average approaches to speculation, "significant" changes in the moving average will follow mainly from persistent and significant changes in the price series. The fact that a change in price will have less than a one-to-one effect on the moving average is taken to mean that an upward trend in the price level will cause the price level to rise more quickly than the trend in the moving average of the price. Hence the moving average will tend to be below the price in a bull market and be above the price in a bear market. From this observation, the obvious trading rule should be: Buy when a rising price crosses above the moving average from below and sell when the declining price crosses the moving average from above.

A moving average system is not as different from the Alexander filter system as it appears. The moving average reacts to a new developing trend in a sluggish fashion and any transitory change in trend will have smaller effects on the moving average than on the price itself. Hence, it is not likely that the moving average will give signals during nondirectional, volatile price movements that are due to noise. This feature is similar to filtering the noise out. Thus, a moving average system may be viewed intuitively as an Alexander filter system where the value of filter changes through time.

As with the Alexander filter, there is a trade-off in the selection of the optimum length of the moving average. A long moving average responds slowly to changes in market trends and hence in many cases tends to give signals when it is too late to make profitable transactions. This may lead to small, repeated losses in a flat market, at least until new, more volatile systematic trends begin. To make a moving average system more sensitive to the start of a new trend, a shorter moving average should be used. This is done, however, at the expense of encouraging wrong signals that may be triggered by mistaking noise for patterns. The trade-off between selecting a longer or shorter moving average length is similar to the choice of the filter size in the Alexander system.

Double Moving Average Rule

This trading rule is an extension of the single moving average rule. The intuition behind the two rules is similar except that now two series of moving averages are used. The longer moving average is used to trace out the long-term trend, and the shorter moving average is used as a timing device to signal when a buy or sell should take place. The long moving average serves the same purpose as the moving average series in the single moving average system, and the short moving average acts as a smoothed proxy for the asset price. The double moving average system smooths out the noise not only in the sluggish (long moving average) trend but also in the fast-responding short moving average. The rule for the double moving average system, therefore, is similar to the rule for the single moving average system: buy when the rising short moving average crosses the long moving average from below and sell when the declining short moving average crosses the long moving average from above.

4B. Formation of Expectations Regarding the Optimum Parameters for Technical Trading Rules

A common view in the academic literature that market inefficiencies are evident if a technical trading rule can consistently outperform the buy-and-hold strategy. The word "consistent," however, needs elaboration. Suppose that experimentation reveals that the Alexander rule with a 0.5 percent filter size outperforms buy-and-hold for three consecutive periods. Is this sufficient to reject the null hypothesis of market efficiency? There must be some ambiguities in the answer. Because analysis is done on an ex post basis and, more important, various values of parameters (filter size, in this case) are usually tried, the fact that the 0.5 percent filter beats the market for three consecutive periods is still an ex post matter. More specifically, the problem is: How would a speculator know to choose a filter size of 0.5 percent in the first place? The possible values of parameters that might reasonably be used for a particular rule are numerous.

This study uses an ex ante expectations approach. Figure 2 is a flow chart describing the general process of expectations formation. The investor gathers the available past data prior to the day s/he starts speculating. The past data are referred to in this book as the prior period. Based on searching over the prior period data, the investor finds the set of optimum parameters that yields the best ex post results for the prior period for the rule considered, for example, the double moving average rule. For each trading rule, best results are chosen in terms of the highest X-statistic adjusted for transaction costs (transactions costs are discussed in Section 4G). As discussed in Chapter 3, the X-statistic is the average return on the trading rule in excess of the comparable average return on buy-and-hold. Further, the X-statistic can be viewed as the average risk-adjusted profit from using the trading rule if the risk premia in asset returns are constant over time, as discussed in Chapter 3. Therefore, the highest adjusted X-statistic implies the highest average profits on the trading rule after adjustment for the average transaction costs incurred. The investor adopts these ex post best rules from the prior period to speculate on the currencies on an ex ante basis in the following test period. This following period of speculation is referred to in this study as a subperiod. At the end of the subperiod, the investor combines this subperiod's data with those from the original prior period to form a new prior period with more data and then revises his expectations regarding the set of best parameter values for each of the rules considered. This new prior period may use all of the data available or may use only some of them; some empirical results on how many data it is optimal to use are discussed in Chapter 10. The revised best parameter values found from the new prior period is used to speculate in the next subperiod. The process continues in this way until the end of the total period studied. The overall period used in this book and how it is divided into subperiods and prior periods are discussed in detail in Section 4E.

Using the ex ante expectations approach just outlined tightens the region for rejecting the null hypothesis of an efficient market. Success in implementing a rule, if it happens, requires that the best rule observed ex post on prior period data must "work" to the extent of generating statistically significant profits when adopted in the following subperiod on an ex ante basis.

Suppose that a particular rule really does give information useful in speculating. To maximize the chances for a trading rule to significantly outperform buy-and-hold in a subperiod, the observed best parameter values for the rule should be the true optimum parameter values for the rule. This may not be the case, however, because the prior period search ranges across numerous parameters and spuriously "best" results may be found. If certain parameters turn out to be ex post best only by chance in a world where there truly are no underlying patterns to be exploited, following the rule with these parameters in the next period will give a performance with profits only randomly different from zero. If the observed best rule is sufficiently close to the true best rule *and* the market is persistently inefficient, however, following the rule should be profitable. Therefore, if the results indicate that trading rules consistently and significantly beat buy-and-hold, it is not likely that this happens by chance. These profit opportunities are truly exploitable because they follow from adopting the best rule based on nonoverlapping prior period data.

The existence of measured profit opportunities, however, cannot lead to decisive rejection of the market efficiency hypothesis. As discussed in Chapter 3, the X-test, like other tests of market efficiency, is inevitably a test of a joint hypothesis. Thus, even if the statistical test leads to rejection of the null hypothesis, one can always preserve the hypothesis of market efficiency by asserting that it is the other components of the joint hypothesis that are violated.

From the investor's standpoint, however, being told that at least one of the components in the joint hypothesis can be decisively rejected is usually not useful unless it is clearly known which one. As far as the investor is concerned, the profit opportunities are there. Thus, in the absence of clear evidence that the profit opportunities are due to factors other than market inefficiency, the investor's best bet is to act on the assumption of inefficiency and to try to exploit these opportunities for profit, as discussed in Chapter 11.

The optimum parameters for each trading rule are selected as follows. For the Alexander filter rule, simulations based on prior period data are performed with different values of filter sizes ranging from 0.1 percent to 10.0 percent with step increments of 0.1 percent. This range is, of course, arbitrary. From past studies, however, it seems unlikely for filter values of higher than 10 percent to be the best rule. In most cases, small filter values tend to perform better. The value of the step increment of 0.1 percent used in this book appears sufficiently small. Later experiments showed that smaller step increments tend to produce results that are not very different from those reported here.

Optimum parameters for the single moving average rule are obtained from simulations on prior period data with different lengths of the moving average ranging from 2 to 50 days with an increment of 1. For the double moving average rule, simulations are based on a short moving average length ranging from 2 to 30 days and a long moving average length ranging from 20 to 50 days, both with a step increment of 1. Cases where the short moving average is longer than the long moving average (e.g., 30 for the shorter and 20 for the longer moving average) are excluded.

4C. Short Sales, the Interest Rate Differential, and Risk

No Short Sales Allowed

Short sales are an integral part of many studies of technical analysis. That is, when a sell signal is triggered, not only does the investor sell his/her long position in the asset, but s/he also goes short on that asset by an amount equal to the long position being closed. The reasoning is that when a sell signal is triggered, the asset's price is expected to go down in the future. Short sales will enhance the profit opportunities for the investor. This book, however, does not take short sales into consideration for two reasons. First, this study deals only with spot exchange rates and assumes that all transactions are done in spot exchange markets where there are no explicit margin or short positions. Second, as Sweeney (1981, 1986a 1988) argues, short sales do not affect the direction but only the magnitude of the results. He argues that short sales essentially magnify profits when the rule is profitable and amplify losses when the rule is not: If an unleveraged, no shorting, rule does (not) beat buy-and-hold, little is learned by having buy-and-hold's inferiority (superiority) magnified by leverage. Further, when the X-statistic in the case where short-sales are allowed is constructed, the associated t-value of this X-statistic is the same as the t-value of the X-statistic under the assumption of no short-sales. That is, short-sales amplify the X-statistic and its standard error to twice their original values and leave the t-value unchanged (Sweeney 1986a).

Adjusting for the Interest Rate Differential

In principle, the speculations reported in later chapters involve switching funds from overnight Euro-dollar deposits (the risk-free asset for a U.S. investor) to Euro-deposits denominated in the currency on which the investor is speculating. In practice, the interest rates on the Euro-deposits are neglected in the results in later chapters. This subsection explains why these rates are neglected and why such neglect is not very important.

Speculation using trading rules generally results in some periods where the speculator is not in the speculative asset. If the funds are simply allowed to lie idle in such periods, no earnings are obtained from these funds. This leads some authors to the rule that when funds are not in the speculative asset, they are always invested in short-term interest–earning assets. In the case of speculation in the foreign exchange market, the speculations reported below are calculated as though the investor holds foreign currency when s/he is in the market and the dollar when out of the market. Both currencies are noninterest earning. Following the above line of reasoning about not letting assets lie idle when they could be earning, funds should be invested in a foreign short-term asset when the investor is in the foreign currency. Similarly, funds should be converted into a dollar short-term asset when the investor is out of the foreign asset. For the type of speculation discussed here, reasonable short-term assets are overnight Eurocurrency deposits.

To obtain results under the assumption that funds in either currency are always invested in Euro-deposits rather than cash requires data on interest rates on such deposits. In terms of daily exchange rate speculation, daily time-series data on overnight Euro-deposit rates would have to be readily available, and ideally they should be quotes for the time of the day corresponding to the exchange rate data. Unfortunately, such data are not readily available. It is hard to gather high quality, matching data on overnight rates for all 15 countries studied here. In this book, therefore, the interest-rate differential effects are omitted.

Past empirical studies show that the results are not economically or statistically significantly different whether or not the interest-rate differentials are incorporated into the X-statistics. These results indicate that including the interest rate differential does not significantly change the *relative* performance between the trading rule and buy-and-hold, although it may substantially change the average return on each of the two. Sweeney (1986a), for instance, finds that interest earnings do not have much effect on filter rule results for the case of the dollar-Deutsche mark exchange rate; an update of Sweeney (1986a) by Mori and Murray (1990) shows that for five currencies where they were able to obtain interest–rate differentials, the profits with and without the differentials were very similar.[1] A similar conclusion can be drawn by comparing the studies by Dooley and Shafer (1976, 1983), which accounted for the effects of interest-rate differentials, with the results reported in Logue, Sweeney, and Willett (1978) and Sweeney (1986a), which assume funds are held in cash.

On a theoretical level, Sweeney (1986a) shows that including the interest-rate differential can affect the X-statistic only when the average differential on days "in" the foreign currency is different from the average differential on total days. In practice, these two average differentials appear to be quite close to each other for exchange rate speculation; thus omitting the differential in empirical work is a great convenience that has no important effects on results.

Can Risk Explain Measured Speculative Profits?

As mentioned in Chapter 2, a number of past studies have found that filter rule profits from the foreign exchange market are significantly greater than those of buy-and-hold, even when transaction costs are taken into account. Some authors argue that the measured profits are spurious because the filter rule returns are riskier than buy-and-hold's. Cornell and Dietrich (1978), for instance, use estimated betas based on the Capital Asset Pricing Model to adjust for these risks. Using the Standard and Poor 500 as a surrogate for a world market portfolio, they found that the estimated betas are extremely small and only one of them is significant. They argue that the risk of implementing filter rules in the foreign exchange market cannot be captured by the model. Levich's (1979) survey article also urges that returns on filter rules in excess of buy-and-hold should be adjusted for the extra risk due to the implementation of the rule; typically the use of CAPM is suggested.

Sweeney (1982, 1986a) points out that the use of the CAPM with constant risk premix to adjust for filter rule riskiness is not relevant. The CAPM can explain the risk attached to both filter rule and buy-and-hold returns. It cannot, however, explain the risk associated with the return on filter rules in excess of buy-and-hold if the currency's beta and the ex ante risk premium on the market are constant. According to the CAPM, the extra risk of implementing the filter rule is unsystematic risk, and the expected return on bearing this risk is zero. Moreover, any significant return on filter rules in excess of buy-and-hold leads to rejection of the CAPM. The X-test described in Chapter 3 is a better test of whether excess returns to speculation are indeed nonzero and, given that a risk premium is time constant, the separate question of a risk premium for speculation does not arise. This general conclusion holds for a wide variety of asset pricing models, including APMs, the Merton (1973) intertemporal CAPM, the Breeden (1979) consumption based asset pricing model, and others as long as risk premia are constant over time.

Time-varying risk premia may, however, be an explanation for measured returns to speculation, as Chapter 11 discusses in some detail.

4D. Transactions Costs

Due to the lack of data on bid and ask prices, estimates of the actual transactions costs reported in later chapters are not obtainable. Following many studies on foreign exchange peculation, transactions costs of one eighth of 1 percent per round trip are assumed throughout this book, and transactions in later chapters are shown as number of round trips (see Sweeney 1986a; Sweeney and Lee 1990). When compared to past studies of transactions costs in the foreign exchange market, this level of transaction cost is probably a good, nonoptimistic estimate of the average transactions cost. McCormick (1975) reports average transactions costs based on bid-ask spreads during 1970 to 1974 to be 0.0243 percent, 0.0400 percent, and 0.0281 percent for the British pound, Deutsche mark, and Canadian dollar, respectively. These are all lower than the one eighth of 1 percent used below. Even the highest bid-ask spread in his period of study, which is 0.0684 for the British pound, is lower than the one used in this study. Transactions costs based on bid-ask spreads during the pre-floating period are even lower. This bid-ask spread, of course, does not include brokerage fees; but the cost of brokerage fees is very small (approximately one–sixteenth of 1 percent per round-trip). Adjusting for the brokerage fee, then, the transactions costs for the British pound, Deutsche mark, and Canadian dollar are 0.03055 percent, 0.04625 percent, and 0.03435 percent, which are still lower than one eighth of 1 percent. Further, large transactors or banks operating on their own account can avoid brokerage fees.

A more recent study of transactions costs is that of Frenkel and Levich (1977). They estimate transactions costs through the concept of triangular arbitrage.[2] According to their interpretation, these estimates incorporate all relevant transactions costs such as brokerage fees, time costs, subscription costs, etc. Based on their method, the transaction costs during the floating period of 1973 to 1975 for British pound are 0.523 percent when Deutsche mark is used as the intermediate currency, and 0.438 percent when the Canadian dollar is alternatively used. These estimates are much bigger than those of other studies.

McCormick (1979) criticizes Frenkel and Levich's estimates on the ground that their data do not satisfy "the simultaneity criterion." That is, the data on these exchange rates were not gathered at exactly the same time. There are nine hours of time-lag between the collection of these data, which introduces biases into their estimates. Using better quality data, where there is no time-lag, McCormick's estimate of transactions costs for the

British pound during April 26, 1976 to October 22, 1976 is only 0.09 percent, using the Canadian dollar as the intermediary. However, due to the lack of simultaneous data when using the Deutsche mark as the intermediate currency, 0.182 percent is the best estimate which still contains one hour time-lag. Sweeney (1986a) interpolates this transactions cost based on McCormick's work when data were collected at exactly the same time, to be approximately 0.104 percent. In these cases, therefore, estimates based on triangular arbitrage are still lower than the one eighth of 1 percent used in this study.

The transactions costs mentioned above are valid for foreign exchange brokers, investors with large accounts, or big companies involved in international trades or multinational firms. For a small investor, however, the level of transactions costs is difficult to estimate. This may vary according to the broker or the bank that the investor deals with as well as the relationship between the investor and the broker. The prices quoted by different brokers may and are likely to vary considerably, depending upon the broker's expectations as well as the broker's position in the currency.[3] It is possible that transactions costs may be so high as to completely eliminate all speculative profits for small investors. For a small investor with a $10,000 investment, for instance, the buying price (i.e., the price at which foreign exchange brokers are willing to buy) for one Deutsche mark on November 20, 1986, was $0.5810, and the selling price (i.e., the price at which a currency is sold by foreign exchange brokers) was $0.6090. The spread between these prices yields the transactions costs of approximately 4.7 percent per round–trip.[4] Similarly, on the same date, the quoted buying and selling prices for one British pound were $1.74 and $1.82, respectively, which amounts to transactions costs of 4.4 percent per round–trip.[5] For smaller investors, transactions costs are undoubtedly higher than this. For a purchase or sale of $500 value, the transactions costs are approximately 0.03 to 0.04 percent higher than those of a purchase or sale of $10,000 value. And for a purchase or sale of less than $500, transactions costs can be expected to be 0.05 percent more.[6] These figures of transactions costs for small investors are so high that it is clearly not fruitful for small investors to engage in foreign exchange speculation.

Although the transactions costs used in this study appear to be quite relevant, it cannot be denied that differences in transactions costs may change the conclusions. Therefore, sensitivity analyses of the effect of changes in transactions costs on the results are performed. The sensitivity analyses look at the range of transactions costs that will not change the significance of the current results. There are two possible ways that changes in transactions costs may alter the results. First, they may change the ex post optimum parameter sets found in the prior periods. Because these optimum parameter sets are used to speculate in the corresponding subperiod, changes in these sets may substantially alter the subperiod results.

Suppose that the optimum parameter set of a trading rule found in the prior period yields adjusted and unadjusted X-statistics of UX and AX with the incurred average transactions cost, computed at one eighth of 1 percent per round trip, of T dollars per $100 investment per day. For any other nonoptimum rule that yields the unadjusted X-statistic of UX' and average transactions cost of T' per day to become the realized optimum, its corresponding adjusted X-statistic should be at least equal to AX. This requires that the per round–trip transactions cost has to be changed (increased or decreased) from T to t such that,

$$UX' - 8\,T't = UX - 8\,Tt.$$

Thus, the sensitivity range of the per round–trip transactions cost can be found by analyzing the corresponding t of all the current nonoptimum parameter sets. The upper bound of the sensitivity range is given by the minimum of t - T for all t > T, because any per round–trip transaction cost higher than this will replace the current optimum by the solution in its neighborhood that yields UX'. Similarly, the lower bound of the sensitivity range is given by the minimum of T - t for all t < T.

The second way that changes in transactions costs may change results is that they may alter the statistical significance of the subperiod test results. Higher transactions costs will, of course, reduce the adjusted X-statistics and hence the statistical significance of the results. The reverse is true for lower transactions costs. In the case of subperiod results, we define Tmax to be the maximum per round-trip transactions cost that will retain the statistical significance of the X-statistics after adjusting for the average transactions cost per $100 investment per day. Let SDX be the standard deviation of X; then Tmax for the 95 percent confidence level is

$$Tmax = (UX - 1.96SDX)/8T.$$

Tmax will be positive for all UX that are statistically significant at the 95 percent confidence level and negative for all UX that are not statistically significant. By comparing Tmax with one eighth of 1 percent, we can measure the sensitivity of the significance of profits to changes in transactions costs per round–trip.

4E. Data and Period of Study

The exchange rate data used in this study were provided by the Board of Governors of the Federal Reserve System. These are noon quotes and are averages of reports for several large U.S. banks. The data were cleaned and double-checked with the data reported in the International Monetary Fund's *International Financial Statistics* monthly bulletin. Fifteen currencies are used in this study: the Australian dollar, Austrian schilling, Belgian franc, British pound, Canadian dollar, Danish krone, Deutsche mark, French franc, Italian lire, Japanese yen, Netherlands guilder, Norwegian krone, Swiss franc, Swedish krona, and Spanish peseta.

For each currency, there are 2,974 daily observations from July 1, 1974, to May 14, 1986. We subdivided these data into prior periods and subperiods before we did any empirical work at all. Thus, the results in Chapters 5–9 are not contaminated by data mining for this study. (Needless to say, the choices made at each step in the study were influenced by previous work on technical analysis; to the extent our data overlap with those of previous studies, there is data mining. In Chapter 10 some experiments are performed to see how sensitive results are to the choices made before any data analysis was done.) The last 2,000 observations are the period over which we look for speculative profits and are divided into two subperiods of 1,000 observations each. Subperiod 1 contains the data from May 22, 1978 (observation number 975), to May 18, 1982 (observation number 1,974). Subperiod 2 contains the data from May 19, 1982 (observation number 1,975), to May 14, 1986 (observation number 2,974). Each subperiod contains data for approximately four years.

Observation numbers 75 to 974, a total of 900 trading days, are used as prior period 1, the data of which are used to generate the ex post optimum parameters that are used as the ex ante optimum parameters for subperiod 1, as described in Section 4B. Observation numbers 1 to 75 are used to generate the moving average necessary to perform moving average trading rule simulations for prior period 1. Prior period 2 contains the data from observation number 1,075 to 1,974, again a total of 900 observations. Chapter 10 discusses how results change if prior periods and subperiods of different lengths are used.

Table 4 summarizes the start and end dates and observation numbers as well as the total number of observations of each subperiod and prior period.

4F. Summary

This book reports on simulations of both single-currency speculation and multi-currency speculation to test for efficiency in spot foreign exchange markets. 15 currencies are used. In Chapter 5 we present results for single-currency speculation for all 15 currencies, using three popular technical trading rules whose parameters are tailored to each currency. Simple averages of these speculations give equally weighted portfolios that are then analyzed in Chapter 5 for each of the rules considered. These individualized rules are also used in Chapter 6 to give buy and sell signals in an alternative portfolio approach that gives variably weighted portfolios.

In Chapter 7 we consider speculation on two types of indexes. First is the optimally weighted index, where the optimum weights are obtained from the Markowitz-Sharpe model in the prior period to form the index for use in the following subperiod. Under this model, a basket of currencies is bought or sold simultaneously when buy or sell signals based on movements in the index are triggered. Best parameters values for each index are found by prior period searches, just as when individual currencies are considered. Second, the same type of approach is also used on an equally weighted index.

In Chapter 8 we explore the portfolio upgrading approach, which uses ranks based on relative strength indices to enhance overall portfolio performance.

Simulations are performed for all of these approaches to speculation. The hypothetical investor searches during the prior period for the best parameter values for each of the technical rules; the prior period does not overlap with the following speculative subperiod. These best rule parameters are used by the investor to speculate in the following subperiod. If the market processes information efficiently, the average return on this simulated speculation should only randomly outperform the average return of a simple buy-and-hold strategy. If the market shows some informational inefficiency that both can be detected and persists into later periods, however, there is some hope of making statistically significant profits from using technical analysis.

Notes

1. The currencies were the British pound, Canadian dollar, Dutch guilder, German mark and Japanese yen. For every currency, the 1, 2 and 3 percent Alexander filters gave significant profits (save for the British pound and the 3 percent rule).

2. For a detailed explanation of triangular arbitrage, see Levich (1979b).

3. It is interesting to note that the variation in prices quoted by different brokers may be substantial. For instance, the selling price of the Japanese yen quoted by Deak International in Los Angeles on November 19, 1987, for $10,000 worth or more was $0.006944, and the buying price posted by L.A. Currency Exchange at Los Angeles International Airport for $500 worth or more was 0.0071. This reflects a substantial difference in the expectations of the two brokers. In this case, assuming

that transactions can be performed without delay, risk-free profits could have been made by buying Yen from Deak International and immediately selling it to L.A. Currency Exchange.

4. The prices for Deutsche marks are based on the quotations given by the American Foreign Exchange in Los Angeles. The transactions costs are computed as percent of the mid-point price.

5. Based on quotations given by the Associated Foreign Exchange Inc. in Beverly Hills.

6. This is approximated by comparing the prices quoted by the American Foreign Exchange and the Associated Foreign Exchange Inc. with the prices posted on the foreign exchange booth in Los Angeles International Airport by L.A. Currency Exchange.

FIGURE 2
Optimum Parameter Search Model

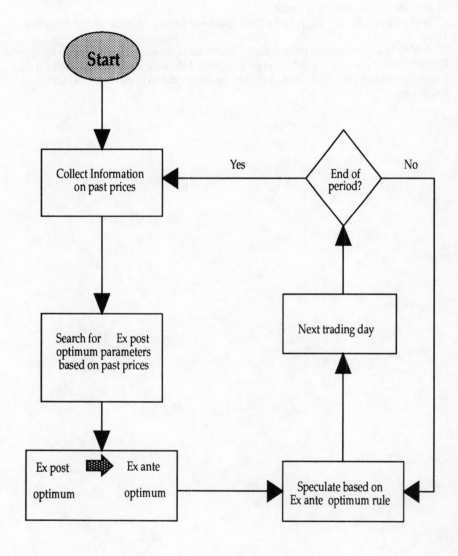

TABLE 4   Number of Observations, Starting and Ending Dates, and
Observation Numbers of the Two Subperiods and Prior Periods.

| PERIOD | DATE | | OBSERVATION NUMBERS | | TOTAL NUMBERS OF |
	START	END	START	END	OBSERVATIONS
Subperiod 1	May 22, 1978	May 18, 1982	975	1974	1000
Subperiod 2	May 19, 1982	May 14, 1986	1975	2974	1000
Prior Period 1	Oct. 16, 1974	May 19, 1978	75	974	900
Prior Period 2	Oct. 13, 1978	May 18, 1982	1075	1974	900

Note: The total number of available observations is 2974.

Source: Board of the Governor of the Federal Reserve System.

PART 3

Performance of Technical Strategies

5

Equally Weighted Portfolios of Currencies, with Rules Tailored for Each Currency

Of the four approaches this book uses to combine individual currencies into portfolios to gain the benefits of diversification, two approaches use rules with parameters individually tailored for each currency—the equally weighted portfolio approach of this chapter and Chapter 6's variably weighted portfolio approach. This chapter presents simulation results for speculation on each of the 15 currencies studied in this book when an individually tailored rule is used on each currency and the buy/sell decision for each currency is independent of what is happening with other currencies' positions. It also discusses the results of forming these single-currency speculations into an equally weighted portfolio of currencies. The single-currency results also form the raw material of Chapter 6's discussion of the variably weighted portfolio approach to speculation, because this portfolio approach uses the same buy/sell signals from rules tailored for each currency but acts on these signals in a way that gives a portfolio with variable weights.

This chapter gives results for speculation under three techniques of technical analysis, namely, the Alexander filter, the double moving average, and the single moving average rules, and compares the performances of these techniques.

For brevity, some technical terms are used throughout in interpreting statistical results; Section 5A discusses and defines these terms. In addition, the section clarifies units of measurement and the general confidence level used for statistical tests.

In Section 5B, we present the ex post best rules for each currency from analysis of the prior period's data. Two points stand out. First, the best rule parameters for a given currency in different prior periods are apparently different. This means either that the true underlying best parameters for given classes of rules are shifting through time or that the exchange markets are so noisy that the true best rules are not easily estimated. Either way, the ex post best rule in one period is not likely to be the realized best rule in the following subperiod where the rule is tested. Second, the ex post best rule parameters obtained from the prior period data are generally not sensitive to small changes in the level of transactions costs.

In Sections 5C, 5D, and 5E we analyze the simulation results for single-currency speculations using the Alexander filter, double moving average, and single moving average techniques, respectively. For some currencies, the prior period best rules still work remarkably well in the subsequent subperiods, and speculation in these currencies is highly profitable. This is particularly true for the first subperiod of the study. The performances of the best rules seem to decline in the second subperiod, however. For the whole period of the study, the average results of speculating in the 15 currencies, as indicated by the equally weighted portfolio, show that these rules significantly outperform the buy-and-hold strategy.

In Section 5F we introduce the concept of the mixed rule, which bases speculation in each currency on the global best rules among the three technical trading techniques, based on prior period searches. As did the three technical trading techniques discussed in Sections 5C to 5E, the mixed-rule technique seems to work very well for some currencies, and the equally weighted portfolio results indicate that the rules are significantly superior to buy-and-hold in the first subperiod and for the whole period.

Section 5G is an analysis of the sensitivity of the statistical significance of the profits in the previous sections to change in the level of transactions costs. The profits' statistical significance is generally insensitive to small changes in transactions costs.

In Section 5H we compare the performances of the different technical trading techniques, using the adjusted X-statistic as the benchmark. In this section the Wilcoxon matched-pair signed-rank test is used to judge the statistical significance of the differences in the performances of these technical trading techniques. On the basis of the equally weighted portfolio, the performances of the mixed rule and the double moving average are significantly better than that of the Alexander filter. Not surprisingly, this superiority disappears when the tests are performed on each individual currency; nonparametric tests find no significant difference between adjusted X-statistics under the single moving average technique and adjusted X-statistics under the other techniques.

Section 5I is a summary of the results and discusses some implications and possible explanations of the results.

5A. Terminology and Scalings

Before turning to the empirical results, it is useful to discuss some of the terminology used in this and the following chapters, as well as the scaling systems of some of the parameters and variables used.

1. For brevity, the term "best rule parameter" or simply "best parameter" is frequently used. This is the ex post best parameter for a given rule, found from searching over prior period data, and it is used as the ex ante best rule parameter in the following subperiod. Thus, the term "best rule parameter" is used in the ex post sense for prior period results and in the ex ante sense in the following subperiod.

2. The term "adjusted X-statistic" is defined as the X-statistic adjusted for the incurred transactions costs. "Unadjusted X-statistic" refers to the actual value of the X-statistic before the deduction of the transactions costs. The level of transactions costs, as discussed in Chapter 4, is assumed to be one eighth of 1 percent per round-trip transaction. In a similar vein, the net profit after adjusting for the transactions costs is called the "adjusted profit." (In the tables below, "Number of Transactions" refers to the number of round–trip transactions.)

3. As previously discussed, the X-statistic can be viewed as the average return on the trading rule in excess of the average return on the comparable buy-and-hold strategy. The phrase "excess return on the trading rule" is used interchangeably with the X-statistic. Following the same line of reasoning, the phrase "excess return on the trading rule, adjusted for transactions costs" is used as equivalent to the adjusted X-statistic. Further, as explained in Chapter 3, the X-statistics can be viewed as risk-adjusted rates of profits and are sometimes so referred to below.

4. All average returns, including the X-statistics, are in percent per trading day. Multiplying the entry by 250 approximately rescales them to percent per year (on average, there are about 252 trading days in a year).

5. Speculative profit is the total profit obtained from speculative activity; it is defined as the difference between the final dollar value of the assets held (i.e., both the U.S. and foreign currencies) at the end of the period and the initial dollar investment. Profit is measured in U.S. dollars, and the initial investment is assumed to be $100. It should be noted, however, that this measure of profit is different from *risk-adjusted* profit, as discussed in Chapter 3. Direct comparison between this speculative profit and the buy-and-hold profit may be misleading because the speculating investor is in the market only a portion of the time; hence, this speculative profit involves only a portion of the risk relative to buy-and-hold.[1]

6. Unless indicated otherwise, the confidence level for statistical tests is 95 percent. Hence, whenever an estimated statistic is stated to be significant without an explicit confidence level, the 95 percent level is tacitly used.

7. Results on X-statistics and profits for the period as a whole are simple averages of results for subperiods save for standard deviations and associated statistics, which are derived from subperiods under the assumption of no serial correlation. In particular, this means that whole period results assume that the speculator sells off his/her position at the end of day 1,000,

changes to the new rule parameters given by the second prior period and buys back in on day 1,001. (Some of the implications of this assumption are discussed in Chapter 10.)

5B. Best Rules in the Prior Periods

Tables 5 to 7 show the prior period results for the ex post best rules (i.e., rules that yield the highest adjusted X- statistics) for all 15 currencies under the three technical trading techniques used in this book. The average returns and the X-statistics are reported in percent per day. Not surprisingly, most of these best rules work quite well, ex post. For the Alexander filter technique, these best rules as judged by the adjusted X–statistic beat buy-and-hold in every case and significantly beat buy-and-hold in 20 out of the 30 cases given by 15 currencies and two prior periods. The results are even better for the best rules under the double moving average technique; the adjusted X-statistics are positive in every case and are statistically significant at the 95 percent confidence level in 25 out of the 30 cases. For the single moving average technique, the ex post best rules seem to perform less well in comparison to the other two trading rules; although all adjusted X–statistics are positive, only 14 out of 30 cases are significant.[2] Most of these best rules under the three technical trading techniques yield positive adjusted profits in both prior periods; the buy-and-hold strategy, as shown in Table 8, mostly yields losses—6 out of 15 currencies in prior period 1 and all of the currencies in prior period 2. In any case, the trading rule profits, net of transactions costs, are considerably higher than buy-and-hold. These results, of course, are not surprising because these best rules were selected from searches over a range of parameters under each technical trading technique, as discussed in Chapter 4.

Note that the fact that many of the foreign currencies fell on net in the first prior period—and all fell on net in the second—by itself has nothing to do with the value of the X- statistic. That is, there is no expectation that the X-statistic should show technical rules beating a market just because it was ex post a down market. Examination of the formulas in Sections 3B or 3E shows that in a falling market the technical trading rules beat buy-and-hold only if on average the rules have the investor out of the market on days when the currency falls more than average and have the investor in on days when the currency falls less than average; indeed, this property is one of the strengths of the X-statistic approach.

With the exception of the Spanish peseta under the Alexander filter technique, the best rules for each currency obtained from the two prior periods are different. In most cases, the first prior period's best rules are those with higher filter sizes or longer lengths of moving averages, which generate fewer transactions and hence lower transactions costs than the best rules in the second prior period. Taking these results at face value, this implies that the profitably exploitable patterns in the first prior period tend to follow cycles that are longer than those of the second prior period. The average number of transactions (in round-trips) of the first prior period's best rules is 17.13, or 34.26 in one-way transactions, which means that the investor will get in and out of the market, on the average, every 900/34.26 = 26.27 trading days. In the second prior period, however, the best rules put the investor in and out of the market, on the average, every 16.75 trading days. This is more than 36 percent more transactions than in the first prior period.

The best rule for one prior period is apparently not the best rule for the other prior period. Nevertheless, simply following these best rules could have earned substantial returns in excess of buy-and-hold if these best rules were known ex ante. Moreover, the fact that one prior period's best rules are different from those of the next prior period does not necessarily imply that they will not work. The problem, then, is whether these best rules still outperform buy-and-hold when used on an ex ante basis in the following subperiods. The next four sections answer this question.

It should also be noted that the best rule parameters generated by different technical trading techniques may substantially differ from each other with regard to the implicit patterns of exploitable profits. The best parameter under the Alexander filter for the Swiss franc in the first prior period, for instance, generates 100 round-trip transactions, and the best parameters under the double moving average generate only eight round-trip transactions. Both of these best rule parameters yield significant adjusted X-statistics at the 95 percent confidence level. This seems to indicate that there is more than one exploitable pattern in this market. Perhaps there is more than one factor that generates the price patterns. For example, one might attribute the shorter cyclical patterns, such as those detected by the Alexander filter in the case of the Swiss franc, to government intervention that "leans against the wind."

Even so, it is apparent that this is not the only cause of profit opportunities in these markets. For instance, the single moving average rule displays a pattern where significant profits can be made from the rule that put the investor in and out of the market for the Canadian dollar every 16 trading days in the first prior period. One might assign these results to the "leaning against the wind" strategy followed by the Canadian authorities. Although this reasoning is plausible, it should be noted that the Alexander filter also displays a profitably exploitable pattern that generates only eight round-trip transactions over the 900 trading days in this market. Thus, the Alexander filter put the investor in and out of the market approximately every 56 trading days, which is almost three months. One might argue that it is not likely, however, that this pattern is generated by the "leaning against the wind" strategy alone, for it is not likely that the Canadian authorities would pursue this strategy for that long a period of time. In this view, it is more likely that these observed profit exploitable patterns are generated by a combination of factors. While trading rules can detect these strikingly different patterns, they are not informative with regard to the factors generating the patterns, nor can they distinguish among the effects of the factors.

It is also worth noting that different exchange rates exhibit different types of patterns, not only on the average length of the cycles across the currencies but regarding the variability of the length of cycles within each currency. For example, the Alexander filter seems to work better for the Australian dollar than the moving average rules, which indicates that the price pattern in this market seems to be of a constant- amplitude cycle—see the interpretation in Chapter 4 of the single moving average rule as an Alexander filter rule with variable filter sizes. The moving average rule, however, tends to perform better for the Belgian franc. Thus, one might interpret the results as saying that the Belgian franc follows a variable-amplitude cycle. Although using the Alexander filter that assumes a fixed filter size works quite well in this market, using the single moving average, which assumes variable-amplitude cycles, works even better. This is also the case for the Danish krone.

Tables 9 to 11 show sensitivity analyses of the effects of transactions costs on these best rules—the issue is whether changes in transactions costs lead to different best rules for the prior periods. Generally speaking, the optimum rules chosen are quite insensitive to the level of transactions costs. Several of the lower bounds are negative; in these cases, the corresponding optimum rules are totally insensitive to the reduction in the level of transactions costs, because negative transactions costs do not make any economic sense. In the cases where the lower bounds are nonnegative, these lower bounds are generally small, which reflects the insensitivity of the best rules to reductions in transactions costs. A small decrease in transactions costs, say from one eighth to one ninth or one tenth of 1 percent will change the optimum rule in only one case: the French franc under the single moving average in prior period 2.

The optimum rules are more sensitive to increases in transactions costs. Nevertheless, the upper bounds of these sensitivity ranges are generally high—some of them can be indefinitely increased. This indicates that small increases in the level of transactions costs in general will not change the optimum rule parameters shown in Tables 5 to 7. For instance, a rise in transactions costs from one eighth to one seventh of 1 percent will change only one out of the 90 best rules given by the three trading techniques, 15 currencies, and two subperiods. In 70 out of the 90 cases, the best rules will not change even when transactions costs are doubled from one eighth to one fourth of 1 percent.

5C. Out-of-Sample Results Using Alexander Filter Rules

Table 12 reports out-of-sample results from speculation under Alexander filter rules in both subperiods and the whole period. Some of the best Alexander filter rule parameters from the prior periods seem to work in the corresponding subperiods. This is true even when transactions costs are taken into account. The rules beat buy-and-hold significantly for four currencies in the first subperiod, as indicated by the positive, significant adjusted X-statistics; these currencies are the Belgian franc, Danish krone, Japanese yen, and Spanish peseta. For the second subperiod, however, there are only two currencies, namely the Belgian franc and Netherlands guilder, for which the best rules significantly outperform buy-and-hold. In most cases, however, the X-statistics, adjusted for transactions costs, are positive. The significant adjusted X-statistics range between 0.02292 and 0.03682, which means that the range of the average profits earned from these speculations, in excess of buy-and-hold, is between 0.02292 percent and 0.03682 percent per day, or approximately 5.738 percent and 9.205 percent per year.

As Table 13 shows, the buy-and-hold strategy yields only small positive dollar profits in 2 out of 15 currencies in the first subperiod. Implementing the filter rule, however, earns positive dollar profits, net of transactions costs, for 12 currencies in the first subperiod, as Table 12 shows. In what was essentially a down market, the filter rules earned substantial, positive dollar profits, and for bearing only about half the risk of buy-and-hold (because the column "Percent of Days out of the Market" in Table 12 averages about 0.5). It might be argued that the filters look good relative to buy-and-hold simply because they get the investor out of what was ex post a down market; this argument, however, implies smaller negative profits, not positive profits. Further, as noted in Section 5B, there is no inherent tendency for the risk-adjusted profits of the X-statistic to be positive in down markets. For the second subperiod, five currencies yield positive dollar profits under the buy-and-hold strategy as opposed to ten currencies under filter techniques. Again, adjusted filter rule profits are, in most cases, higher than those of buy-and-hold.

When the results of the two subperiods are pooled, as indicated by the whole-period results in Table 12, 6 of the 15 currencies yield significant profits, net of transactions costs, in excess of buy-and-hold, as measured by the adjusted X-statistic. These currencies are the Austrian schilling, Belgian franc, Deutsche mark, French franc, Japanese yen, and Netherlands guilder.

The average returns on speculating in these currencies range from 0.01585 percent to 0.02423 percent per day or 3.963 percent to 6.058 percent per year. For the Belgian franc, this is not surprising because filter rules outperform buy-and-hold in both subperiods. For the other five currencies, however, the whole period results imply that even though the rules do not seem to beat buy-and-hold significantly for some subperiods, the positive X-statistics are high enough that they are marginally nontrivial. This is particularly true in the case of the Austrian schilling, for which neither of the two subperiod results are significant at the 95 percent level, but the whole period result indicates that the rules outperform buy-and-hold significantly.

The variance of percentage rates of change of exchange rates generally increased from subperiod 1 to subperiod 2, as Table 13 shows. The variance rose for every currency save the Austrian schilling and the Japanese yen, and the average variance rose from 0.40066 to 0.54316, or by a factor of 1.36, so that the average standard deviation rose by a factor of 1.16. The increase in variance would by itself reduce t-statistics on average by about one sixth. This result applies to the other technical rules discussed below.

Results on single-currency speculation can be aggregated by forming an equally weighted portfolio, as in Sweeney (1986a, 1988). The X-statistic of this portfolio is simply the average of the X-statistics of the individual currencies. The variance of this portfolio X-statistic is given by

$$\sigma_X^2 = (1/N^2)\, I'\, (VCX)I,$$

where VCX is the variance-covariance matrix of the X-statistics of individual currencies, n the number of currencies in the portfolio, and I the unit column vector. This portfolio X-test gives a more powerful test than the simple X-test for individual currencies in the sense that the sampling variability of individual currencies tends to cancel out through portfolio formation. Further, the number of observations in the portfolio X-tests is amplified by the number of currencies held in the portfolio, which tends to reduce the sampling variance of the portfolio X-statistics as long as the co-movements of these X-statistics are less than perfectly correlated.

Table 12's results on an equally weighted portfolio of these single-currency speculations indicate that following these best rules for all 15 currencies is highly profitable on average in both subperiods and the period as a whole, as measured by adjusted X-statistics. The average yearly rates of risk-adjusted profit on the portfolio of these single-currency speculations are 3.578 percent, 2.561 percent, and 3.070 percent for subperiods 1 and 2 and the whole period, respectively. The risk-adjusted profits are statistically significant in the first subperiod, but not in the second subperiod. For the whole period, however, following these rules gives highly significant profits.

It is interesting to decompose the fall in portfolio t-statistics between the two subperiods, from 2.94 to 1.47. The adjusted X-statistic is approximately 40 percent higher in the first subperiod [(.0143 /.0102 - 1) 100], and the standard error is approximately 43 percent higher in the second [(.00696/ .004864 - 1) 100]. If the standard error had stayed the same from the first to second subperiod, the t-statistic in the second subperiod would have been 2.10. In general, the fall in significance noted in this book for the second subperiod is due in part to the higher standard errors of the second subperiod.

5D. Out-of-Sample Results Using Double Moving Average Rules

Speculative results under double moving average rules in the first subperiod are highly inconsistent with the market efficiency hypothesis. As Table 14 shows, the adjusted X-statistics of all currencies are positive. These positive adjusted X-statistics are statistically significant for 7 out of the 15 currencies studied, 3 of them at the 99 percent level and the other 4 at the 95 percent level. These currencies include the Austrian schilling, Belgian franc, Deutsche mark, French franc, Japanese yen, Netherlands guilder, and Spanish peseta. The average returns from speculating in these currencies, in excess of the corresponding buy-and-hold returns, range from 0.01901 percent to 0.03259 percent per day or approximately 4.753 percent to 8.148 percent per year. In all cases, the trading rules' dollar profits are higher than the profits obtained from simple buy-and-hold strategies, even when transactions costs are taken into account, as can be seen by comparing the "Filter Rule Profit" column in Table 14 with the "Buy-and-Hold Profit" column in Table 13.

The speculative profits in the second subperiod, however, are less impressive. Although the adjusted X-statistics are positive in 13 out of 15 currencies, only one of these adjusted X-statistics is significant at the 95 percent level. This is the case of the Belgian Franc, with the adjusted X-statistic of 0.02437 percent per day, which amounts to a 6.093 percent average annual return in excess of buy-and-hold.

For the whole period, signs of inefficiencies still persist. Following the rules beats buy-and-hold significantly in seven currencies, namely, the Belgian franc, Deutsche mark, French franc, Italian lire, Japanese yen, Netherlands guilder, and Norwegian krone. The significant X-statistics range from 0.01660 percent to 0.02848 percent per day, or 4.15 percent to 7.12 percent per annum. Note that there are two currencies (the Italian lire and Norwegian krone) where the subperiods' results are not significant at the 95 percent level, but the whole period's results indicate significant, positive X-statistics. This is not very surprising because the positive X-statistics of these two currencies in both subperiods, even though not significant, are marginally nontrivial. The t-statistics of these two currencies in the first subperiod, for instance, are higher than 1.8. Therefore, when the results of the two subperiods are pooled, the higher degrees of freedom enable the test to reject the null hypothesis.

There are two currencies (the Austrian schilling and Spanish peseta), however, where the results in the first subperiod indicate significant X-statistics and the whole period results are not statistically significant at the 95 percent level. The reason for this is that the performance of the trading rules in these two currencies is so weak (though positive) in the second subperiod that the strong performances in the first subperiod are offset when the two subperiods are pooled.

The equally weighted portfolio under double moving average rules yields a significant X-statistic of 0.0179768 percent per day, or 4.494 percent per year in the first subperiod. This points out that following the rules to speculate in these 15 currencies is highly profitable on average in the first subperiod. For the second period, however, the average return on the trading rule, although it is about 2.7114 percent per year higher than that of buy-and-hold, is not statistically significant at the 95 percent level. Nevertheless, when the results in both subperiods are pooled, the adjusted X-statistic of .0144111 percent per day, or 3.603 percent per year, still shows that the double moving average rule significantly outperforms buy-and-hold for the average of these speculations.

5E. Out-of-Sample Results Using Single Moving Average Rules

Speculative returns from single moving average rules are less impressive than those from double moving average rules. These rules, however, would have performed remarkably well in a world with no transactions costs. Table 15 shows that in markets without transactions costs, the single moving average rule would have beaten buy-and-hold in 7 out of 15 currencies in both subperiods. As in past studies regarding trading rules (for example, Fama and Blume 1966), and unlike the cases of the Alexander filter and double moving average above, the single moving average technique generates so many transactions that the speculative profits obtained are eaten up by transactions costs. An important implication is that if we can constrain the single moving average rules to generate fewer transactions and at the same time yield approximately the same level of gross profits, we might be able to make profits even when transactions costs are taken into account. This is important when these single moving average rules are applied to speculation under the variably weighted portfolio approach in the next chapter.

After deducting transactions costs, following the single moving average rules yields significant profits in excess of buy-and-hold for only three currencies in the first subperiod and one currency in the second subperiod. As shown in Table 15, the adjusted X-statistics are significantly nonzero at the 99 percent level for the Belgian franc and the Japanese yen in the first subperiod. The excess returns from following the rules are, respectively, 0.03164 percent and 0.03092 percent per day, or 7.66 percent and 7.73 percent on an annual basis. The results for these two currencies in the second subperiod, although not significant, are positive and marginally nontrivial. The associated t-statistic for the Japanese yen, for instance, is 1.8794 which is close to the borderline of the 95 percent critical region. Thus, it is not surprising that the whole period results for these two currencies show that single moving average rules significantly beat buy-and-hold. The adjusted X-statistics for speculation in these two currencies are 0.02472 percent and 0.02446 percent per day for the Belgian franc and Japanese yen, respectively. These amount to an annual excess return of 6.18 percent and 6.12 percent and, according to the associated t-statistics, are highly significant even at the 99 percent confidence level.

For the French franc, single moving average rules significantly beat buy-and-hold for both subperiods. The X-statistics, adjusted for transactions costs, are 0.02012 percent and 0.02550 percent per day for subperiods 1 and 2. These amount to 5.155 percent and 6.375 percent per year and are statistically significant at the 95 percent level. For the whole period, the rules yield an X-statistic of 0.02281 percent per day, or 5.70 percent annually. This X-statistic is statistically significant at the 99 percent level.

The Deutsche mark and Netherlands guilder are the other two currencies that have significant X-statistics for the whole period results, even though subperiod results for the two currencies are statistically insignificant. This is not surprising because the subperiod results for these two currencies show that the associated t-statistics of the corresponding adjusted X-statistics are close to the borderline of the 95 percent critical region. Pooling the data from the two subperiods strengthens the tests through the increase in the degrees of freedom and hence allows us to reject the null hypothesis.

The equally weighted portfolio, following single moving average rules for all 15 currencies, is significantly profitable in the first subperiod. The average daily excess return on speculation in these 15 currencies, adjusted for transactions costs, is 0.01824 percent, which is equivalent to an average annual excess return of 3.467 percent. In the second subperiod, however, the average return on trading rule speculations in excess of buy-and-hold, even though it is 3.09 percent annually, is not statistically significant at the

95 percent level. In this case, the drop in significance is largely due to an increase in the standard error. For the whole period, the adjusted X-statistic is highly significant. The portfolio earns daily profits 0.01312 percent higher than buy-and-hold. This amounts to 3.28 percent excess returns per year.

5F. Out-of-Sample Speculation Using Mixed Rules

The previous three sections assume that the investor adopts only one kind of technical trading technique at a time. Section 5 C, for instance, assumes that for every currency the investor chooses the best rule parameters under the Alexander filter technique from the results in the prior period to speculate with in the subsequent subperiod, regardless of how well the other two techniques perform in the prior period for some of the currencies. This section, however, assumes that the investor uses all three types of technical analysis to search for the best rules. That is, if the prior period's best rule parameter under the Alexander filter technique yields a higher adjusted X-statistic than the other two techniques, the investor chooses this best rule under the Alexander filter technique to use in the following subperiod. In this case, therefore, the best rules used by the investor are actually the global best rules in the sense that they are the rules that perform the best in the prior period among all the rules under the three technical approaches. Hence, the technical trading approach used for a currency in one subperiod may be different from the technique used for the same currency in the other subperiod, and will generally differ across currencies for any one subperiod. Call this the "mixed-rule" technique.

Table 16 shows the results of these mixed rules. These global best rules tend to perform quite well, particularly in the first subperiod. Six currencies have significant adjusted X-statistics in the first subperiod and two currencies in the second subperiod. It should be noted that the two currencies that have significant adjusted X-statistics in the second subperiod also have significant adjusted X-statistics in the first subperiod, which may indicate the persistence of profit opportunities in these currencies. These two currencies are the Netherlands guilder and, once again, the Belgian franc. The significant adjusted X-statistics of these currencies range from 0.02720 percent to 0.03682 percent per day, or 6.8 percent to 9.205 percent per year, in subperiod 1, and 0.02437 percent to 0.02511 percent per day, or 6.093 percent to 6.278 percent per year, in subperiod 2.

The whole-period results indicate that when transactions costs are taken into consideration, mixed rules significantly outperform buy-and-hold for six currencies: the Belgian franc, British pound, Deutsche mark, French franc, Japanese yen, and Netherlands guilder. The daily speculative profits range from 0.01664 percent to 0.02801 percent higher than the daily profits from buy-and-hold. These are equivalent to excess returns of 4.16 percent to 7.0 percent per year.

The results under the mixed-rule technique for the equally weighted portfolio indicate that this approach works remarkably well in the first subperiod. The X-statistics, adjusted for transactions costs, are significantly positive at the 99 percent level. The average return on following the rules is 0.01861 percent per day, or 4.65 percent per year higher than the average return on buy-and-hold. For the second subperiod, however, the rules tend to generate so many transactions that the significant (unadjusted) X-statistic is substantially reduced due to transaction costs. Although the adjusted X-statistic is not statistically significant, it is marginally nontrivial; it is not surprising that when the results of the two subperiods are pooled the whole-period results strongly show that following the mixed rules beats the buy-and-hold strategy significantly. Following the rule for the whole period, on the average across the currencies, yields profits significantly higher than buy-and-hold at the 99 percent level. This excess profit amounted to 0.01463 percent per day, or 3.66 percent per year.

5G. The Effects of Changes in Transactions Costs on the Significance of the X–Statistics

Table 17 shows the results of sensitivity analysis of the effect of transactions costs on the statistical significance of the X-statistics. Each entry in Table 17 shows the maximum transactions costs (MTC) that gives statistical significance for the corresponding adjusted X-statistic at the 95 percent confidence level. A negative MTC implies that the X-statistic is not significant at 95 percent even before deducting the transactions costs. We therefore should be concerned only with the positive MTCs.

The asterisks in Table 17 indicate the cases where the adjusted X-statistics are significant at the 95 percent confidence level, with transactions costs evaluated at the base case one eighth of 1 percent per round–trip. Most of the MTCs of the cases with significant adjusted X-statistics are quite high. In the case of the Belgian franc in the first subperiod, for instance, the transactions costs can be larger than one third of 1 percent under the single moving average and one half of 1 percent under the Alexander filter and double moving average rule. Most impressive is the MTC for the Spanish peseta under the Alexander filter in the first subperiod; even transactions costs as high as 1.5 percent per round–trip leave the results significant. Broadly speaking, then, the sensitivity analysis results indicate that the statistical results from speculation are generally insensitive to small changes in transactions costs. If the transactions costs rise from one eighth to one sixth of 1 percent, for instance, only 3 out of these 50 significant results become insignificant.

For the equally weighted portfolio for the whole period, transactions costs can rise to as much as .34 of 1 percent for the double moving average, or .21 of 1 percent for the single moving average, rule and the trading rule profits are still statistically significant.

5H. Comparison of the Performance of Trading Techniques

The statistical significance of the adjusted X-statistics is summarized in Table 18. Out of the 15 cases given for 15 currencies, the trading rules under the Alexander filter, double moving average, single moving average, and mixed rule significantly outperform buy-and-hold, respectively, in four, seven, three and six cases in the first subperiod, and two, one, one and two cases in the second subperiod. The results tend to indicate that the double moving average and the mixed rule seem to perform better than the other two techniques, with the single moving average having the worst performance.

In addition, some techniques work for some currencies but other techniques do not work for the same currencies. For instance, in the first subperiod, the double moving average is the only technique that yields significant results for the Austrian schilling, and the Alexander filter works well for the Danish krone. Given these results, one might conclude that there are some differences in the performance between these technical trading techniques. Further analysis shows that these conjectures are at least partially correct. Based on the results from matched-pair nonparametric tests discussed below, the mixed rule and the double moving average techniques perform significantly better, in terms of the adjusted X-statistics, than the Alexander filter for the equally weighted portfolio results. These significant superiorities, however, vanish when the tests are conducted within each individual currency. The individual exchange rates are very noisy, however, so it is perhaps not surprising that differences in performance that can be detected for the equally weighted portfolio cannot be noticed in results for individual currencies.

Time series of the adjusted X-statistics of the speculations in each currency under the four techniques for the whole period were collected.[3] For each currency, one-on-one comparison between these four techniques requires the comparison of six matched pairs of the time series of the adjusted X-statistics. Wilcoxon matched-pair signed rank tests are conducted to see if the excess returns on speculation under each pair of techniques are different. In addition, a Friedman ANOVA is performed to test the joint hypothesis of no difference between the adjusted X-statistics obtained from these four technical trading rules.

Table 19 shows the results. The figures in parentheses indicate the significance level of the associated statistics. For all currencies, the Wilcoxon Z-scores indicate that there is no significant difference between the four technical trading techniques when applied to any single currency.[4] This is confirmed by the Chi-square tests given by the Friedman ANOVA. That is, even though there seem to be some differences between the performance of these trading techniques when applied to a currency, these differences are superficial from the statistical standpoint.

For the equally weighted portfolio of the 15 currencies, however, the differences between some of these technical trading techniques are nontrivial. The Wilcoxon Z–scores between the pairs of Alexander filter and double moving average rules and Alexander filter and mixed rules are significant at the 95 percent level (two-tailed p-value = 0.0165 and 0.0232 respectively). These results imply that for equally weighted portfolios of these 15 currencies, the double moving average and the mixed rule tend to perform significantly better than the Alexander filter.[5] On the face of it, it appears advisable for an investor to adopt the mixed rule or the double moving average techniques rather than the Alexander filter technique. In other words, even though significant differences between the performances are not found in the speculation in any single currency, a Bayesian investor, being informed about the average results, would be inclined to bet on the chance that adopting the mixed rule or double moving average techniques is better than the Alexander filter.

5I. Conclusion

In the period considered in this book, speculation in the spot foreign exchange market using technical analysis seems to be profitable, particularly in the first subperiod studied. For some markets, the results appear highly inconsistent with the efficient markets hypothesis. In the case of the Belgian franc, for instance, most of the best trading rules beat the market significantly in both subperiods. The whole-period results indicate that there are 24 out of 60 cases, given by 15 currencies and four trading techniques, where the trading rule beats buy-and-hold significantly (see Table 18; of course, the results for the different rules for the same currency are not independent, so we give no formal test of whether this fraction of 24 out of 60 cases is itself significant). That is, on the average, about 40 percent of these markets seem to show exploitable profits.

Further, for the whole period the equally weighted portfolio produces profits that are significant at the 99 percent confidence level for each of the four technical trading techniques.

In the first subperiod, for the equally weighted portfolio approach all of the technical trading techniques give risk-adjusted profits significant at the 99 percent confidence level, save the single moving average rule where the profits are significant at the 95 percent level, with risk-adjusted profits measured by the adjusted X-statistic. In the second subperiod, for the equally weighted portfolio approach not one of the rules gives profits significant at the 95 percent level, but all give positive risk-adjusted profits after transactions costs.

The first subperiod shows more significant excess returns than the second. The lower profits in the second subperiod may mean that the exchange rate patterns change between the second prior period and the second subperiod. This is consistent with the results noted in Section 5B that the prior periods' best rules seem to shift through time.[6] In one interpretation, changes in the exchange rate patterns between the first prior period and the first subperiod are not very large, so that the prior-period best rules still work consistently despite the fact that the best rules in the first prior period may no longer be the best rules in the first subperiod.[7] In this interpretation, shifts in the best rules occur in a continuous fashion. That is, the patterns from the first prior period still persist to a useful extent in the first subperiod while new patterns slowly and continuously develop and eventually dominate the old patterns. The old patterns may fade away in the long run, so it may be advisable to update the set of best rules periodically.

There are a number of possible reasons why the second prior period best rules might work less well out of sample in the second subperiod, giving alternative interpretations of how technical patterns vary over time. (1) Changes in the patterns are so substantial that they quickly dominate the old patterns. This points out the need to update the set of best rules rapidly enough to detect a new substantial shift in trend. (2) The old patterns that are detected may simply fade away very quickly. This indicates a disadvantage of updating the set of best rules too often. It may be that the updated set of best rules will simply detect short–term or medium-term dominant patterns that fade away quickly, but will neglect persistent long-term trends that might be exploited over long time periods. (3) The changes in best rules may be due to noise and wholly spurious.[8]

In any case, it seems likely that exchange rates do not follow the same patterns in the long run. Substantial profits, however, can be made if the patterns do not change too quickly or in too substantial a fashion. In Chapter 10 we report the results of some explorations of these issues of the stability of speculative profits over time.

There are some markets where none of these rules outperform buy-and-hold significantly. Table 18 shows these are the markets for the Australian dollar, Canadian dollar, Swiss franc, and Swedish krona. These results may seem to contradict past studies. Sweeney (1986a), for instance, reports some profitable filter rules in these markets during the period of 1975 to 1980. This book uses only the best rule from the prior period; one of Sweeney's experiments uses the three best rules from his equivalent of our prior period. More generally, the results here seem consistent with past studies. For instance, knowing that a rule beats the market on an ex post basis in a prior period cannot assure the profitability of the rule in the future.[9] As an example, the results in Sweeney's (1986a) paper show that the filter rule with a 2 percent filter size is the only rule that significantly beat the market for the Canadian dollar in the first 610 observations of his data. This rule, however, performs poorly in his final 1,220 observations. Similarly, the rules that work well in the Canadian dollar market in the final 1,220 observations do not outperform buy-and-hold significantly in the first 610 observations. Thus, an investor using the best rule from the first 610 observations will not be able to beat the market significantly in the final 1,220 observation. This is consistent with the results of this study.

Table 18 also shows that the significant profits are not clustered in markets that necessarily have small volume or are thin. For example, for the whole period all four portfolio approaches show significant profits for the Deutsche mark, French franc, Italian lire, Japanese yen and Netherlands guilder.

In general, this chapter's empirical results suggest that there are opportunities for measured profits from speculation in some of the markets investigated. These profits raise two substantial intellectual issues. One issue is whether these measured profits are economic profits or can instead be explained by, for example, time-varying risk premia. Assuming for purposes of discussion that these measured profits are economic profits, another issue is why these profits exist and, especially, persist. Unfortunately, the results shed no light on these issues and past studies suggest different possible answers. In Chapter 6 we find similar, indeed greater, profits by using an alternative portfolio approach, and this raises the same issues. These issues in some detail in Chapter 11.

Notes

1. For instance, suppose that the trading rule keeps the investor in the market 50 percent of the time and yields a profit of $20, while the profit on buy-and-hold is $30.

Direct comparison of these two profits may lead to a mistaken conclusion that buy-and-hold is superior to the trading rule. This is not correct, however. Since the investor is in the market only 50 percent of the time, he bears only 50 percent of the risk attached to the buy-and-hold strategy. Hence, to perform just as well as buy-and-hold, the trading rule is expected to earn only $30x0.5 = $15. The difference between the actual and the expected profits on the trading rule of $20 - $15 = $5 is the risk-adjusted profit. In this case case, therefore, the trading rule is better than buy-and-hold. This type of misleading conclusion rarely happens in this study, however, because the profits on buy-and-hold of most currencies are either negative and/or lower than the trading rule profits. For a precise, detailed explanation of risk-adjusted profits, see Richard J. Sweeney (1987a) or Marc A. Bremer and Richard J. Sweeney (1988).

2. Note that the best rule is chosen as the rule that yields the highest adjusted X-statistic. The statistical significance of the best rule, however, is not guaranteed by this criterion. On the other hand, one might suggest the criterion of choosing the best rule according to the highest t-statistic to raise the likelihood of the significance of the best rule. It can be argued that this is probably not a good approach, however. Using the t-statistic as a criterion is subject to two spurious effects. In addition to possible spurious results in the X-statistics (i.e., the rule happens to have a good X-statistic by chance) discussed in the previous chapter, the t-statistic criterion may yield a spurious best rule due to the spuriously low sample variance of the X-statistic. That is, it may yield a best rule that gives a small excess return, with a spuriously small variance that makes it the best rule. For instance, suppose that the rule puts the investor in the market only one day and yields a huge positive return (say, four standard deviations away from the mean return), while the average return on buy-and-hold is negative. The X-statistic in such case will be small but positive. Given the large sample, however, the variance of the X-statistic is extremely small due to the fact that the rule keeps the investor out of the market almost all the time. This rule may yield the highest t-statistic due to the extremely low variance, but the return on this rule is also low, so that it should not be considered the best rule in the general sense.

3. The analysis is presented for the whole period data (i.e., data in both subperiods 1 and 2 combined). Analyses on each individual subperiod essentially yield the small same results as the whole period.

4. As Chapter 4 discussed, the Wilcoxon signed-rank test may be inappropriate when the distribution is skewed. As a result, one might argue that the use of the Wilcoxon signed-rank test in this case may be inappropriate since Chapter 4 shows that some exchange rates have return distributions that are significantly skewed. The problem, however, is not severe in this case. Even if the distributions of the X-statistics of both rules are skewed, the difference between the two X-statistics need not have a skewed distribution. If both rules are profitable by providing the right timing for going in and out of the market, then it is likely that the two rules will be highly correlated. That is, the periods in and out of the market provided by the two rules will be much the same. Thus, despite the skewness in the X-statistics of the two rules, the difference between these X-statistics is not necessarily skewed. As a confirmation of this argument, the parametric tests yield the same results in terms of statistical significance (i.e., the acceptance or the rejection of the hypothesis) as the

Wilcoxon signed-rank test.

5. It should be noted, however, that these results do not necessarily conflict with each other. The differences between the adjusted X-statistics of these technical trading techniques may not be obvious for any single currency. In terms of the Wilcoxon test, there may be roughly as many periods when the differences between the two adjusted X-statistics are negative as when they are positive so that the observed sum-rank does not diverge considerably from its expected value of zero. When the time-series of the adjusted X-statistics are averaged across currencies, however, the differences become more apparent in two ways. The first way is through the number of positive or negative counts in the signed-rank. If the performances of the two technical trading techniques are really different, the difference of these average series will show more of the observations with negative values than positive values, or vice versa. The second way is through changes in the rankings of the difference. The ambiguous observations will have smaller values through the averaging process, and the more clear-cut observations will have the relatively bigger values. This will result in a chosen sum-rank that is substantially smaller than the expected value and, hence, enhance the power of the test. The same effect happens in the parametric t-test, except that the power of the t-test is enhanced through the reduction in the variance caused by the sample-moment effects.

6. It might be argued that the best rules do not actually change through time. That is, the true best rules in the second prior period are the same as those of the first. The observed different best rules in the second prior period are spurious due to noise in the data. Further analysis does not support this argument, however. The performances of the first prior period best rules in the second subperiod are even worse than those of the second prior period.

7. Strictly speaking, this is not correct. We only observe that the best rules in the two prior periods are different. However, since 90 percent (900 observations) of the data in the first subperiod are the data in the second prior period, we can regard this statement as roughly correct.

8. As a footnote above points out, in the second subperiod the best rules from the first prior period in fact work less well than those from the second prior period.

9. Another possibility is that the prior period best rules for these currencies my be spurious (i.e., they happen to yield the highest X-statistics by chance). In such circumstances, the fact that following these rules in the associated subperiod does not beat the market is not surprising.

TABLE 5 Results on the Best Alexander Filter Rules
for Each Individual Currency Found in the Two Prior Periods,
To Be Used as Ex Ante Rules for Single Currency Simulations
in the Corresponding Subperiods.

CURRENCY	PRIOR PERIOD NO.	PERCENT OF FILTER		AVERAGE RETURN ON FILTER RULE	PERCENT OF DAY OUT OF MARKET
		UP	DOWN		
Australian Dollar	1	2.7	2.7	0.011560	0.4033
	2	1.0	1.0	0.008745	0.4989
Austrian Schilling	1	4.8	4.8	0.023410	0.2544
	2	1.8	1.8	0.016420	0.5556
Belgian Franc	I	4.6	4.6	0.026560	0.3433
	2	1.3	1.3	0.017660	0.5967
British Pound	1	2.3	2.3	0.017420	0.4211
	2	1.7	1.7	0.024440	0.4733
Canadian Dollar	1	1.1	1.1	0.004597	0.4389
	2	1.6	1.6	0.002991	0.5044
Danish Krone	1	1.4	1.4	0.013370	0.4878
	2	2.1	2.1	0.006036	0.6222
Deutche Mark	1	4.6	4.6	0.031100	0.2422
	2	1.6	1.6	0.022650	0.5367
French Franc	1	3.6	3.6	0.016930	0.4811
	2	1.8	1.8	0.015150	0.6200
Italian Lire	1	0.6	0.6	0.016480	0.5544
	2	1.6	1.6	0.000207	0.5833
Japanese Yen	1	1.1	1.1	0.028200	0.4344
	2	0.8	0.8	0.029890	0.6011
Netherland Guilder	1	4.7	4.7	0.026780	0.3322
	2	1.0	1.0	0.026700	0.5689
Norwegian Krone	1	3.4	3.4	0.010960	0.3911
	2	1.1	1.1	0.015540	0.5333
Spanish Peseta	1	1.7	1.7	0.004400	0.4144
	2	1.7	1.7	0.011520	0.4578
Swedish Krona	1	3.7	3.7	0.012760	0.3333
	2	4.4	4.4	-0.004769	0.5367
Swiss Franc	1	0.3	0.3	0.060930	0.4889
	2	1.8	1.8	0.024160	0.5189

TABLE 5 (CONTINUED)

FILTER RULE PROFIT		X STATISTICS		DEVIATION OF	T STATISTICS		NO. OF
UNADJ.	ADJ.	UNADJ.	ADJ.	X	UNADJ.	ADJ.	TRANS.
10.8086	10.5498	0.020370	0.020090	0.010250	1.9870	1.9599	2.
8.0598	6.4757	0.013990	0.012330	0.003875	3.6112	3.1810	12.
22.2234	21.8209	0.005748	0.005331	0.009382	0.6127	0.5683	3.
14.1922	11.0718	0.024480	0.021280	0.013140	1.8630	1.6199	23.
26.1965	25.9204	0.014480	0.014200	0.006803	2.1284	2.0876	2.
16.2157	11.6523	0.034170	0.029730	0.012060	2.8326	2.4642	32.
16.4673	15.9318	0.033180	0.032620	0.007605	4.3624	4.2893	4.
23.3660	20.2144	0.028580	0.025530	0.010970	2.6056	2.3271	22.
4.1337	3.1200	0.012230	0.011120	0.003616	3.3821	3.0749	8.
2.5942	1.7134	0.005225	0.004253	0.004124	1.2669	1.0312	7.
12.2217	10.3308	0.010130	0.008183	0.007164	1.4138	1.1424	14.
4.5204	2.2256	0.022390	0.019890	0.011330	1.9758	1.7551	18.
31.2892	31.0099	0.013840	0.013560	0.006528	2.1197	2.0772	2.
21.4756	18.0190	0.032420	0.029090	0.011520	2.8149	2.5254	24.
15.7536	15.1945	0.015500	0.014950	0.007334	2.1137	2.0380	4.
13.6718	11.0038	0.028880	0.026100	0.010690	2.7017	2.4419	20.
15.6479	12.4088	0.028970	0.025640	0.008051	3.5985	3.1844	24.
-0.4793	-2.8638	0.020440	0.017800	0.010080	2.0281	1.7663	19.
28.4203	26.7855	0.010720	0.009196	0.006278	1.7083	1.4649	11.
29.3202	20.6918	0.039490	0.031160	0.011810	3.3434	2.6378	60.
26.5057	26.2290	0.014450	0.014170	0.006496	2.2243	2.1815	2.
26.0652	20.0864	0.036990	0.031300	0.011560	3.1999	2.7074	41.
9.6245	9.2160	0.009628	0.009211	0.007582	1.2699	1.2150	3.
14.3789	10.6299	0.024160	0.020410	0.009582	2.5210	2.1296	27.
3.8904	3.3883	0.025770	0.025210	0.010390	2.4799	2.4264	4.
10.2739	8.3991	0.033870	0.031920	0.009602	3.5270	3.3245	14.
11.6812	11.2746	0.016270	0.015860	0.007783	2.0908	2.0373	3.
-4.5792	-5.1975	0.009245	0.008551	0.009511	0.9720	0.8990	5.
70.9240	54.1718	0.037760	0.023870	0.011350	3.3254	2.1021	100.
22.5743	18.9363	0.035780	0.032030	0.013240	2.7028	2.4195	27.

1. The rules chosen as best were those which yielded the highest X-statistics, adjusted for transactions costs, in each prior period. Filter size ranged from 0.1 percent to 10.0 percent with step increments of 0.1 percent.

2. Unit of X-statistics is percent per day.

3. Profits are based on $100 initial investment. Adjusted profits are profits net of total transactions costs; transactions costs of one-eighth of 1 percent per round trip are assumed.

4. Adjusted X-statistics were computed by deducting average transactions costs per day from the X-statistics.

TABLE 6 Results on the Best Double Moving Average
Rules for Each Individual Currency Found in the Two Prior
Periods, To Be Used as Ex Ante Rules for Single Currency
Simulations in the Corresponding Subperiods.

CURRENCY	PRIOR PERIOD NO.	PERCENT OF FILTER SHORT	LONG	AVERAGE RETURN ON FILTER RULE	PERCENT OF DAY OUT OF MARKET
Australian Dollar	1	14.0	32.	0.006665	0.4756
	2	3.0	25.	0.008788	0.5733
Austrian Schilling	1	7.0	23.	0.038640	0.3389
	2	12.0	25.	0.027430	0.5800
Belgian Franc	1	3.0	30.	0.036900	0.3367
	2	7.0	21.	0.025660	0.6156
British Pound	1	15.0	33.	0.018090	0.5089
	2	2.0	20.	0.025770	0.4989
Canadian Dollar	1	7.0	20.	0.008129	0.5689
	2	3.0	20.	0.007681	0.5467
Danish Krone	1	3.0	39.	0.021600	0.4511
	2	4.0	23.	0.013470	0.6300
Deutche Mark	1	2.0	38.	0.039550	0.3033
	2	7.0	23.	0.023770	0.5600
French Franc	1	7.0	23.	0.026530	0.4689
	2	8.0	22.	0.024060	0.6267
Italian Lire	1	17.	21.	0.011810	0.5244
	2	4.	25.	0.005648	0.6200
Japanese Yen	1	6.	21.	0.040870	0.4244
	2	11.	26.	0.024050	0.6333
Netherland Guilder	1	5.	24.	0.036910	0.3522
	2	6.	26.	0.025630	0.5822
Norwegian Krone	1	7.	24.	0.016390	0.4389
	2	2.	24.	0.013260	0.5644
Spanish Peseta	1	9.	20.	0.008134	0.5556
	2	19.	23.	0.009621	0.6311
Swedish Krona	1	2.	28.	0.020320	0.4467
	2	6.	30.	-0.000185	0.5911
Swiss Franc	1	22.	41.	0.058970	0.3156
	2	3.	24.	0.022320	0.5556

TABLE 6 (CONTINUED)

FILTER RULE PROFIT		X STATISTICS		DEVIATION OF	T STATISTICS		NO. OF
UNADJ.	ADJ.	UNADJ.	ADJ.	X	UNADJ.	ADJ.	TRANS.
6.0728	4.5307	0.01441	0.01275	0.010440	1.3808	1.2211	12.
8.1144	5.2462	0.01325	0.01020	0.003833	3.4584	2.6611	22.
40.3433	37.6616	0.02298	0.02048	0.010200	2.2537	2.0085	18.
26.4418	24.2384	0.03504	0.03282	0.013050	2.6851	2.5148	16.
38.5227	36.9260	0.02469	0.02316	0.006771	3.6463	3.4207	11.
24.8225	22.7004	0.04141	0.03933	0.011960	3.4612	3.2871	15.
17.2367	16.0826	0.03146	0.03021	0.007700	4.0856	3.9232	9.
24.9115	20.8289	0.02972	0.02597	0.010990	2.7051	2.3637	27.
7.5172	5.2155	0.01399	0.01149	0.003609	3.8776	3.1849	18.
7.0285	3.2130	0.00972	0.00570	0.004106	2.3680	1.3871	29.
20.7298	19.0553	0.01812	0.01645	0.007131	2.5408	2.3071	12.
11.8297	9.5045	0.02948	0.02698	0.011280	2.6128	2.3912	18.
41.7002	40.1083	0.02367	0.02214	0.007004	3.3796	3.1615	11.
22.5330	19.7717	0.03304	0.03027	0.011460	2.8822	2.6399	20.
26.2891	24.2484	0.02507	0.02313	0.007325	3.4233	3.1578	14.
23.1646	20.7871	0.03754	0.03518	0.010650	3.5250	3.3033	17.
10.9347	7.7330	0.025140	0.021800	0.008089	3.1073	2.6953	24.
4.6130	1.9357	0.024100	0.021180	0.009923	2.4288	2.1349	21.
43.6789	41.3415	0.023090	0.020730	0.006260	3.6887	3.3115	17.
22.9635	21.0579	0.032870	0.030930	0.011620	2.8280	2.6607	14.
38.6404	35.8132	0.024950	0.022310	0.006587	3.7876	3.3870	19.
24.5190	22.2571	0.035610	0.033390	0.011510	3.0931	2.9001	16.
15.1136	12.8312	0.015160	0.012940	0.007710	1.9660	1.6778	16.
11.9803	9.1164	0.021300	0.018240	0.009523	2.2367	1.9158	22.
7.5062	5.3197	0.024350	0.021990	0.010480	2.3235	2.0982	17.
8.4792	5.3774	0.024830	0.021490	0.009300	2.6697	2.3113	24.
19.4871	17.4945	0.023240	0.021290	0.008208	2.8311	2.5942	14.
-0.9439	-2.9823	0.012180	0.009960	0.009377	1.2991	1.0622	16.
66.9599	65.6939	0.027930	0.026820	0.010560	2.6463	2.5410	8.
20.4881	17.5527	0.033060	0.030000	0.013170	2.5108	2.2787	22.

1. The rules chosen as best were those which yielded the highest X-statistics, adjusted for transactions costs, in each prior period. Short-term moving averages ranged in length from 2 to 30 days, long-term from 20 to 50 days, in increments of 1 day; cases where the short is longer than the long moving average are excluded.

2. Unit of X-statistics is percent per day.

3. Profits are based on $100 initial investment. Adjusted profits are profits net of total transactions costs; transactions costs of one-eighth of 1 percent per round trip are assumed.

4. Adjusted X-statistics were computed by deducting average transactions costs per day from the X-statistics.

TABLE 7 Results on the Best Single Moving Average
Rules for Each Individual Currency Found in the Two Prior
Periods, To Be Used as Ex Ante Rules for Single Currency
Simulations in the Corresponding Subperiods.

CURRENCY	PRIOR PERIOD NO.	DEGREE OF MOVING AVERAGE	AVERAGE RETURN ON FILTER RULE	PERCENT OF DAY OUT OF MARKET
Australian Dollar	1	34.0	0.004035	0.4856
	2	11.0	0.011740	0.5622
Austrian Schilling	1	32.0	0.027670	0.3200
	2	27.0	0.013000	0.5756
Belgian Franc	1	28.0	0.038880	0.3422
	2	27.0	0.019220	0.6200
British Pound	1	28.0	0.018000	0.5167
	2	13.0	0.033300	0.4933
Canadian Dollar	1	27.0	0.006993	0.5822
	2	24.0	0.007267	0.5500
Danish Krone	1	42.0	0.019400	0.4456
	2	48.0	0.008145	0.6678
Deutche Mark	1	37.0	0.040700	0.3122
	2	26.0	0.017660	0.5922
French Franc	1	46.0	0.012870	0.4611
	2	20.0	0.014890	0.6078
Italian Lire	1	47.0	0.007396	0.5022
	2	12.0	0.000088	0.5844
Japanese Yen	1	18.0	0.040540	0.4322
	2	15.0	0.021330	0.6189
Netherland Guilder	1	31.0	0.032680	0.3667
	2	10.0	0.023820	0.5600
Norwegian Krone	1	21.0	0.014470	0.4389
	2	25.0	0.009255	0.5689
Spanish Peseta	1	29.0	0.005502	0.5733
	2	50.0	-0.001185	0.6078
Swedish Krona	1	28.0	0.018580	0.4489
	2	14.0	-0.000574	0.5800
Swiss Franc	1	50.0	0.052100	0.2778
	2	26.0	0.017640	0.5689

TABLE 7 (CONTINUED)

FILTER RULE PROFIT		X STATISTICS		STANDARD DEVIATION OF	T STATISTICS		NO. OF
UNADJ.	ADJ.	UNADJ.	ADJ.	X	UNADJ.	ADJ.	TRANS.
3.6008	0.6483	0.011630	0.008441	0.010450	1.1139	0.8081	23.
11.0256	4.9037	0.016320	0.009933	0.003845	4.2454	2.5836	46.
27.2423	24.4027	0.011550	0.008637	0.010050	1.1499	0.8596	21.
10.8508	6.2414	0.020690	0.015970	0.013070	1.5835	1.2222	34.
41.0233	38.1098	0.026780	0.024000	0.006798	3.9389	3.5303	20.
17.8349	14.4317	0.034780	0.031310	0.011940	2.9138	2.6229	25.
17.1069	13.5714	0.031150	0.027400	0.007697	4.0473	3.5601	27.
33.7031	26.2112	0.037290	0.030480	0.010980	3.3946	2.7750	49.
6.4286	2.8786	0.012680	0.008788	0.003594	3.5272	2.4452	28.
6.6323	1.7921	0.009295	0.004156	0.004104	2.2651	1.0128	37.
18.3551	15.3409	0.015880	0.012830	0.007123	2.2298	1.8008	22.
6.6192	4.8681	0.022520	0.020580	0.011010	2.0463	1.8696	14.
43.1833	40.9836	0.025030	0.022940	0.007061	3.5444	3.2493	15.
16.0923	11.5050	0.026250	0.021530	0.011350	2.3132	1.8971	34.
11.7821	9.0038	0.011390	0.008613	0.007317	1.5569	1.1772	20.
13.4141	9.4114	0.029060	0.025030	0.010750	2.7028	2.3281	29.
6.6812	4.4959	0.021350	0.018990	0.008099	2.6361	2.3445	17.
-0.5569	-7.2205	0.020270	0.013050	0.010070	2.0117	1.2948	52.
43.3044	38.4157	0.023000	0.018000	0.006274	3.6664	2.8694	36.
19.8191	14.2636	0.030510	0.024810	0.011710	2.6040	2.1179	41.
33.4468	30.6026	0.020990	0.018210	0.006646	3.1586	2.7406	20.
22.6391	14.8084	0.034330	0.026550	0.011590	2.9623	2.2911	56.
13.3070	6.9093	0.013240	0.006849	0.007710	1.7170	0.8884	46.
8.0225	4.3415	0.017220	0.013190	0.009511	1.8099	1.3865	29.
4.9926	1.3397	0.021070	0.017040	0.010430	2.0199	1.6338	29.
-1.5229	-4.9237	0.014980	0.011230	0.009410	1.5922	1.1937	27.
17.6378	14.6851	0.021490	0.018570	0.008211	2.6173	2.2621	21.
-1.3809	-8.0468	0.012130	0.004908	0.009414	1.2885	0.5213	52.
56.9312	53.8084	0.019350	0.016570	0.010170	1.9022	1.6291	20.
15.5628	11.0907	0.028050	0.023330	0.013120	2.1380	1.7781	34.

1. The rules chosen as best were those which yielded the highest X-statistics, adjusted for transaction cost, in each prior period. Degree of moving average ranged from 2 days to 50 days with step increments of 1 day.

2. Unit of X-statistics is percent per day.

3. Profits are based on $100 initial investment. Adjusted profits are profits net of total transactions costs; transactions costs of one-eighth of 1 percent per round trip are assumed.

4. Adjusted X-statistics were computed by deducting average transactions costs per day from the X-statistics.

TABLE 8 Information on Buy-and-Hold of Each Currency in Both Prior Periods.

CURRENCY	PRIOR PERIOD 1			PRIOR PERIOD 2		
	BUY-AND-HOLD PROFIT	AVERAGE RETURN ON BUY-AND-HOLD	VARIANCE	BUY-AND-HOLD PROFIT	AVERAGE RETURN ON BUY-AND-HOLD	VARIANCE
Australian Dollar	-13.96286	-0.015269	0.417457	-9.097153	-0.009667	0.048679
Austrian Schilling	21.448332	0.019432	0.379966	-17.582360	-0.019152	0.569887
Belgian Franc	16.763026	0.015729	0.166731	-32.921820	-0.039320	0.491947
British Pound	-22.569357	-0.025463	0.193047	-8.685731	-0.009036	0.392224
Canadian Dollar	-11.706948	-0.012461	0.043132	-4.38138	-0.004332	0.055117
Danish Krone	5.371152	0.004870	0.166822	-34.178294	-0.041176	0.444021
Deutche Mark	21.139425	0.019565	0.188445	-19.702205	-0.021140	0.433228
French Franc	1.279570	0.001604	0.174273	-29.312625	-0.034479	0.394022
Italian Lire	-23.226265	-0.026297	0.213153	-36.614772	-0.045410	0.339390
Japanese Yen	31.160233	0.027155	0.128728	-21.643828	-0.024015	0.469730
Netherland Guilder	16.671089	0.015845	0.154426	-21.357913	-0.023706	0.442990
Norwegian Krone	1.104872	0.000988	0.197675	-17.147612	-0.018115	0.299782
Spanish Peseta	-29.368917	-0.034759	0.395452	-32.010047	-0.038610	0.300778
Swedish Krona	-6.083217	-0.005881	0.230348	-25.294089	-0.028722	0.301666
Swiss Franc	46.376812	0.038712	0.418841	-22.689269	-0.024594	0.569774

1. Profits are based on $100 initial investment. Adjusted profits are profits net of total transaction costs; transactions costs of one-eighth of 1 percent per round trip are assumed.

2. Average returns are presented in percent per day.

TABLE 9 Sensitivity Ranges of Transactions Costs on Ex Ante Optimum Rules for Individual Currencies using Alexander Filter.

CURRENCY	PRIOR PERIOD 1		PRIOR PERIOD 2	
	LOWER BOUND	UPPER BOUND	LOWER BOUND	UPPER BOUND
Australian Dollar	-0.163563	8320.500000	0.031334	0.785132
Austrian Schilling	0.048074	6.716394	-0.135895	0.767027
Belgian Franc	0.001592	7541.500000	-0.165794	0.285385
British Pound	-0.067226	2.809863	-0.002333	0.725278
Canadian Dollar	0.003609	1.010558	0.030952	0.617095
Danish Krone	-0.054285	0.209720	0.117457	0.148481
Deutche Mark	0.000117	12548.250000	0.074432	0.162953
French Franc	-0.019422	1.294250	0.064973	0.455214
Italian Lire	-0.036316	0.321791	-0.053831	0.429871
Japanese Yen	0.009119	0.199312	-0.126721	0.311910
Netherland Guilder	-0.000995	52746.374999	-0.108974	0.279328
Norwegian Krone	0.013632	5.155708	-0.191564	0.166951
Spanish Peseta	-0.125734	2.023491	-0.211768	1.350079
Swedish Krona	0.059246	10.955870	0.089911	0.878684
Swiss Franc	-0.001171	0.209447	0.051151	0.649933

1. Sensitivity range is defined as the range over which transactions costs can be varied without changing the ex post optimum rule in the prior period.

2. The base case of transactions costs used in the simulation is one-eighth of 1 percent per round trip.

3. Transactions costs ranges are presented in terms of percent per round trip.

TABLE 10 Sensitivity Ranges of Transactions Costs on
Ex Ante Optimum Rules for Individual Currencies Using
Double Moving Average.

CURRENCY	PRIOR PERIOD 1		PRIOR PERIOD 2	
	LOWER BOUND	UPPER BOUND	LOWER BOUND	UPPER BOUND
Australian Dollar	0.067792	0.283534	-0.114278	0.378361
Austrian Schilling	-0.317558	0.197548	-0.233604	0.731104
Belgian Franc	0.027462	0.152936	-0.459605	1.022708
British Pound	0.043843	0.349066	-0.029223	0.659509
Canadian Dollar	-0.141399	0.165266	-0.098885	0.263143
Danish Krone	-0.021170	3.222676	-0.408379	0.618768
Deutche Mark	-0.006360	0.228591	-0.216643	0.700536
French Franc	-0.013959	1.267111	-0.705342	0.935453
Italian Lire	0.113875	0.216577	-0.291755	0.470415
Japanese Yen	0.046683	0.411340	-0.137515	0.403485
Netherland Guilder	-0.038460	0.163538	-0.427056	1.030934
Norwegian Krone	0.068685	0.232522	-0.069913	0.385701
Spanish Peseta	-0.052278	0.406068	-0.040470	0.183576
Swedish Krona	-0.028084	0.494879	-0.013885	0.578159
Swiss Franc	-0.147856	1.548408	-0.343118	0.782429

1. Sensitivity range is defined as the range over which transactions costs
can be varied without changing the ex post optimum rule in the prior period.

2. The base case of transactions costs used in the simulation is one-eighth
of 1 percent per round trip.

3. Ranges of transactions costs are presented in terms of percent per round trip.

TABLE 11 Sensitivity Ranges of Transactions Costs on
Ex Ante Optimum Rules for Individual Currencies Using
Single Moving Average.

CURRENCY	PRIOR PERIOD 1		PRIOR PERIOD 2	
	LOWER BOUND	UPPER BOUND	LOWER BOUND	UPPER BOUND
Australian Dollar	0.030430	0.532544	0.100291	0.177599
Austrian Schilling	-0.042763	0.288970	-0.129588	0.498585
Belgian Franc	-0.096754	0.397308	-0.023783	0.764376
British Pound	-0.048760	0.246556	-0.091477	0.304554
Canadian Dollar	0.112406	0.141697	0.005842	0.632310
Danish Krone	-0.037485	0.350658	0.110023	Infinity
Deutche Mark	-0.062022	0.706438	0.104010	0.285846
French Franc	0.090699	Infinity	0.120162	0.519037
Italian Lire	0.029683	Infinity	-0.057067	0.156341
Japanese Yen	-0.039006	0.219436	-0.032706	0.497768
Netherland Guilder	0.112505	1.536657	0.007624	0.136484
Norwegian Krone	-0.026336	0.181544	-0.046909	0.132326
Spanish Peseta	-0.067752	0.193692	0.003181	Infinity
Swedish Krona	-0.032001	0.704484	-0.015536	0.379212
Swiss Franc	0.072083	Infinity	0.094925	0.905413

1. Sensitivity range is defined as the range over which transactions costs
can be varied without changing the ex post optimum rule in the prior period.

2. The base case of transactions costs used in the simulation is one-eighth
of 1 percent per round trip.

3. Ranges of transactions costs are presented in terms of percent per round trip.

TABLE 12 Simulation Results on Single Currency Speculation Using Alexander Filter Rule.

CURRENCY/PERIOD	RULE	PERCENT FILTER SIZE UP	DOWN	FILTER RULE PROFIT	AVERAGE RETURN ON FILTER	PERCENT OF DAYS OUT OF MARKET	X STAT. UNADJ.	STD. DEV. OF X	T STAT UNADJ	ADJ. FILTER PROFIT	ADJ. X STAT.	ADJ. T STAT.	NO. OF TRANS.
Australian Dollar													
Subperiod No. 1	ALEX	2.7	2.7	3.2690	0.00334	0.5440	0.006033	0.003630	1.66223	2.7560	0.00553	1.52448	4
Subperiod No. 2	ALEX	1.0	1.0	-4.7991	-0.004042	0.4850	0.014817	0.012217	1.21284	-10.7314	0.00857	0.70126	50
Whole Period				-1.5301	-0.000351	0.5145	0.010425	0.006372	1.63601	-7.9754	0.00705	1.10639	54
Austrian Schilling													
Subperiod No. 1	ALEX	4.8	4.8	13.9633	0.014535	0.4070	0.017203	0.012077	1.42445	12.8317	0.01620	1.34165	8
Subperiod No. 2	ALEX	1.8	1.8	30.6001	0.02806	0.5170	0.023644	0.011896	1.98759	26.5111	0.01952	1.64083	33
Whole Period				44.5634	0.021297	0.4620	0.020423	0.008476	2.40960	39.3428	0.01786	2.10727	41
Belgian Franc													
Subperiod No. 1	ALEX	4.6	4.6	11.1884	0.01173	0.4210	0.026537	0.011226	2.36395	10.0767	0.02554	2.27486	8
Subperiod No. 2	ALEX	1.3	1.3	31.1648	0.028489	0.5550	0.028291	0.011386	2.48476	25.6282	0.02292	2.01268	43
Whole Period				42.3532	0.020109	0.4880	0.027414	0.007995	3.42907	35.7049	0.02423	3.03036	51
British Pound													
Subperiod No. 1	ALEX	2.3	2.3	20.0625	0.019266	0.5050	0.018076	0.010107	1.78846	17.2683	0.01570	1.55347	19
Subperiod No. 2	ALEX	1.7	1.7	8.6470	0.009824	0.5780	0.015513	0.011911	1.30242	4.4345	0.01114	0.93512	35
Whole Period				28.7095	0.014545	0.5415	0.016795	0.007811	2.15021	21.7028	0.01342	1.71812	54
Canadian Dollar													
Subperiod No. 1	ALEX	1.1	1.1	-2.9771	-0.002903	0.6000	0.001298	0.003770	0.34419	-4.9679	-0.00070	-0.18625	16
Subperiod No. 2	ALEX	1.6	1.6	-0.5818	-0.000447	0.4970	0.004731	0.004013	1.17874	-1.5768	0.00373	0.92957	8
Whole Period				-3.3589	-0.001675	0.5485	0.003014	0.002753	1.09476	-6.5447	0.00151	0.54996	24
Danish Krone													
Subperiod No. 1	ALEX	1.4	1.4	14.4728	0.014759	0.5710	0.027281	0.010680	2.55435	10.0125	0.02328	2.17983	32
Subperiod No. 2	ALEX	2.1	2.1	-12.6384	-0.009267	0.5850	-0.011706	0.021074	-0.55548	-15.4556	-0.01508	-0.71563	27
Whole Period				1.8343	0.002746	0.5780	0.007787	0.011813	0.65922	-5.4431	0.00410	0.34707	59

Deutche Mark														
Subperiod No. 1	ALEX	4.6	4.6	8.6381	0.009468	0.3700	0.013366	0.010389	1.28657	7.3749	0.01224	1.17828	9	
Subperiod No. 2	ALEX	1.6	1.6	30.4586	0.027959	0.5460	0.024086	0.011460	2.10175	25.7347	0.01946	1.69817	37	
Whole Period				39.0967	0.018713	0.4580	0.018726	0.007734	2.42126	33.1096	0.01585	2.04952	46	
French Franc														
Subperiod No. 1	ALEX	3.6	3.6	7.5271	0.008186	0.5250	0.019184	0.010192	1.88219	6.0725	0.01781	1.74728	11	
Subperiod No. 2	ALEX	1.8	1.8	16.0834	0.016223	0.5690	0.021204	0.012073	1.75635	12.3177	0.01720	1.42504	32	
Whole Period				23.6104	0.012205	0.5470	0.020194	0.007900	2.55622	18.3902	0.01751	2.21603	43	
Italian Lire														
Subperiod No. 1	ALEX	0.6	0.6	-2.5748	-0.001940	0.5550	0.014537	0.009312	1.56121	-11.7806	0.00579	0.62152	70	
Subperiod No. 2	ALEX	1.6	1.6	16.9504	0.016855	0.5510	0.022807	0.010936	2.08549	12.9955	0.01868	1.70830	33	
Whole Period				14.3756	0.007458	0.5530	0.018672	0.007182	2.59999	1.2149	0.01223	1.70362	103	
Japanese Yen														
Subperiod No. 1	ALEX	1.1	1.1	40.5788	0.035427	0.5650	0.036017	0.011368	3.16821	31.9828	0.02927	2.57446	54	
Subperiod No. 2	ALEX	0.8	0.8	46.2095	0.038973	0.4990	0.019340	0.009579	2.01892	38.2328	0.01209	1.26210	58	
Whole Period				86.7883	0.037200	0.5320	0.027679	0.007433	3.72371	70.2156	0.02068	2.78198	112	
Netherland Guilder														
Subperiod No. 1	ALEX	4.7	4.7	3.1129	0.004308	0.3700	0.010688	0.010442	1.02357	1.8874	0.00956	0.91584	9	
Subperiod No. 2	ALEX	1.0	1.0	40.4472	0.035269	0.5530	0.032108	0.011150	2.87960	32.9459	0.02511	2.25181	56	
Whole Period				43.5601	0.019789	0.4615	0.021398	0.007638	2.80149	34.8333	0.01734	2.26962	65	
Norwegian Krone														
Subperiod No. 1	ALEX	3.4	3.4	2.6923	0.003412	0.4780	0.007087	0.009038	0.78415	1.5066	0.00596	0.65968	9	
Subperiod No. 2	ALEX	1.1	1.1	5.1456	0.006221	0.5440	0.015483	0.010435	1.48379	-0.1363	0.00998	0.95671	44	
Whole Period				7.8379	0.004817	0.5110	0.011285	0.006902	1.63496	1.3703	0.00797	1.15506	53	
Spanish Peseta														
Subperiod No. 1	ALEX	1.7	1.7	28.0501	0.025380	0.4120	0.038573	0.008750	4.40854	25.8831	0.03682	4.20853	14	
Subperiod No. 2	ALEX	1.7	1.7	-18.6749	-0.017556	0.6010	-0.007965	0.016964	-0.46954	-22.3186	-0.01234	-0.72745	35	
Whole Period				9.3751	0.003912	0.5065	0.015304	0.009544	1.60359	3.5645	0.01224	1.28269	49	

(Continues)

TABLE 12 (CONTINUED)

CURRENCY/PERIOD	RULE	PERCENT FILTER SIZE UP	DOWN	FILTER RULE PROFIT	AVERAGE RETURN ON FILTER	PERCENT OF DAYS OUT OF MARKET	X STAT. UNADJ.	STD. DEV. OF X	T STAT. UNADJ.	ADJ. FILTER PROFIT	ADJ. X STAT.	ADJ. T STAT.	NO. OF TRANS.
Swedish Krona													
Subperiod No. 1	ALEX	3.7	3.7	-9.5930	-0.009139	0.3480	0.003877	0.008403	0.46135	-10.6107	0.00288	0.34234	8
Subperiod No. 2	ALEX	4.4	4.4	1.5935	0.002169	0.6500	0.008540	0.009427	0.90594	0.7675	0.00767	0.81312	7
Whole Period				-7.9995	-0.003485	0.4990	0.006208	0.006314	0.98326	-9.8432	0.00527	0.83478	15
Swiss Franc													
Subperiod No. 1	ALEX	0.3	0.3	32.8555	0.030177	0.5420	0.028447	0.013166	2.16070	9.2672	0.00882	0.67006	157
Subperiod No. 2	ALEX	1.8	1.8	13.8888	0.015113	0.5620	0.009738	0.014022	0.69451	9.4375	0.00499	0.35575	38
Whole Period				46.7442	0.022645	0.5520	0.019092	0.009617	1.98530	18.7047	0.00690	0.71800	195
Equally Weighted Portfolio													
Subperiod No. 1				11.4178	0.011067	0.4809	0.017880	0.004877	3.66610	7.3041	0.01431	2.93480	
Subperiod No. 2				13.6330	0.012923	0.5528	0.014709	0.006989	2.10450	0.5528	0.01024	1.46550	
Whole Period				25.5254	0.011995	0.5168	0.016295	0.004261	3.82390	16.5566	0.01228	2.88130	

1. Unit of X-statistics is percent per day

2. Profits are based on $100 initial investment. Adjusted profits are profits net of total transactions costs. Adjusted X-statistics were computed by deducting average transactions costs per day from the X-statistics. Transaction costs of one-eighth of 1 percent per round trip are assumed.

3. Adjusted X-statistics were computed by deducting average transactions costs per day from the X-statistics.

4. Whole period results were computed using averages or summation, depending upon result entries. Standard deviations were computed from the sample moment formula, assuming no serial correlation between the X-statistics in the two subperiods.

5. Equally weighted portfolio is the portfolio with equal weights on every currency speculation. This is equivalent to the arithmetic average of speculations in all currencies. The standard deviations of the X-statistics are computed from the variance-covariance matrices of the individual X-statistics.

TABLE 13 Information on Buy-and-Hold of Each Currency in Both Subperiods.

CURRENCY	SUBPERIOD 1			SUBPERIOD 2		
	BUY-AND-HOLD PROFIT	AVERAGE RETURN ON BUY-AND-HOLD	VARIANCE	BUY-AND-HOLD PROFIT	AVERAGE RETURN ON BUY-AND-HOLD	VARIANCE
Australian Dollar	-5.859295	-0.006171	0.053159	-32.542685	-0.039671	0.615126
Austrian Schilling	-6.364857	-0.007530	0.608154	6.194029	0.006316	0.565440
Belgian Franc	-24.120906	-0.028166	0.519127	-1.879213	-0.002171	0.523152
British Pound	0.016629	0.000359	0.409965	-14.305593	-0.016380	0.579322
Canadian Dollar	-10.266590	-0.010799	0.059249	-10.261274	-0.010617	0.064433
Danish Krone	-26.956056	-0.031526	0.467506	-2.550494	-0.003092	0.788746
Deutche Mark	-8.249838	-0.008504	0.464255	6.134141	0.005889	0.528175
French Franc	-22.415754	-0.025240	0.417994	-13.029400	-0.014531	0.595588
Italian Lire	-32.063721	-0.038791	0.352026	-14.238207	-0.015670	0.482963
Japanese Yen	-3.547720	-0.003978	0.524240	46.325785	0.037353	0.365293
Netherland Guilder	-11.784241	-0.012470	0.469487	4.690326	0.004564	0.501444
Norwegian Krone	-8.012381	-0.008680	0.328435	-19.638263	-0.022515	0.441981
Spanish Peseta	-21.050058	-0.024018	0.315893	-25.923278	-0.030026	0.899695
Swedish Krona	-19.135094	-0.021542	0.318280	-17.568004	-0.020181	0.39211
Swiss Franc	0.031132	0.00288	0.699073	8.665697	0.008285	0.797792

1. Profits are based on $100 initial investment. Adjusted profits are profits net of total transaction costs; transactions costs of one-eighth of 1 percent per round trip are assumed.

2. Average returns are presented in percent per day.

114

TABLE 14 Simulation Results on Single Currency Speculation Using Double Moving Average Rule.

CURRENCY/PERIOD	RULE	MOVING AVERAGE		FILTER RULE PROFIT	AVERAGE RETURN ON FILTER	PERCENT OF DAYS OUT OF MARKET	X STAT. UNADJ.	STD. DEV. OF X	T STAT. UNADJ.	ADJ. FILTER PROFIT	ADJ. X STAT.	ADJ. T STAT.	NO. OF TRANS.
		SHORT	LONG										
Australian Dollar													
Subperiod No.1	DMOV	14.0	32.0	3.5178	0.003578	0.5650	0.006147	0.003613	1.70137	1.5820	0.00427	1.18239	15
Subperiod No.2	DMOV	3.0	25.0	4.3981	0.005032	0.5610	0.021108	0.012131	1.73999	1.3860	0.01823	1.50300	23
Whole Period				7.9159	0.004305	0.5630	0.013628	0.006329	2.15322	2.9680	0.01125	1.77796	38
Austrian Schilling													
Subperiod No.1	DMOV	7.0	23.0	32.1113	0.029301	0.5360	0.031389	0.012260	2.56037	29.1037	0.02889	2.35645	20
Subperiod No.2	DMOV	12.0	25.0	8.2706	0.009280	0.5330	0.005011	0.011877	0.42192	6.1709	0.00276	0.23247	18
Whole Period				40.3819	0.019291	0.5345	0.018200	0.008535	2.13251	35.1746	0.01582	1.85423	38
Belgian Franc													
Subperiod No.1	DMOV	3.0	30.0	26.0251	0.024118	0.5760	0.034961	0.011236	3.11144	23.2870	0.03259	2.90007	19
Subperiod No.2	DMOV	7.0	21.0	29.6483	0.027321	0.5410	0.027116	0.011417	2.37515	26.9464	0.02437	2.13427	22
Whole Period				55.6734	0.025719	0.5585	0.031039	0.008009	3.87533	50.2334	0.02848	3.55539	41
British Pound													
Subperiod No.1	DMOV	15.0	33.0	12.6279	0.012865	0.4750	0.011603	0.010095	1.14938	10.3954	0.00960	0.95126	16
Subperiod No.2	DMOV	2.0	20.0	0.9186	0.002317	0.6090	0.007589	0.011769	0.64480	-3.5463	0.00271	0.23057	39
Whole Period				13.5465	0.007591	0.5420	0.009596	0.007753	1.23774	6.8491	0.00616	0.79434	55
Canadian Dollar													
Subperiod No.1	DMOV	7.0	20.0	1.1387	0.001254	0.5780	0.005686	0.003801	1.49585	-2.1565	0.00244	0.64083	26
Subperiod No.2	DMOV	3.0	20.0	-2.4301	-0.002342	0.5610	0.002177	0.003983	0.54657	-6.8154	-0.00220	-0.55173	35
Whole Period				-1.2914	-0.000544	0.5695	0.003932	0.002753	1.42810	-8.9719	0.00012	0.04324	61
Danish Krone													
Subperiod No.1	DMOV	3.0	39.0	6.3555	0.007150	0.6270	0.018037	0.010436	1.72839	4.0418	0.01579	1.51278	18
Subperiod No.2	DMOV	4.0	23.0	-6.5955	-0.002939	0.5440	-0.005619	0.021303	-0.26376	-9.7485	-0.00924	-0.43393	29
Whole Period				-0.2400	0.002105	0.5855	0.006209	0.011861	0.52351	-5.7067	0.00327	0.27584	47

Deutche Mark												
Subperiod No. 1	DMOV	2.0	38.0	22.7658	0.021608	0.5610	0.024324	0.010678	2.27793	19.9136	0.02182	2.04380	20
Subperiod No. 2	DMOV	7.0	23.0	24.5968	0.023249	0.5350	0.019282	0.011481	1.67955	21.9511	0.01653	1.44001	22
Whole Period				47.3627	0.022428	0.5480	0.021803	0.007839	2.78121	41.8647	0.01918	2.44637	42
French Franc												
Subperiod No. 1	DMOV	7.0	23.0	25.6249	0.023757	0.5930	0.033180	0.010027	3.30912	23.0308	0.03093	3.08473	18
Subperiod No. 2	DMOV	8.0	22.0	17.1529	0.017136	0.5490	0.022348	0.012131	1.84224	14.4083	0.01947	1.60524	23
Whole Period				42.7778	0.020446	0.5710	0.027764	0.007869	3.52819	37.4392	0.02520	3.20255	41
Italian Lire												
Subperiod No. 1	DMOV	17.0	21.0	4.0317	0.004556	0.5820	0.020033	0.009242	2.16774	0.6582	0.01678	1.81607	26
Subperiod No. 2	DMOV	4.0	25.0	12.9979	0.013317	0.5880	0.018779	0.010822	1.73525	10.4436	0.01615	1.49269	21
Whole Period				17.0296	0.008937	0.5850	0.019406	0.007116	2.72729	11.1018	0.01647	2.31446	47
Japanese Yen												
Subperiod No. 1	DMOV	6.0	21.0	35.1390	0.031316	0.5800	0.031885	0.011318	2.81723	32.0199	0.02939	2.59634	20
Subperiod No. 2	DMOV	11.0	26.0	41.3437	0.035606	0.4740	0.014994	0.009567	1.56732	38.5255	0.01237	1.29293	21
Whole Period				76.4826	0.033461	0.5270	0.023440	0.007410	3.16336	70.5454	0.02088	2.81753	41
Netherland Guilder												
Subperiod No. 1	DMOV	5.0	24.0	26.8151	0.025013	0.5370	0.029702	0.010785	2.75412	23.9404	0.02720	2.52231	20
Subperiod No. 2	DMOV	6.0	26.0	14.3375	0.014625	0.5310	0.011309	0.011192	1.01042	11.6790	0.00843	0.75354	23
Whole Period				41.1526	0.019819	0.5340	0.020505	0.007771	2.63862	35.6194	0.01782	2.29279	43
Norwegian Krone												
Subperiod No. 1	DMOV	7.0	24.0	16.6357	0.016116	0.5310	0.019418	0.009029	2.15052	14.0346	0.01704	1.88749	19
Subperiod No. 2	DMOV	2.0	24.0	9.9363	0.010676	0.5520	0.019776	0.010419	1.89808	6.4121	0.01615	1.55015	29
Whole Period				26.5720	0.013396	0.5415	0.019597	0.006893	2.84279	20.4461	0.01660	2.40760	48
Spanish Peseta												
Subperiod No. 1	DMOV	9.0	20.0	12.5405	0.012418	0.5670	0.022133	0.008808	2.51281	8.9277	0.01901	2.15802	25
Subperiod No. 2	DMOV	19.0	23.0	-6.8712	-0.002895	0.6060	0.006576	0.016927	0.38847	-9.9243	0.00320	0.18908	27
Whole Period				5.6693	0.004761	0.5865	0.014354	0.009541	1.50454	-0.9966	0.01110	1.16389	52

(Continues)

TABLE 14 (CONTINUED)

CURRENCY/PERIOD	RULE	PERCENT FILTER SIZE UP	DOWN	FILTER RULE PROFIT	AVERAGE RETURN ON FILTER	PERCENT OF DAYS OUT OF MARKET	X STAT. UNADJ.	STD. DEV. OF X	T STAT. UNADJ.	ADJ. FILTER PROFIT	ADJ. X STAT.	ADJ. T STAT.	NO. OF TRANS.
Swedish Krona													
Subperiod No. 1	DMOV	2.0	28.0	-0.7993	0.000054	0.5550	0.008937	0.008767	1.01946	-5.2754	0.00469	0.53468	34
Subperiod No. 2	DMOV	6.0	30.0	12.9809	0.012881	0.5530	0.021018	0.009826	2.13897	10.9024	0.01889	1.92271	17
Whole Period				12.1816	0.006468	0.5540	0.014978	0.006584	2.27476	5.6270	0.01179	1.79066	51
Swiss Franc													
Subperiod No. 1	DMOV	22.0	41.0	11.4534	0.012580	0.5390	0.010838	0.013172	0.82282	9.7023	0.00921	0.69945	13
Subperiod No. 2	DMOV	3.0	24.0	23.8213	0.024006	0.5400	0.018361	0.014085	1.30356	20.3697	0.01486	1.05508	28
Whole Period				35.2747	0.018293	0.5395	0.014600	0.009642	1.51412	30.0710	0.01204	1.24837	41
Equally Weighted Portfolio													
Subperiod No. 1				15.7323	0.015046	0.5601	0.020552	0.006064	3.38890	12.8804	0.01798	2.96430	
Subperiod No. 2				12.3004	0.012485	0.5518	0.013988	0.007600	1.84050	9.2774	0.01085	1.42690	
Whole Period				28.1578	0.013765	0.5560	0.017270	0.004862	3.55230	22.1578	0.01441	2.96420	

1. Unit of X-statistics is percent day.

2. Profits are based on $100 initial investment. Adjusted profits are profits net of total transactions costs; transaction costs of one-eighth of 1 percent per round trip are assumed.

3. Adjusted X-statistics were computed by deducting average transactions costs per day from the X-statistics.

4. Whole period results were computed using averages or summation, depending upon result entries. Standard deviations were computed from the sample moment formula, assuming no serial correlation between the X-statistics in the two subperiods.

5. Equally weighted portfolio is the portfolio with equal weights on every currency speculation. This is equivalent to the arithmetic average of speculations in all currencies. The standard deviations of the X-statistics are computed from the variance-covariance matrices of the individual X-statistics.

TABLE 15 Simulation Results on Single Currency Speculation Using Single Moving Average Rule.

CURRENCY/PERIOD	RULE	DEGREE OF MOVING AVERAGE	FILTER RULE PROFIT	AVERAGE RETURN ON FILTER	PERCENT OF DAYS OUT OF MARKET	X STAT. UNADJ.	STD. DEV. OF X UNADJ.	T STAT. UNADJ.	ADJ. FILTER PROFIT	ADJ. X STAT.	ADJ. T STAT.	NO. OF TRANS.
Australian Dollar												
Subperiod No. 1	SMOV	34.0	6.1020	0.006045	0.5400	0.008762	0.003632	2.41236	1.9499	0.00476	1.31109	32
Subperiod No. 2	SMOV	11.0	7.2402	0.007797	0.5460	0.024422	0.012171	2.00665	-1.9197	0.01567	1.28771	70
Whole Period			13.3423	0.006921	0.5430	0.016592	0.006351	2.61271	0.0302	0.01022	1.60887	102
Austrian Schilling												
Subperiod No. 1	SMOV	32.0	13.4582	0.014174	0.5430	0.016230	0.012246	1.32536	7.9784	0.01136	0.92726	39
Subperiod No. 2	SMOV	27.0	26.3416	0.024714	0.5340	0.020454	0.011875	1.72244	20.8150	0.01483	1.24876	45
Whole Period			39.7998	0.019444	0.5385	0.018342	0.008529	2.15055	28.5934	0.01309	1.53500	84
Belgian Franc												
Subperiod No. 1	SMOV	28.0	26.8314	0.024769	0.5750	0.035638	0.011240	3.17069	22.2133	0.03164	2.81481	32
Subperiod No. 2	SMOV	27.0	23.4657	0.022363	0.5670	0.022170	0.011352	1.95295	19.2836	0.01779	1.56756	35
Whole Period			50.2971	0.023566	0.5710	0.028904	0.007987	3.61864	41.4969	0.02472	3.09438	67
British Pound												
Subperiod No. 1	SMOV	28.0	16.0218	0.015862	0.4650	0.014576	0.010083	1.44560	10.8966	0.01020	1.01169	35
Subperiod No. 2	SMOV	13.0	20.2043	0.019881	0.6050	0.025206	0.011790	2.13796	12.6984	0.01758	1.49122	61
Whole Period			36.2261	0.017872	0.5350	0.019891	0.007757	2.56437	23.5950	0.01389	1.79085	96
Canadian Dollar												
Subperiod No. 1	SMOV	27.0	2.4567	0.002546	0.5880	0.006873	0.003788	1.81431	-2.8969	0.00162	0.42839	42
Subperiod No. 2	SMOV	24.0	0.7000	0.000817	0.5750	0.005192	0.003968	1.30858	-5.8146	-0.00118	-0.29803	51
Whole Period			3.1567	0.001681	0.5815	0.006033	0.002743	2.19933	-8.7115	0.00022	0.08024	93
Danish Krone												
Subperiod No. 1	SMOV	42.0	4.8119	0.005725	0.6230	0.016729	0.010458	1.59963	1.1830	0.01323	1.2496	28
Subperiod No. 2	SMOV	48.0	-17.0149	-0.014519	0.5870	-0.016947	0.021059	-0.80471	-19.7877	-0.02020	-0.95904	26
Whole Period			-12.2030	-0.004397	0.6050	-0.000109	0.011757	-0.00926	-18.6047	-0.00348	-0.29633	54

(Continues)

118

TABLE 15 (CONTINUED)

CURRENCY/PERIOD	RULE	DEGREE OF MOVING AVERAGE	FILTER RULE PROFIT	AVERAGE RETURN ON FILTER	PERCENT OF DAYS OUT OF MARKET	X STAT. UNADJ.	STD. DEV. OF X	T STAT. UNADJ.	ADJ. FILTER PROFIT	ADJ. X STAT.	ADJ. T STAT.	NO. OF ADJ. TRANS.
Deutsche Mark												
Subperiod No. 1	SMOV	37.0	20.3481	0.019607	0.5540	0.022366	0.010696	2.09113	15.9865	0.01849	1.72883	31
Subperiod No. 2	SMOV	26.0	33.4830	0.030183	0.5360	0.026225	0.011479	2.28462	28.3264	0.02110	1.83815	41
Whole Period			53.8311	0.024895	0.5450	0.024295	0.007845	3.09702	44.3129	0.01980	2.52339	72
French Franc												
Subperiod No. 1	SMOV	46.0	13.8373	0.013744	0.6060	0.022866	0.009973	2.29278	10.8237	0.02012	2.01703	22
Subperiod No. 2	SMOV	20.0	27.1939	0.025379	0.5460	0.030626	0.012138	2.52317	22.2625	0.02550	2.10094	41
Whole Period			41.0312	0.019561	0.5760	0.026746	0.007855	3.40506	33.0862	0.02281	2.90377	63
Italian Lire												
Subperiod No. 1	SMOV	47.0	-0.4104	0.000139	0.6030	0.014838	0.009168	1.61856	-3.7616	0.01159	1.26405	26
Subperiod No. 2	SMOV	12.0	12.0572	0.012570	0.5610	0.018390	0.010911	1.68533	3.1728	0.00939	0.86052	72
Whole Period			11.6468	0.006354	0.5820	0.016614	0.007126	2.33153	-0.5888	0.01049	1.47197	98
Japanese Yen												
Subperiod No. 1	SMOV	18.0	40.7310	0.035476	0.5770	0.036050	0.011329	3.18211	34.2192	0.03092	2.72973	41
Subperiod No. 2	SMOV	15.0	57.0783	0.046264	0.4860	0.026122	0.009576	2.72790	47.5803	0.01800	1.87940	65
Whole Period			97.8094	0.040870	0.5315	0.031086	0.007417	4.19124	81.7995	0.02446	3.29800	106
Netherland Guilder												
Subperiod No. 1	SMOV	31.0	16.7128	0.016577	0.5550	0.021084	0.010749	1.96154	12.4696	0.01721	1.60103	31
Subperiod No. 2	SMOV	10.0	32.3271	0.029275	0.5420	0.026036	0.011174	2.33012	21.2299	0.01566	1.40161	83
Whole Period			49.0398	0.022926	0.5485	0.023560	0.007752	3.03915	33.6995	0.01644	2.12005	114
Norwegian Krone												
Subperiod No. 1	SMOV	21.0	12.3804	0.012416	0.5330	0.015705	0.009027	1.73971	6.4321	0.01008	1.11659	45
Subperiod No. 2	SMOV	25.0	10.0757	0.010775	0.5530	0.019853	0.010416	1.90597	5.3248	0.01485	1.42596	40
Whole Period			22.4560	0.011595	0.5430	0.017779	0.006892	2.57971	11.7569	0.01247	1.80887	85

Spanish Peseta											
Subperiod No. 1	SMOV	29.0	10.5684	0.010626	0.5410	0.020925	0.008858	2.36214	5.1928	0.01630	1.84003	37
Subperiod No. 2	SMOV	50.0	8.2549	0.012101	0.6540	0.020418	0.016479	1.23908	5.2259	0.01729	1.04944	25
Whole Period			18.8233	0.011364	0.5975	0.020672	0.009354	2.20983	10.4187	0.01680	1.79559	62
Swedish Krona											
Subperiod No. 1	SMOV	28.0	-6.2387	-0.005584	0.5520	0.003359	0.008772	0.38295	-12.5847	-0.00277	-0.31526	49
Subperiod No. 2	SMOV	14.0	13.9335	0.013766	0.5440	0.022067	0.009844	2.24170	5.3552	0.01332	1.35280	70
Whole Period			7.6948	0.004091	0.5480	0.012713	0.006593	1.92834	-7.2295	0.00528	0.80020	119
Swiss Franc											
Subperiod No. 1	SMOV	50.0	19.0873	0.019223	0.5800	0.017636	0.013042	1.35223	14.1149	0.01326	1.01677	35
Subperiod No. 2	SMOV	26.0	16.3760	0.017279	0.5360	0.011585	0.014094	0.82200	11.1588	0.00584	0.41403	46
Whole Period			35.4633	0.018251	0.5580	0.014611	0.009601	1.52173	25.2737	0.00955	0.99446	81
Equally Weighted Portfolio											
Subperiod No. 1			13.1133	0.012756	0.5623	0.018243	0.006337	2.87870	8.2812	0.013867	2.18830	
Subperiod No. 2			18.1145	0.017243	0.5581	0.018788	0.007396	2.54030	11.6608	0.012363	1.67160	
The Whole Period			31.2277	0.015000	0.5602	0.018515	0.004870	3.80210	19.8340	0.013115	2.69315	

1. Unit of X-statistics is percent per day

2. Profits are based on $100 initial investment. Adjusted profits are profits net of total transactions costs; transaction costs of one-eighth of 1 percent per round trip are assumed.

3. Adjusted X-statistics were computed by deducting average transactions costs per day from the X-statistics.

4. Whole period results were computed using averages or summation, depending upon result entries. Standard deviations were computed from the sample moment formula, assuming no serial correlation between the X-statistics in the two subperiods.

5. Equally weighted portfolio is the portfolio with equal weights on every currency speculation. This is equivalent to the arithmetic average of speculations in all currencies. The standard deviations of the X-statistics are computed from the variance-covariance matrices of the individual X-statistics.

TABLE 16 Simulation Results on Single Currency Speculation Using Mixed Rules.

CURRENCY/PERIOD	RULE	PERCENT FILTER AND MOV. AVG. UPSHRT	DNLONG	FILTER RULE PROFIT	AVERAGE RETURN ON FILTER	PERCENT OF DAYS OUT OF MARKET	X STAT. UNADJ.	STD. DEV. OF X	T STAT. UNADJ.	ADJ. FILTER PROFIT	ADJ. X STAT.	ADJ. T STAT.	NO. OF TRANS.
Australian Dollar													
Subperiod No. 1	ALEX	2.7	2.7	3.2690	0.003340	0.5440	0.006033	0.003630	1.66223	2.7560	0.0055	1.52448	4
Subperiod No. 2	SMOV	1.0	11.0	7.2402	0.007797	0.5460	0.024422	0.012171	2.00665	-1.9197	0.0157	1.28771	70
Whole Period				10.5092	0.005569	0.5450	0.015228	0.006350	2.39789	0.8363	0.0106	1.66919	74
Austrian Schilling													
Subperiod No. 1	DMOV	7.0	23.0	32.1113	0.029301	0.5360	0.031389	0.012260	2.56037	29.1037	0.0289	2.35645	20
Subperiod No. 2	DMOV	12.0	25.0	8.2706	0.009280	0.5330	0.005011	0.011877	0.42192	6.1709	0.0028	0.23247	18
Whole Period				40.3819	0.019291	0.5345	0.018200	0.008535	2.13251	35.2746	0.0158	1.85423	38
Belgian Franc													
Subperiod No. 1	SMOV	1.0	28.0	26.8314	0.024769	0.5750	0.035638	0.011240	3.17069	22.2133	0.0316	2.81481	32
Subperiod No. 2	DMOV	7.0	21.0	29.6483	0.027321	0.5410	0.027116	0.011417	2.37515	26.9464	0.0244	2.13427	22
Whole Period				56.4797	0.026045	0.5580	0.03377	0.008010	3.91698	49.1597	0.0280	3.49566	54
British Pound													
Subperiod No. 1	ALEX	2.3	2.3	20.0625	0.019266	0.5050	0.018076	0.010107	1.78846	17.2683	0.0157	1.55347	19
Subperiod No. 2	SMOV	1.0	13.0	20.2043	0.019881	0.6050	0.025206	0.011790	2.13796	12.6984	0.0176	1.49122	61
Whole Period				40.2668	0.019574	0.5550	0.021641	0.007765	2.78714	29.9667	0.0166	2.14306	80
Canadian Dollar													
Subperiod No. 1	DMOV	7.0	20.0	1.1387	0.001254	0.5780	0.005686	0.003801	1.49585	-2.1565	0.00244	0.64083	26
Subperiod No. 2	DMOV	3.0	20.0	-2.4301	-0.002342	0.5610	0.002177	0.003983	0.54657	-6.8154	-0.00220	-0.55173	35
Whole Period				-1.2914	-0.000544	0.5695	0.003932	0.002753	1.42810	-8.9719	0.00012	0.04324	61
Danish Krone													
Subperiod No. 1	DMOV	3.0	39.0	6.3555	0.007150	0.6270	0.018037	0.010436	1.72839	4.0418	0.01579	1.51278	18
Subperiod No. 2	DMOV	4.0	23.0	-6.5955	-0.002939	0.5440	-0.005619	0.021303	-0.26376	-9.7485	-0.00924	-0.43393	29
Whole Period				-0.2400	0.002105	0.5855	0.006209	0.011861	0.52351	-5.7067	0.00327	0.27584	47

Deutsche Mark													
Subperiod No. 1	SMOV	1.0	37.0	20.3481	0.019607	0.5540	0.022366	0.010696	2.09113	15.9865	0.01849	1.72883	31
Subperiod No. 2	DMOV	7.0	23.0	24.5968	0.023249	0.5350	0.019282	0.011481	1.67955	21.9511	0.01653	1.44001	22
Whole Period				44.9949	0.021428	0.5445	0.020824	0.007845	2.65431	37.9376	0.01751	2.23209	53
French Franc													
Subperiod No. 1	DMOV	7.0	23.0	25.6249	0.023757	0.5930	0.033180	0.010027	3.30912	23.0308	0.03093	3.08473	18
Subperiod No. 2	DMOV	8.0	22.0	17.1529	0.017136	0.5490	0.022348	0.012131	1.84224	14.4083	0.01947	1.60524	23
Whole Period				42.7778	0.020446	0.5710	0.027764	0.007869	3.52819	37.4391	0.02520	3.20255	41
Italian Lire													
Subperiod No. 1	ALEX	0.6	0.6	-2.5748	-0.001940	0.5550	0.014537	0.009312	1.56121	-11.7806	0.00579	0.62152	70
Subperiod No. 2	SMOV	4.0	25.0	12.9979	0.013317	0.5880	0.018779	0.010822	1.73525	10.4436	0.01615	1.49269	21
Whole Period				10.4231	0.005689	0.5715	0.016685	0.007138	2.33356	-1.3370	0.01097	1.53675	91
Japanese Yen													
Subperiod No. 1	DMOV	6.0	21.0	35.1390	0.031316	0.5800	0.031885	0.011318	2.81723	32.0199	0.02939	2.59634	20
Subperiod No. 2	ALEX	0.8	0.8	46.2095	0.038973	0.4990	0.019340	0.009579	2.01892	38.2328	0.01209	1.26210	58
Whole Period				81.3485	0.035145	0.5395	0.025813	0.007414	3.45473	70.2527	0.02074	2.79750	78
Netherland Guilder													
Subperiod No. 1	DMOV	5.0	24.0	26.8151	0.025013	0.5370	0.029702	0.010785	2.75412	23.9404	0.02720	2.52231	20
Subperiod No. 2	ALEX	1.0	1.0	40.4472	0.035269	0.5530	0.032108	0.011150	2.87960	32.9459	0.02511	2.25181	56
Whole Period				67.2623	0.030141	0.5450	0.030905	0.007756	3.98452	56.8863	0.02616	3.37211	76
Norwegian Krone													
Subperiod No. 1	DMOV	7.0	24.0	16.6357	0.016116	0.5310	0.019418	0.009029	2.15052	14.0346	0.01704	1.88749	19
Subperiod No. 2	ALEX	1.1	1.1	5.1456	0.006221	0.5440	0.015483	0.010435	1.48379	-0.1363	0.00998	0.95671	44
Whole Period				21.7813	0.011169	0.5375	0.017451	0.006900	2.52924	13.8983	0.01351	1.95811	63
Spanish Peseta													
Subperiod No. 1	ALEX	1.7	1.7	28.0501	0.025380	0.4120	0.038573	0.008750	4.40854	25.8831	0.03682	4.208530	14
Subperiod No. 2	ALEX	1.7	1.7	-18.6749	-0.017556	0.6010	-0.007965	0.016964	-0.46954	-22.3186	-0.01234	-0.727450	35
Whole Period				9.3752	0.003912	0.5065	0.015340	0.009544	1.60355	3.5645	0.01224	1.282500	49

(Continues)

122

TABLE 16 (CONTINUED)

CURRENCY/PERIOD	RULE	PERCENT FILTER AND MOV. AVG. UPSHRT	DNLONG	FILTER RULE PROFIT	AVERAGE RETURN ON FILTER	PERCENT OF DAYS OUT OF MARKET	X STAT. UNADJ.	STD. DEV. OF X	T STAT. UNADJ.	ADJ. FILTER PROFIT	ADJ. X STAT.	ADJ. T STAT.	NO. OF TRANS.
Swedish Krona													
Subperiod No. 1	DMOV	2.0	28.0	-0.7993	0.000054	0.5550	0.008937	0.008767	1.01946	-5.2754	0.00469	0.534680	34
Subperiod No. 2	DMOV	6.0	30.0	12.9809	0.012881	0.5530	0.021018	0.009826	2.13897	10.9024	0.01889	1.922710	17
Whole Period				12.2084	0.006468	0.5540	0.014978	0.006584	2.27474	5.6270	0.01179	1.790630	51
Swiss Franc													
Subperiod No. 1	ALEX	0.3	0.3	32.8555	0.030177	0.5420	0.028447	0.013166	2.16070	9.2672	0.00882	0.670060	157
Subperiod No. 2	ALEX	1.8	1.8	13.8888	0.015113	0.5620	0.009738	0.014022	0.69451	9.4375	0.00499	0.355750	38
Whole Period				46.7443	0.022645	0.5520	0.019093	0.009617	1.98525	18.7047	0.00691	0.717987	195
Equally Weighted Portfolio													
Subperiod No. 1				18.1243	0.016971	0.5483	0.022794	0.005679	4.01370	13.3556	0.01861	3.277100	
Subperiod No. 2				14.0722	0.013574	0.5543	0.015230	0.006901	3.27710	9.5466	0.01065	1.543900	
Whole Period				32.1963	0.015272	0.5513	0.019012	0.004469	4.25450	22.9022	0.01463	3.274500	

1. Unit of X-statistics is percent per day.

2. Profits are based on $100 initial investment. Adjusted profits are profits net of total transactions costs; transaction costs of one-eighth of 1 percent per round trip are assumed.

3. Adjusted X-statistics were computed by deducting average transactions costs per day from the X-statistics.

4. The mixed rule strategy exploits the best of all types of trading rules found in the prior periods.

5. Whole period results were computed using averages or summation, depending upon result entries. Standard deviations were computed from the sample moment formula, assuming no serial correlation between the X-statistics in the two subperiods.

6. Equally weighted portfolio is the portfolio with equal weights on every currency speculation. This is equivalent to the arithmetic average of speculations in all currencies. The standard deviations of the X-statistics are computed from the variance-covariance matrices of the individual X-statistics.

TABLE 17 Sensitivity Analysis of the Maximum Transactions Costs
Allowable for Statistical Significance of the Adjusted X-Statistics.

CURRENCY/SUBPERIOD	ALEXANDER FILTER	DOUBLE MOVING AVERAGE	SINGLE MOVING AVERAGE	MIXED RULE
Australian Dollar				
Subperiod No. 1	-0.268837	-0.062232	0.051327	-0.268837
Subperiod No. 2	-0.182654	-0.115912	0.008096	0.008096
Whole Period	-0.076449	0.064296	0.081294	0.075140
Austrian Schilling				
Subperiod No. 1	-0.806072	0.368117*	-0.199491	0.368117*
Subperiod No. 2	0.009937	-1.014434	-0.062700	-1.014434
Whole Period	0.185819*	0.077279	0.038680	0.077605
Belgian Franc				
Subperiod No. 1	0.568460*	0.682119*	0.425450*	0.425450*
Subperiod No. 2	0.139044*	0.215708*	-0.002281	0.215708*
Whole Period	0.461047*	0.749383*	0.395838	0.582024*
British Pound				
Subperiod No. 1	-0.091210	-0.510684	-0.148157	-0.091210
Subperiod No. 2	-0.223890	-0.396553	0.034382	0.034382
Whole Period	0.055016	-0.203721	0.097635	0.160508*
Canadian Dollar				
Subperiod No. 1	-0.381081	-0.067928	-0.013123	-0.067928
Subperiod No. 2	-0.391419	-0.160775	-0.050716	-0.160775
Whole Period	-0.197962	-0.048002	0.014122	-0.048002
Danish Krone				
Subperiod No. 1	0.198332*	-0.134488	-0.134634	-0.134488
Subperiod No. 2	-1.963954	-1.635352	-2.237267	-1.635352
Whole Period	-0.520968	-0.724675	-0.858526	-0.724675
Deutche Mark				
Subperiod No. 1	-0.776692	0.169485*	0.045209	0.045209
Subperiod No. 2	0.043893	-0.146292	0.090882	-0.146292
Whole Period	0.155049*	0.306832*	0.248020*	0.205484*
French Franc				
Subperiod No. 1	-0.072082	0.751504*	0.151080*	0.751504*
Subperiod No. 2	-0.076769	-0.062055	0.166687*	-0.062055
Whole Period	0.219355*	0.601636*	0.360461*	0.601636*
Italian Lire				
Subperiod No. 1	-0.053083	0.073727	-0.120508	-0.053083
Subperiod No. 2	0.041569	-0.115639	-0.041605	-0.115639
Whole Period	0.089166	0.232401*	0.054030	0.058935
Japanese Yen				
Subperiod No. 1	0.254478*	0.486058*	0.337358*	0.486058*
Subperiod No. 2	0.009744	-0.178988	0.113165	0.009744
Whole Period	0.234146*	0.435371*	0.312192*	0.27798*
Netherland Guilder				
Subperiod No. 1	-1.083590	0.427828*	0.000515	0.427828*
Subperiod No. 2	0.183159*	-0.461415	0.049814	0.183159*
Whole Period	0.197989*	0.245523*	0.146876*	0.413679*
Norwegian Krone				
Subperiod No. 1	-1.178736	0.090473	-0.044176	0.090473
Subperiod No. 2	-0.112884	-0.022244	-0.014051	-0.112884
Whole Period	-0.084575	0.253867*	0.100553	0.124556

(Continues)

124

TABLE 17 (CONTINUED)

CURRENCY/SUBPERIOD	ALEXANDER FILTER	DOUBLE MOVING AVERAGE	SINGLE MOVING AVERAGE	MIXED RULE
Spanish Peseta				
Subperiod No. 1	1.527596*	0.194898*	0.096306	1.527596*
Subperiod No. 2	-1.177555	-0.984927	-0.474778	-1.177555
Whole Period	-0.138799	-0.166962	0.075483	-0.135735
Swedish Krona				
Subperiod No. 1	-1.578847	-0.242710	-0.282145	-0.242710
Subperiod No. 2	-1.427718	0.103327	0.039624	0.103327
Whole Period	-0.821887	0.081295	-0.003519	0.081295
Swiss Franc				
Subperiod No. 1	0.016824	-1.150117	-0.226415	0.016824
Subperiod No. 2	-0.467174	-0.330106	-0.348983	-0.467174
Whole Period	0.002488	-0.209879	-0.103906	0.002500
Equally Weighted Portfolio				
Subperiod No. 1	0.291600*	0.420682*	0.166332*	0.348528*
Subperiod No. 2	0.028273	-0.036127	0.083499	0.046539
Whole Period	0.247182*	0.338464*	0.207643*	0.292662*

1. Allowable Maximum Transactions Costs (MTC) are computed from:

$$MTC = \frac{X - 1.96\ SDX}{8\ T}$$

where X is the X-statistic (unadjusted for transactions costs), SDX is the standard deviation of X, and T is the estimated average transactions costs per 100 dollars of investment per day evaluated using transactions costs of one-eighth of one percent per round trip. Thus, MTC is the maximum transactions costs per round trip that will make the adjusted X-statistics significant at the 95 percent confidence level. Any per-round-trip transactions costs higher than MTC will make the trading rule return insignificantly better than buy-and-hold.

2. Figures with an asterisk are the cases where the adjusted X-statistics are significant at the 95 percent level, when transactions costs of one-eighth of 1 percent are used.

TABLE 18 Summary of the Statistical Significance of the Adjusted X-Statistics of Each Currency under Various Trading Rules.

CURRENCY	SUBPERIOD 1				SUBPERIOD 2				WHOLE PERIOD			
	A	D	S	M	A	D	S	M	A	D	S	M
Australian Dollar												
Austrian Schilling		X		X					X			
Belgian Franc	X	XX	XX	XX	X			X	XX	XX	XX	XX
British Pound						X						X
Canadian Dollar	X											
Danish Krone		X										
Deutsch Mark		XX	X						X	X	X	X
French Franc				XX			X		X	XX	XX	XX
Italian Lire											X	
Japanese Yen	X	XX	XX	XX					XX	XX	XX	XX
Netherland Guilder		X			X				X	X	X	XX
Norwegian Krone								X			X	
Spanish Peseta	XX	X		XX								
Swedish Krona												
Swiss Franc												
TOTAL NUMBER OF CASES	15	15	15	15	15	15	15	15	15	15	15	15
CASES SIGNIFICANT AT 95% CONFIDENCE LEVEL	4	7	3	6	2	1	1	2	6	7	5	6
Equally Weighted Portfolio	XX	XX	X	XX					XX	XX	XX	XX

1. A = Alexander filter, D = Double moving average, S = Single moving average, M = Mixed rule.
2. X and XX indicate that the adjusted X-statistics are significantly non-zero at 95 and 99 percent confidence levels respectively.

TABLE 19 Nonparametric Results for the Difference in the Adjusted X-statistics of Implementing Various Technical Trading Rules on Each Single Currency.

CURRENCY	WILCOXON MATCHED-PAIR SIGNED-RANK Z-SCORE						FRIEDMAN CHI-SQUARE TEST OF JOINT HYPOTHESIS
	ALEX-DMOV	ALEX-SMOV	ALEX-MIX	DMOV-SMOV	DMOV-MIX	SMOV-MIX	
Australian Dollar	-0.6488	-1.2567	-1.0471	-0.8579	-0.2394	-0.9137	4.0394
	(0.5165)	(0.2089)	(0.2951)	(0.3909)	(0.8108)	(0.3609)	(0.2572)
Austrian Schilling	-0.1109	-1.0615	-0.1109	-1.1519	0.0000	-1.1519	1.9898
	(0.9117)	(0.2885)	(0.9117)	(0.2493)	(1.0000)	(0.2493)	(0.5745)
Belgian Franc	-0.6938	-0.4422	-0.3235	-0.2200	-1.3697	-0.3807	1.1642
	(0.4878)	(0.6584)	(0.7463)	(0.8258)	(0.1708)	(0.7034)	(0.7616)
British Pound	-1.5082	-0.5403	-0.5123	-0.7885	-1.6232	-0.2633	11.5190
	(0.1315)	(0.5890)	(0.6085)	(0.4304)	(0.1046)	(0.7923)	(0.0092)
Canadian Dollar	-0.6610	-0.0519	-0.6610	-1.4386	0.0000	-1.4386	3.2414
	(0.5086)	(0.9586)	(0.5086)	(0.1503)	(1.0000)	(0.1503)	(0.3559)
Danish Krone	-0.5737	-1.6449	-0.5737	-0.1160	0.0000	-0.1160	1.0532
	(0.5662)	(0.1000)	(0.5662)	(0.9076)	(1.0000)	(0.9076)	(0.7884)
Deutche Mark	-0.8389	-0.5112	-0.5079	-0.1613	-0.2215	-0.3403	2.2490
	(0.4015)	(0.6092)	(0.6115)	(0.8719)	(0.8247)	(0.7336)	(0.5224)
French Franc	-1.4298	-1.1851	-1.4298	-0.5314	0.0000	-0.5314	4.5392
	(0.1528)	(0.2360)	(0.1528)	(0.5951)	(1.0000)	(0.5951)	(0.2088)
Italian Lire	-0.2410	-0.2614	-0.4468	-0.1759	-0.7440	-0.3652	0.3350
	(0.8096)	(0.7938)	(0.6550)	(0.8604)	(0.4569)	(0.7150)	(0.9533)
Japanese Yen	-0.2832	-0.7349	-0.7484	-0.3730	-0.3860	-0.4108	1.6448
	(0.7770)	(0.4624)	(0.4542)	(0.7092)	(0.6995)	(0.6812)	(0.6493)

Netherland Guilder	-0.5151	-0.3740	-1.1621	-1.6247	-0.2031	-1.6204	1.6442
	(0.6065)	(0.7084)	(0.2452)	(0.1042)	(0.8390)	(0.1052)	(0.6494)
Norwegian Krone	-0.3355	-0.5486	-0.4777	-1.4099	-0.8744	-1.2826	2.3324
	(0.7372)	(0.5833)	(0.6329)	(0.1586)	(0.3819)	(0.1996)	(0.5063)
Spanish Peseta	-1.7485	-1.5637	0.0000	-0.7679	-1.7485	-1.5637	6.7004
	(0.0804)	(0.1179)	(1.0000)	(0.4425)	(0.0804)	(0.1179)	(0.0821)
Swedish Krona	-0.7196	-0.2698	-0.7196	-0.6160	0.0000	-0.6160	0.0602
	(0.4717)	(0.7873)	(0.4717)	(0.5379)	(1.0000)	(0.5379)	(0.9961)
Swiss Franc	-0.6525	-0.8501	-0.0378	-1.2186	-0.6233	-0.7885	2.6468
	(0.5141)	(0.3953)	(0.9698)	(0.2230)	(0.5331)	(0.4321)	(0.4493)
Equally Weighted Portfolio	-2.3979	-1.5806	-2.2697	-0.4566	-0.2184	-0.4407	4.6958
	(0.0165)	(0.1140)	(0.0232)	(0.6480)	(0.8271)	(0.6594)	(0.1955)

1. The figures in the parentheses are the corresponding two-tailed p-values.

6

Variably Weighted Portfolios of Currencies, with Rules Tailored for Each Currency

In Chapter 5 we discussed the results for speculating on an equally weighted portfolio of currencies. Each currency had parameters specially tailored for it within each class of technical rules considered. Forming these currencies into equally weighted portfolios was simply a device to diversify risk; decisions to take speculative positions in one currency had nothing to do with positions taken in other currencies. It seems reasonable, however, to consider portfolio strategies where the positions across currencies show interaction. There are, of course, many ways in which to integrate the decisions across currencies. This chapter focuses on one approach that leads to variably weighted portfolios. If technical analysis has some predictive power, this variably weighted portfolio approach should tend to do better than the equally weighted portfolio approach, because it leads to more intensive use of funds, with funds lying idle less often in the risk-free but zero-excess-return Euro-dollar account. The results reported below support the view that the variably weighted approach used here gives superior performance. Not only is this approach highly profitable, it has the highest X-statistics of all the approaches tried in this book. A drawback of this approach is that it increases risk, as indicated by increased standard errors relative to equally weighted portfolios. This risk may be diversifiable, however; if this is so, the higher profits from this chapter's approach come with essentially no cost in terms of risk.

There are many other ways of carrying out multi-currency speculation, even if we agree to stick with rules with parameters tailored for each individual currency. The main complication in moving from single- to multiple-currency speculation is that there are many ways of allocating the available funds to each currency.

Under the approach adopted here, trading rules are used to find buy and sell signals on each currency in isolation without any constraints on how investment in each currency is to be allocated. The realized weights of the

currencies are the result of how many dollars are available to be allocated
to a particular currency when its trading rule gives a buy signal. Figure 3
is a flow chart detailing the steps for this type of speculation. First, in a prior
period, optimal ex post parameters are chosen for each currency for the class
of rule being used (for example, double moving average). At the beginning
of the following subperiod, the investor puts an equal amount of funds in
all currencies. On successive days, if there are sell signals for some
currencies, those currencies are sold. Funds obtained from sales of these
currencies are used to purchase a currency that triggers a buy signal that
day. If there is more than one currency with a buy signal that day, funds
obtained from currency sales are equally allocated to buy these currencies.
If there is no currency with a buy signal that day, however, funds are held
in the form of Euro-dollar deposits (which this book uses as the risk-free
asset) until there is a currency with a buy signal.

Another possibility under this approach is the case where there are buy
signals without any sell signals. In this case, if there are dollars remaining
from sales in previous periods that have not been used, these dollars are
spent to buy the currencies with buy signals. If, on the contrary, there are
no dollars from previous sales available, then those currencies are not
bought because the investor has no available funds. The investor is
assumed to have no other source of funds and, for tractability, levered
speculation is not considered here. Note that the possibility of receiving buy
signals that cannot be acted on means that the number of transactions can
be noticeably smaller than under the equally weighted portfolio approach,
where there are always funds available to buy; under the equally weighted
portfolio approach of Chapter 5, each currency is in effect a separate mutual
fund, with any available funds either fully invested in that currency or in a
Euro-dollar account waiting to be invested once again in the particular
currency.

As this discussion suggests, the approach presented in this chapter
typically leaves funds lying idle less often in the zero-excess-return Euro-
dollar account as compared to the equally weighted portfolio approach. It
should also be clear that there is more possibility of getting an undiversified
portfolio and hence higher risk. For example, if there are sell signals on the
same day for all currencies save (say) the French franc, which gets a buy
signal, the investor ends up with all funds in this one currency until that
currency gets a sell signal.

6A. Best Rules in the Prior Periods

The variably weighted portfolio approach uses the buy and sell signals
of each individual currency to speculate in the 15 currencies simultane-

ously. Hence, the sets of best rules used under this approach are the same sets of best rules used for both the single-currency speculations and for the equally weighted portfolio approach discussed in the previous chapter. For the review of these sets of best rules, see Section 5B.

The differences in results for the variably weighted and equally weighted portfolio approaches have nothing to do with any differences in underlying rules or parameters for the individual currencies. Instead, the differences result solely in how the weights of the portfolios are chosen. This portfolio formation procedure is outlined in Figure 3.

6B. Results of Speculation

Table 20 shows the simulation results using the variably weighted portfolio approach. The tests using the rebalancing X-statistics yield the same results, in terms of statistical significance, as the no-rebalancing X-tests in all cases except the mixed rule in subperiod 2, and even here the t-statistics are very close (1.91 versus 1.98). (See Chapter 3 for a discussion of the differences in X-tests using rebalancing and no-rebalancing benchmark portfolios.) The discussion focuses on the no-rebalancing benchmark portfolio case, because it requires fewer transactions costs to maintain this benchmark and hence this benchmark may be viewed intuitively as more realistic. The Wilcoxon Z-scores for rebalancing buy-and-hold are exactly the same in all cases as those for no rebalancing. This indicates that the signed rank of the two X-statistics is identical. This in turn implies that the difference between these X-statistics is only a matter of degree rather than order. In addition, the Wilcoxon matched-pair signed-rank tests generally yield the same statistical results as the parametric X-tests.

The Alexander filter technique performs extraordinarily well in the first subperiod. After adjusting for transactions costs, the portfolio X-statistics are significant at the 99 percent level. The averaged daily return from speculation is 0.024796 percent higher than the comparable buy-and-hold strategy. This amounts to a return of 6.24 percent per year in excess of buy-and-hold. Out of a $100 initial investment, the net profit (after deducting the transactions costs) from this speculation is $15.38.

In the second subperiod, however, the Alexander filter technique is not significantly superior to buy-and-hold. The adjusted X-statistic of 0.0074989 percent per day, or 0.6942 percent per year, even though positive, is extremely small and not statistically different from zero.

Following the double moving average technique also yields significant profits in the first subperiod. After transactions costs, the adjusted X-statistic is 0.0232553 percent per day, or 5.81383 percent per year, and is statistically significant at the 95 percent level. The total profit, net of transactions costs, from this speculation is $18.68 on an initial investment of $100.

In the second subperiod, speculation under the double moving average rule still yields a return, net of transactions costs, of 0.0200645 percent per day or 5.01612 percent per year higher than buy-and-hold. The standard error of these excess returns is also higher, however, so the adjusted X-statistic is not statistically significant at the 95 percent level.

Speculation using the single moving average technique is significantly profitable in both subperiods. The adjusted X-statistics in both subperiods are significantly positive at the 95 percent level, and these adjusted X-statistics are higher than the adjusted X-statistics obtained from the other technical trading techniques. After adjusting for transactions costs, the average returns on speculation are 0.0232553 percent per day (6.57 percent per year) and 0.0238703 percent per day (5.97 percent per year) higher than the average returns on buy-and-hold in subperiods 1 and 2. The profits net of transactions costs in the first and the second subperiods are $20.28 and $21.01.

There is one point worth mentioning here. Speculation under the variably weighted and equally weighted portfolio approaches uses the same sets of best rules. The single moving average technique seems to work very well in the variably weighted portfolio approach; it works less well in the equally weighted portfolio approach. As noted in the previous chapter, the best rules under the single moving average technique, although profitable, generate frequent transactions that substantially reduce the potential profits. In the variably weighted portfolio approach, however, there are cases when some of the rules trigger buy signals, but these currencies cannot be purchased due to the fact that all funds are fully invested in other currencies. The reduced number of transactions indirectly imposed by the variably weighted portfolio approach, together with the underlying profitability of the trading rules and the fact that the funds are used more intensively, enables this technique to produce larger profits than the equally weighted portfolio approach.

The mixed-rule strategy yields an average daily return, net of transactions costs, 0.0174693 percent higher than buy-and-hold in the first subperiod. Even though this excess return amounts to 4.357 percent per year, it is not statistically significant at the 95 percent level. In the second subperiod, however, the mixed-rule strategy yields a net excess return on speculation of 0.0212486 percent per day or 5.312 percent per year. The adjusted X-statistic is significant at the 95 percent level.

Table 21 shows the results of speculation using the variably weighted portfolio approach for the whole period. The whole-period speculations are highly profitable for all of the trading techniques used. The adjusted X-statistics are significant at the 95 percent level for the Alexander filter and mixed rules, and at the 99 percent level for the double moving average and single moving average. The average daily returns in excess of buy-and-hold returns are 0.0137864 percent, 0.216599 percent, 0.0250599 percent, and 0.0193590 percent for the Alexander filter, double moving average, single moving average, and mixed rules. These amount to 3.45 percent, 5.41 percent, 6.27 percent, and 4.84 percent of excess annual returns. The results generally indicate that speculation using the variably weighted portfolio approach is highly profitable. In fact, Chapter 9 shows that speculation using the variably weighted portfolio approach generally yields the highest excess return over buy-and-hold among all the types of speculation considered in this book.

Nevertheless, enthusiasm for the variably weighted portfolio approach should be tempered with the knowledge that it is riskier than the equally weighted portfolio approach. From Chapter 5, Tables 12, 14, 15, and 16, the whole-period standard errors for the results under the equally weighted portfolio approach for the Alexander, double moving average, single moving average and mixed rules are .004261, .004862, .004698, and .004686, with an average of .004627 (or 1.1568/year); under the variably weighted approach, from Table 21 the standard errors are .007995, .007701, .007636, and .007572, with an average of .007479 (or 1.8698/year). The ratio of the average whole-period standard for the variably weighted relative to the whole–period standard error for the equally weighted portfolio approach is 1.616. This is an indication of the relative risks of the two strategies. Although the variably-weighted portfolio approach offers higher expected rewards according to the above simulations, the investor can expect ultimately to face some unpleasant periods with bad outcomes as indicated by the standard errors.

It is possible that the risk represented by the portfolio standard error can be diversified away. For example, it is well known that estimates of market betas of currencies tend to be relatively close to zero and unstable. If the true betas on currencies are taken as zero and beta is assumed to be the appropriate measure of risk, this would imply that this chapter's portfolio risk is wholly diversifiable. Intuitively, if the investor puts, say, 5 percent of his/her funds in the speculative currency portfolio of this chapter, most of the risk of this currency portfolio gets diversified away. Put another way, the standard error of the portfolio almost surely overstates its risk for any investor who holds assets beyond the portfolio.

6C. Sensitivity of the Statistical Results to the Level of Transactions Costs

Table 22 shows the maximum transactions costs (MTC) allowable that retain the statistical significance of the adjusted X-statistics. Again, the asterisk indicates where the X-statistics, adjusted for transactions costs of one eighth of 1 percent (.0125%), are significant at the 95 percent level. In the first subperiod, the results are generally not sensitive to small changes (increases or decreases) in transactions costs. Transactions costs can be as high as one fifth of 1 percent, or as low as one thirteenth of 1 percent without changing the statistical significance of these results.

In the second subperiod, most of the statistical results are still insensitive to small changes in transactions costs, except for the mixed rule where a small increase in transactions costs from one eighth to one seventh of 1 percent makes the statistical results insignificant. Finally, for the whole period, the statistical results are not sensitive to small increases in transactions costs, with the exception of the Alexander filter. Transactions costs can rise to one fifth of 1 percent without changing the statistical significance of the results under the double moving average, single moving average, and mixed rules.

6D. Some Conclusions

The results in this chapter and Chapter 5 provide some startling evidence of the possibility of making profits by speculating in foreign exchange markets. The profits seem both economically and statistically significant, and they seem consistent in the sense that rule parameters found by searching in prior periods seem to lead to profits when applied in later periods. These results pose two major intellectual challenges. First, are the measured profits economic profits? Second if they are economic profits, why do such profits exist and, especially, why do they persist? These issues are discussed in detail in Chapter 11.

FIGURE 3

Flow Chart for Speculation Under the
Variably-Weighted Portfolio Approach

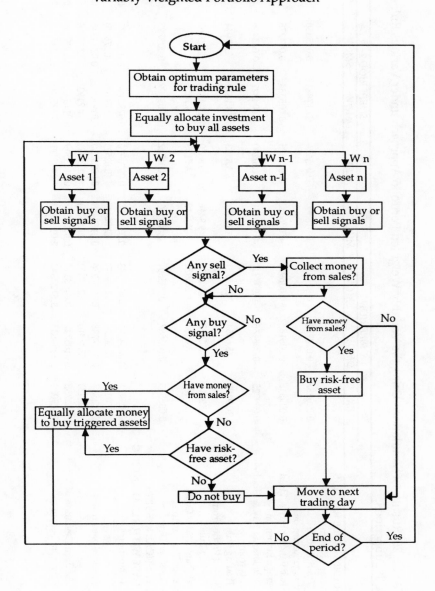

TABLE 20 Rusults of Simulations Using the Variably Weighted Portfolio Approach under Various Rules in Both Subperiods.

	SUBPERIOD 1				SUBPERIOD 2			
	ALEX	DMOV	SMOV	MIXED	ALEX	DMOV	SMOV	MIXED
TRADING RULE RESULTS								
Average Return on Trading Rule	0.020287	0.018274	0.024358	0.018300	0.005424	0.017881	0.025850	0.024094
Average Return on Rebalancing Buy & Hold	-0.009515	-0.008187	-0.006970	-0.006612	-0.001673	-0.005334	-0.004278	-0.001703
Average Return on No Rebalancing Buy & Hold	-0.009725	-0.008486	-0.007310	-0.006951	-0.000200	-0.004327	-0.003436	-0.000591
Profits from Trading Rule	20.9197	18.6854	25.8781	18.0994	3.8523	18.1472	27.7944	25.2705
Adjusted Profits from Trading Rule	15.3819	15.0017	20.2830	9.9446	-0.8650	14.4416	21.0065	20.0982
Total Transactions Costs	5.5378	3.6837	5.5951	8.1548	4.7173	3.7056	6.7879	5.1723
Average Transactions Costs per Day	0.005543	0.003687	0.005601	0.08163	0.004722	0.003709	0.006795	0.005177
STATISTICAL RESULTS CASE WITH REBALANCING								
X-statistics	0.0298021	0.0264612	0.0313283	0.0249118	0.0070970	0.0232154	0.0301283	0.0257970
	(3.6013)	(2.5028)	(2.8977)	(2.3241)	(0.6252)	(2.0462)	(2.7555)	(2.3910)
Adjusted X-statistics	0.0242588	0.0227738	0.0257276	0.0167488	0.0023750	0.0195062	0.0233335	0.0206196
	(2.9315)	(2.1540)	(2.3797)	(1.5626)	(0.2092)	(1.7193)	(2.1340)	(1.9111)
Standard Deviation of X	0.0082753	0.0105727	0.0108114	0.0107187	0.0113509	0.0113457	0.0109339	0.0107894
Wilcoxon Z-score	-3.2479060	-2.8964635	-3.6120842	-2.0185709	-1.2445411	-2.7295805	-3.1297703	-2.9035999

CASE WITH NO REBALANCING

X-statistics	0.0303394	0.0269427	0.0318789	0.0256323	0.0074989	0.0237737	0.0306651	0.0264260
Adjusted X-statistics	0.0247960	0.0232553	0.0262783	0.0174693	0.0027768	0.0200645	0.0238703	0.0212486
	(3.0297)	(2.1810)	(2.4526)	(1.6374)	(0.2442)	(1.7782)	(2.1936)	(1.9773)
Standard Deviation of X	0.0081843	0.0104842	0.0107144	0.0106692	0.0113695	0.0112839	0.0108819	0.010746
Wilcoxon Z-score	-3.2479060	-2.8964635	-3.6120842	-2.0185709	-1.2445411	-2.7295805	-3.1297703	-2.9035999

1. Average returns are presented as percent per day.

2. Profits are based on $100 initial investment. Adjusted profits are profits net of total transaction costs. Transaction costs of one-eighth of 1 percent per round trip are assumed.

3. Rebalancing cases are those where the weights of the buy-and-hold benchmark portfolios are held constant through rebalancing. No rebalancing Buy & Hold are the cases with strict buy-and-hold, where the weights of the buy-and-hold benchmark portfolios change through time as the prices of currencies evolve.

4. Units of X-statistics and average returns are in percent per day.

5. Adjusted X-statistics were computed by deducting average transactions costs per day from the corresponding X-statistics. Transactions costs of one-eighth of 1 percent per round trip are assumed.

6. Figures in the parentheses are the t-values of the corresponding estimated X-statistics.

TABLE 21 Results of Simulations Using the Variably Weighted
Portfolio Approach under Various Rules for the Whole Period.

	TRADING RULES IMPLEMENTED			
	ALEX	DMOV	SMOV	MIXED
TRADING RULE RESULTS				
Average Return on				
Trading Rule	0.012856	0.018078	0.025104	0.021197
Average Return on				
Rebalancing Buy & Hold	-0.005594	-0.006761	-0.005624	-0.004158
Average Return on No				
Rebalancing Buy & Hold	-0.004963	-0.006407	-0.005373	-0.003771
Trading Rule Profits	24.772	36.8326	53.6725	43.3699
Adjusted Trading Rule				
Profits	14.5169	29.4433	41.2895	30.0428
Total Transactions Costs	10.2551	7.3893	12.383	13.3271
Average Transactions				
Costs per Day	0.005133	0.003698	0.006198	0.006670
STATISTICAL RESULTS				
CASE WITH REBALANCING				
X-statistics	0.0184496	0.0248383	0.0307283	0.0253544
	(2.6268)	(3.2032)	(3.9968)	(3.3342)
Adjusted X-statistics	0.0133619	0.0211400	0.0245306	0.0186842
	(1.8960)	(2.7263)	(3.1907)	(2.4571)
Standard Deviation of X	0.0070236	0.0077541	0.0076882	0.0076043
CASE WITH NO REBALANCING				
X-statistics	0.0189192	0.0253582	0.0312720	0.0260292
	(2.7010)	(3.2927)	(4.0955)	(3.4378)
Adjusted X-statistics	0.0137864	0.0216599	0.0250743	0.0193590
	(1.9682)	(2.8125)	(3.2838)	(2.5568)
Standard Deviation of X	0.0070040	0.0077014	0.0076357	0.0075715

1. Average returns are presented in percent per day.

2. Profits are based on $100 initial investment. Adjusted profits are profits net of total transactions costs. Transactions costs of one-eighth of 1 percent per round trip are assumed.

3. Rebalancing cases are those cases where the weights of the buy-and-hold benchmark portfolios are held constant through rebalancing. No rebalancing Buy & Hold are the cases with strict buy-and-hold, where the weights of buy-and-hold benchmark portfolios change through time as the prices of currencies evolve.

4. X-statistics are presented in percent per day.

5. Adjusted X-statistics were computed by deducting average transactions costs per day from the corresponding X-statistics. Transactions costs of one-eighth of one percent per round trip is assumed.

6. Figures in the parentheses are the associated t-values of the estimated X-statistics.

7. Whole period results were computed using the averages or the sums of the subperiod results, depending upon each result entry. Standard deviations were computed with the sample moment formula, assuming no serial-correlation between the X-statistics between the two subperiods. Wilcoxon Z-scores are not computable since combining the results in the two subperiods implies changes in the ranking order.

TABLE 22 Sensitivity Analysis Results on the Maximum Transactions Costs Allowable for Statistical Significance of the Adjusted X-Statistics under the Variably Weighted Portfolio Approach Using Various Rules.

RULE	SUBPERIOD 1	SUBPERIOD 2	WHOLE PERIOD
Alexander Filter	0.32241431*	-0.39138625	0.12642612*
Double Moving Average	0.21674039*	0.05584951	0.34689776*
Single Moving Average	0.24280157*	0.17175958*	0.32887257*
Mixed Rule	0.07228758	0.12950129*	0.20268375*

1. Allowable Maximum Transactions Costs (MTC) are computed from

$$MTC = \frac{x - 1.96\ SDX}{8\ T}$$

where X is the X-statistic (unadjusted for transactions costs), SDX is the standard deviation of X, and T is the estimated average transactions cost per 100 dollars of investment per day evaluated using transactions costs of one-eighth of 1 percent per round trip. Thus, MTC is the maximum transactions costs per round trip that will make the adjusted X-statistics significant at the 95 percent confidence level. Any per-round-trip transactions costs higher than MTC will make the trading rule return insignificantly better than buy-and-hold.

2. Figures with an asterisk are the cases where the adjusted X-statistics are significant at the 95 percent level when transactions costs of one-eighth of 1 percent are used.

7

Speculating on Indexes of Currencies

In Chapters 5 and 6 we looked at speculation based on analysis of individual currencies. In this chapter we focus on the results of speculating on indexes of currencies, using two approaches to forming the indexes. The first approach uses currency weights that appear optimal on the basis of prior period results. The second approach simply uses an equally weighted index of all of the 15 currencies.

Speculating on indexes involves a trade-off between reducing the noise in the price series that gives buy-sell signals versus foregoing tailoring parameters separately for each currency considered. In Chapters 5 and 6, if, say, a double moving average rule was used for each currency, the lengths of the lags in both the long and short averages were chosen separately for each currency by experiments in the prior periods. The thought was that currencies are different enough that they warrant separate treatment. Exchange rates are very noisy series, however. It may be that particular lag lengths selected for a currency owe more to noise than to underlying pattern. Further, in later periods, noisy movements in a rate may trigger false signals or obscure true signals.

Cross-asset averages of noisy price series are well known to be less noisy than the underlying series are because of the smoothing properties of diversification. This suggests that focusing on an index of currencies may give the advantage of providing better estimates in prior periods of the underlying optimal parameters for use with a particular rule and may filter out more noise in subperiods than using parameters tailored to each currency. Which approach—individual currencies aggregated to a portfolio or an index—works better is an empirical issue.

In Section 7A we discuss the procedure for choosing weights in the optimally weighted indexes used in the empirical work and also why it might make sense to use an equally weighted index. The mean-variance optimum portfolios in both prior periods and the best ex ante technical trading rules for these portfolios and for equally weighted index portfolios are discussed in Section 7B. Sensitivity analyses suggest that these best rules are quite sensitive to changes in the level of transactions costs. The simulation results

141

in Section 7C indicate that speculating on an optimal index is significantly profitable in the first subperiod but not in the second subperiod. This poor result for the second subperiod arises because the mean-variance optimum portfolios in the second subperiod include only two currencies; further, in the single-currency speculation results in Chapter 5, these two currencies offered only small profit opportunities in the second subperiod. Speculating on an equally weighted index is profitable in both subperiods for all rules but is often not significantly profitable for some rules in some subperiods; for the whole period, the profits are significant for every rule. Section 7D shows that the speculation results are generally not sensitive to decreases in transactions costs but show somewhat greater sensitivity to increases in transactions costs.

7A. Choosing Indexes for Speculation

In this section we discuss two types of indexes for speculation, indexes with ex ante optimal weights and equally weighted indexes.

Choosing an Index Through Risk-Return Optimization

The index approach allocates speculative funds according to some weight vector. This weight vector is set before beginning speculation. For an individual investor, the obvious choice is to select the weight vector according to the individual's utility function. To simplify the problem, this study assumes that the individual investor is risk averse and, in particular, possesses a quadratic von Neumann-Morgenstern utility function with respect to rates of return. Thus, the problem can be modeled using a Markowitz-Sharpe formulation, giving the quadratic programming problem

$$\text{Max} \ h\,W'R - W'VW \qquad (7.1)$$

subject to

$$W'I = 1 \qquad (7.2)$$

and

$$w_j \geq 0 \qquad (7.3)$$

for all j, where R is the column vector of expected asset returns, W the column vector of weights, V the variance-covariance matrix of asset returns, and

I the unit column vector (Markowitz 1952; Sharpe 1963). The non-negativity constraint, (7.3), reflects the fact that all transactions are performed in spot markets where there is no short position.[1] The scalar h shows the degree of risk aversion. The possible values of h vary within the boundary of [0,] inclusive. The value of h is infinite if the investor is risk neutral and is zero if the investor is risk phobic. The lower the value of h, the higher is the degree of risk aversion. By varying the value of h, various weight vectors can be obtained as optimum values, given fixed R and V. There is an infinite number of solutions to this problem, depending upon the value of h chosen. Fortunately, it can be shown that 50 percent of possible solutions lie within the values of h ranging from 0.4142 to 2.4142 inclusive.

The maximization problem in (7.1) to (7.3) implies that h is the inverse of the slope of the efficient frontier at the optimum solution. As the investor is assumed to be risk averse, h cannot take on a negative value, and hence we are concerned only with the upper-right quadrant of the problem. Figure 4 shows the possible values of h. Because h is the inverse of the slope of the efficient frontier, the interval [0, ∞] of h can be represented by the interval [0,90] of degrees in angles. The cotangents of these angles, in turn, yield the values for h. By drawing lines dividing the right angle of the quadrant into four equilateral segments, the cotangents of the angles produced by these lines exhibit the values of h. It is obvious that 50 percent of the possible solutions lie within the h range of [0.4142, 2.4142]. This book uses the values of 0.4142, 1, and 2.4142 for h as they are the mid-boundaries of the four quartiles of all possible solutions. An infinite value for h collapses the problem into a one-asset speculation, because only the asset with the highest expected return will be chosen. In contrast, an h value of 0 is a very restrictive case where the investor wants to minimize variance regardless of expected return.

Following the general expectations formation model explained in Chapter 4, the maximization problem is performed prior to the period of speculation. Data from the prior period are used to compute the vector of expected returns and the variance-covariance matrix. Optimization is done using Wolfe's (1959) modification of the simplex algorithm, and the weight vector obtained from the ex post optimal solution is used as the ex ante weight vector for the index on which the investor speculates in the following subperiod. Figure 5 outlines the procedure for finding an optimally weighted index.

The weights obtained from quadratic programming are directly dependent on the risk-return structures of the assets studied. Therefore, it may turn out that only a few assets are chosen simply because they have better risk-return structures than the other assets. This is particularly true for speculation in currencies, where the risk-return structures are not as uniform as those of stocks (i.e., in a particular period, a currency with a higher average return may easily have a lower variance than a currency with a lower average return). Some currencies may yield negative returns in some period with higher variances than some other currencies that have positive returns. Given high positive correlation between the two currencies (as is often observed with exchange rates), the former will be completely dominated by the latter and will never enter into the basis of the optimal solution.   Under the index approach, the investor puts funds into every currency j at weight w_j whenever there is a buy signal. Buy and sell signals are triggered by movements of the price of the portfolio of currencies that has weight w_j for stock j. Therefore, buy or sell signals cause the basket of assets to be bought or sold simultaneously. The steps for speculation under the optimally weighted index approach are shown in Figure 6 and can be explained as follows.

Before the initial period of speculation, the investor gathers information on the past prices of all currencies in which he wants to speculate. Based on these past prices, he computes the ex post optimum weight vector (Figure 5). He then forms a time series based on past prices and the optimum weight vector and performs a simulation to search for the best parameters of rules for this index, using the process described in Section 4B. All three trading rules described in Section 4A are used—the Alexander filter, the double moving average and the single moving average rules. During the period of speculation, the index always gives each currency its optimum weight as found in the prior period. Then trading rules are applied to this index to see if there is any buy or sell signal noted. If there is a buy signal, the investor will buy all currencies according to the optimum weight vector and hold these currencies until there is a sell signal. Therefore, in every buying period, the weights of the currencies invested in are exactly equal to the ex ante optimum weights (which are also the weights of the index). As the investor holds these currencies in the later periods, however, and the prices of these currencies change over time, the actual weights of his portfolio will no longer exactly match the target optimum weights (or the weights of the index). The deviations from the ex ante optimum weights depend upon the length of the period these currencies are held, as well as exchange rate changes over the period. Normally, these deviations should be quite small. Nevertheless, to avoid the costs of transactions involved, there is no adjustment (buying or selling) to rebalance these weights. If there is a sell signal, all the currencies are sold.

The optimally weighted index method seems similar to the equally weighted portfolio formed from single-currency speculation described in Chapter 5. There are, however, differences between the two methods. First, because the optimally weighted index approach uses the optimum weight to allocate investments and transactions are done on the basket-of-currencies basis, this ensures that whenever the investor is in the market the weight of each currency in his/her portfolio will be close to the ex ante risk-return optimum rather than the foreign currency's weight simply being approximately one fifteenth when the currency is held. Therefore, the investor will hold a portfolio with what he views as a good risk-return structure, at least on an ex ante basis.

Second, under the optimally weighted index method, buy and sell signals are triggered based on the price of the index, not on the prices of individual currencies. When individual currencies are formed into an index, the price patterns generated by idiosyncratic disturbances of these currencies tend to cancel out. This leaves the portfolio price series with the more repetitive patterns that technical analysts look for, if the patterns are indeed there. Therefore, if the trading rule triggers some signals on the index, the hope is that it is more likely that these signals come from significant trend patterns rather than noise. Using an index of prices instead of prices of individual currencies, however, implies throwing away some information regarding currency-specific patterns that may be exploitable. Because transactions under the optimally weighted index approach are performed on the basket (all-or-nothing) basis, there may be instances where some currencies in the basket are bought even though the trading rule signals for these individual currencies strongly suggest selling. That is, the superiority of holding the portfolio with a good risk-return structure in the index approach and trying to filter out noise with the index is bought at the expense of having to buy some currencies when it is not perhaps a good time to do so.

An Equally Weighted Index

In addition to the weight vectors obtained from quadratic programming, the equally weighted vector is also used. Using this weight vector, funds are equally allocated to speculation in each currency. This weight vector is not necessarily optimal from the standpoint of portfolio theory. The use of this weight vector, however, assures that we have an index where all the currencies are speculated in. Moreover, this equally weighted vector might be motivated as consistent with the speculation of a firm that concentrates its business activities equally among foreign countries. The advantage of an equally weighted index over the equally weighted portfolio approach of Chapter 5 is that the index uses signals where aggregation reduces the noise of individual currencies' movements; its weakness is precisely its disregard of whatever information might be extracted from these individual currencies' movements. It is an empirical issue as to whether the benefits outweigh the gains.

7B. Best Rules in the Prior Periods

Table 23 shows the ex ante optimum weight vectors for both subperiods; these might be compared to an equal weight across the 15 currencies of 0.066667. These optimum weight vectors are the ex post optimum weight vectors obtained from prior periods' data. The returns and variances reported in Table 23 are those of the portfolios with the optimum weights during the prior periods. These ex post weights are used on an ex ante basis for speculation in the successive subperiods.

As should be expected, the optimum portfolio for the investor with a high degree of risk aversion (low value of h) yields a lower mean return with a lower variance in the prior periods. In the first prior period, the optimum portfolios for h values of 0.414, 1, and 2.414 contain 11, 9, and 6 currencies, respectively; even when the portfolio includes 11 currencies, the weights are often notably different from equal weights based either on 15 or 11 currencies. In the second prior period all the optimum portfolios contain only two currencies: the Australian dollar and the Canadian dollar. The dramatic differences between the optimum weight vectors of these two prior periods imply that the ex post risk-return structures of the 15 currencies change substantially between the two periods. This is a very common problem when Markowitz portfolio methods are applied to ex post data. One way around the problem is to find the optimal solutions using techniques that replace the actual data with data that are adjusted to capture the investigator's prior beliefs. Instead of imposing prior beliefs, we simply use the ex post data and the implied weights.

The ex post risk-return structures of the 15 currencies in the first prior period are more uniform in the sense that the currencies with a higher return tend to have a higher variance (see Table 8). In the second prior period, however, the ex post risk-return structures of the currencies are somewhat out of line. The feasibility of all the currencies other than the Australian dollar to enter into the optimal basis solution is ruled out by the fact that they all have higher variances than the Canadian dollar and yet yield smaller average returns. Therefore, the risk-return trade-off can only be found by changing the mixtures of the Canadian dollar and the Australian dollar. In terms of the critical line methodology, the results suggest that there are only two corner portfolios in the second prior period, with the Canadian dollar being the first variable to enter into the basis.

Using these optimum weight vectors from the prior periods, we formed price indices and applied trading rules to these indices to find the rules that gave the best results in the prior periods. Tables 24 to 26 report the ex post best rules for these indexes for speculation under the Alexander filter, double moving average, and single moving average rules. As with the single-currency speculations, the best rules in the two prior periods are not the same, which might be taken to indicate that the price patterns tend to change over time. Most of these ex post best rules perform extremely well in the second prior period. Their performances in the first prior period, however, are less impressive.

Table 27 presents sensitivity analyses of the effect of transactions costs on the best rules found in the prior periods. The sensitivity ranges of transactions costs indicate that some of the best rules are sensitive to the level of transactions costs. A small increase in transactions costs from one eighth to one seventh of 1 percent will change three of the four best rules for the double moving average in the second prior period. An additional increase in transactions costs to one sixth of 1 percent will change another three best rules for the Alexander filter in the first prior period. Some of the best rules under the single moving average, however, are sensitive to reductions in transactions costs. These rules are the case where h = 0.414 and h = 1.0 in the first prior period. Because 8 out of the total 12 best rules are quite sensitive to changes (increases or decreases) in the level of transactions costs, it should be clear that the results of speculation reported in this chapter may change substantially if the actual level of transactions costs are different from one eighth of one percent.

7C. Results of Speculation

When the ex post best rules found in the prior periods are used for speculation in the following subperiods, the speculative profits obtained from these rules are quite substantial, particularly for the first subperiod. Tables 28 to 31 report the results for the Alexander filter, double moving average, single moving average, and mixed rules. The tables give X-statistics for both the rebalancing and no-rebalancing buy-and-hold benchmark portfolio cases. These X-statistics and average returns are reported in percent per day. In all cases, the X-statistics for the no-rebalancing buy-and-hold case are slightly higher than under the rebalancing case. This indicates that in these samples, the strict buy-and-hold strategy performs less well than holding a constant-weight portfolio through rebalancing. In terms of statistical significance, however, the two X-statistics are similar, with the exception for the speculation under double moving average technique with h = 1.0 in the first subperiod.[2] As in previous chapters, the interpretations of the results in this chapter are based mainly on the adjusted X-statistic for the no-rebalancing benchmark case.

Speculation using the Alexander filter technique is highly profitable in comparison to buy-and-hold in the first subperiod, as judged by the adjusted X-statistic. Among the three classes of risk aversion, Alexander filter rule speculation yields excess returns over buy-and-hold that are statistically significant at the 95 percent level, even when transactions costs are taken into account. Speculations of investors with higher degrees of risk aversion yield higher excess returns.

In the case of the equally weighted index, speculation also yields higher, though not significant, profits than buy-and-hold.

The Alexander filter technique seems to perform less well in the second subperiod. Before deduction of transactions costs, these rules beat the market significantly. The frequent transactions created by these rules, however, eliminate much of the available profits when transactions costs are taken into account.

Under the double moving average technique, the best rules outperform buy-and-hold significantly in all cases, including the equally weighted index case, in the first subperiod. The adjusted X-statistics are significant at the 95 percent level. In the second subperiod, however, the performance of the best rules is not significantly superior to buy-and-hold; after adjusting for transactions costs, the adjusted X-statistics are small (ranging from 0.0044155 percent to 0.0119003 percent per day, or 1.103875 percent to 2.975075 percent per year) and are not statistically different from zero at the 95 percent level.

The single moving average technique yields average daily returns that are higher than those of buy-and-hold for all cases in the first subperiod. After adjusting for transactions costs, the adjusted X-statistics are significant at the 95 percent level in three out of the four cases. In the second subperiod, speculation on the equally weighted portfolio is still significantly profitable, with the return in excess of buy-and-hold of 0.0249302 percent per day or 6.23255 percent per year. Speculation on the other indexes, however, does not yield significant profits.

In previous chapters, the mixed–rule technique involved using potentially different rules on each currency that was then part of a portfolio. Here the mixed–rule technique uses potentially a different rule for each of the indexes in a particular subperiod. Similar to the results of the other technical trading strategies used on indexes, the mixed–rule technique works remarkably well in the first subperiod. For all of the indexes, the mixed–rule strategy provides the investor with significant profits in excess of buy-and-hold in the first subperiod; the adjusted X-statistics in all cases are significant at the 95 percent level.

In the second subperiod, the mixed–rule results are equivalent to those of the Alexander filter and, hence, need not be repeated here. The Alexander filter technique was used in the second subperiod because it yields the highest adjusted X-statistics in all cases in the second prior period. Hence all the ex ante global best rules in the second subperiod are simply the best rules under the Alexander filter technique.

Tables 32 to 35 show the speculation results for the whole period (i.e., subperiods 1 and 2 combined). For all of the optimally weighted indexes, the Alexander filter technique significantly outperforms buy-and-hold, yielding significant profits net of transactions costs. In the equally weighted index case, however, the excess return on speculation, although substantial

(.0147191 percent per day, or 3.679775 percent per year), is not statistically significant.

Following the double moving average rule for the whole period does not beat buy-and-hold significantly for the optimal indexes based on h = 0.414 and h = 1.0. In the other optimally weighted case (for h = 2.414) and in the equally weighted case, the adjusted X-statistics are significant at the 95 percent level.

In three out of four cases, the whole period results indicate that using the single moving average technique yields an average return significantly superior to buy-and-hold. The positive adjusted X-statistics are significantly nonzero at the 95 percent level for the optimally weighted indexes for the cases where h = 1.0 and h = 2.414, and at the 99 percent level for the equally weighted index case.

The mixed–rule technique seems to perform remarkably well for the whole period. The rules significantly beat buy-and-hold for all indexes. The adjusted X-statistics are statistically significant at 95 percent for the indexes based on the three classes of risk aversion, and at 99 percent for the equally weighted index case.

In sum, the results indicate that speculation using the index approach is highly profitable in the first subperiod. Out of 16 cases given by four technical trading techniques and four types of indexes, 14 cases yield daily profits that are significant (these results are not, however, statistically independent). Contrarily, the speculative performances in the second subperiod are not significant. The adjusted X-statistic is significant in only one case—for the equally weighted index using the single moving average rule. For the three optimally weighted indexes based on the three classes of risk aversion studied, which account for 12 of the total 16 cases, the insignificance of the results is not surprising. The ex ante optimum weight vectors used in the second subperiod constrain the investor to speculate in only two currencies—the Australian dollar and the Canadian dollar. As indicated by the results for single-currency speculation in Chapter 5, the profits from speculation in these two currencies are positive but not significant in the two subperiods.[3] Hence, the use of optimally weighted indexes to ensure the ex ante efficiency of the risk-return trade-off limits the investor to speculation in the currencies that have little profit opportunity.

7D. Sensitivity of the Statistical Results
to the Level of Transactions Costs

Table 36 reports the sensitivity of the above statistical tests to the level of transactions costs. Each entry in the table represents the maximum transactions costs (MTC) in terms of percent per round-trip that retain the statistical significance of the adjusted X-statistics at the 95 percent level. A negative MTC implies that the corresponding adjusted X-statistic will never be significant for any non-negative transactions costs. The asterisks indicate cases where the adjusted X-statistics are significant at 95 percent for a level of transactions costs of one eighth of 1 percent.

The results generally are not sensitive to reductions in transactions costs. Small decreases in transactions costs will not make significant the currently insignificant cases. The results, however, are more sensitive to increases in transactions costs, particularly the whole-period results. Nevertheless, these sensitivities are not overwhelming. Out of 11 significant cases in the whole period, 3 cases (the Alexander filter with h = 0.414 and h = 2.414, and the mixed rule with h = 0.414) turn out to be insignificant if the transactions cost rises from one eighth of 1 percent to one seventh of 1 percent. The same increase in transactions costs will render insignificant only 2 out of 14 significant cases in the first subperiod. Finally, in the second subperiod, where there is only one significant case, the significant result will not change even if the transactions costs are doubled.

Notes

1. For some applications, for example, a firm managing a currency portfolio and cash flows from manufacturing and import/export operations, the constraints in (7.3) might be nonzero numbers, through, say, not hedging scheduled payments in foreign currency.

2. Note that the conflict between the two X-tests happens in the case of adjusted X-statistics but not the unadjusted X-statistics. In all cases studied in this book, the (unadjusted) X-statistics of the rebalancing and no-rebalancing cases always yield the same results in terms of statistical tests and significance.

3. The fact that only the Australian dollar and the Canadian dollar are in the portfolios in the second subperiod may also explain the dramatic differences between the Wilcoxon signed-rank test results and the X-test results in this subperiod. As mentioned in Chapter 3, the Wilcoxon signed-rank test requires symmetry in the time-series of the X-statistics. This assumption is not satisfied in these cases, however, because the return distribution of the Australian dollar, as shown in Chapter 3, is positively skewed, though not that of the Canadian dollar. As a result, the return on the portfolio also has a distribution that is positively skewed. In such cases, we should rely on the X-test results rather than the Wilcoxon test.

FIGURE 4

Possible Values of the Degree of Risk-Aversion (h) in Risk-Return Space

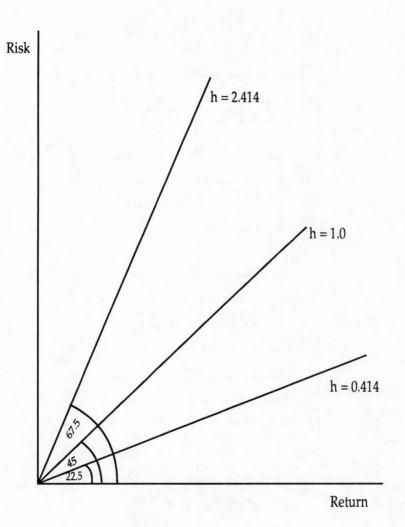

FIGURE 5

Optimum Weight Search Model

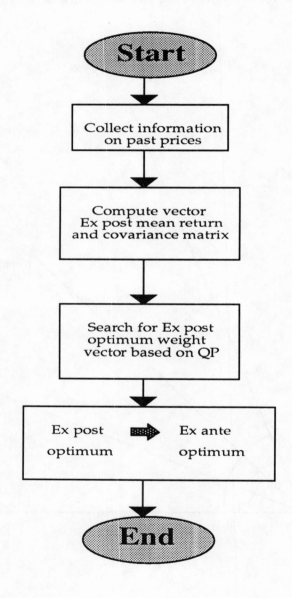

FIGURE 6
Flow Chart for Speculation under the
Index Approach

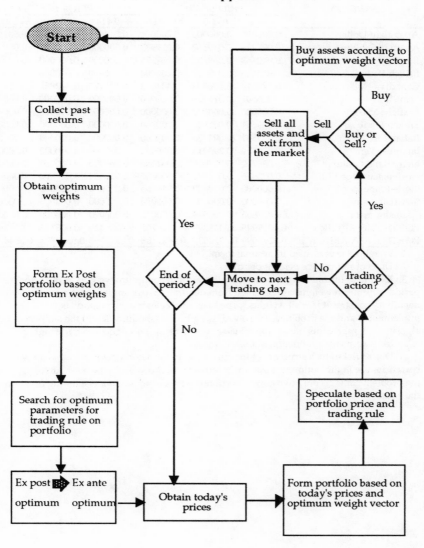

TABLE 23 Ex Ante Optimum Weights of Currencies under Various Degrees of Risk Aversion.

CURRENCY	PRIOR PERIOD 1			PRIOR PERIOD 2		
	$h=0.414$	$h=1.0$	$h=2.414$	$h=0.414$	$h=1.0$	$h=2.414$
Australian Dollar	0.000000	0.000000	0.000000	0.544825	0.557168	0.581852
Austrian Schilling	0.007228	0.019569	0.029933	0.000000	0.000000	0.000000
Belgian Franc	0.040463	0.069733	0.067776	0.000000	0.000000	0.000000
British Pound	0.035415	0.000000	0.000000	0.000000	0.000000	0.000000
Canadian Dollar	0.548118	0.520393	0.404463	0.455175	0.442832	0.418148
Danish Krone	0.026501	0.015576	0.000000	0.000000	0.000000	0.000000
Deutche Mark	0.000000	0.000000	0.000000	0.000000	0.000000	0.000000
French Franc	0.009681	0.001513	0.000000	0.000000	0.000000	0.000000
Italian Lire	0.033581	0.001738	0.000000	0.000000	0.000000	0.000000
Japanese Yen	0.229759	0.293913	0.390082	0.000000	0.000000	0.000000
Netherland Guilder	0.038712	0.071050	0.061580	0.000000	0.000000	0.000000
Norwegian Krone	0.002876	0.000000	0.000000	0.000000	0.000000	0.000000
Swiss Franc	0.000000	0.000000	0.046165	0.000000	0.000000	0.000000
Swedish Krona	0.000000	0.000000	0.000000	0.000000	0.000000	0.000000
Spanish Peseta	0.027665	0.006514	0.000000	0.000000	0.000000	0.000000
PORTFOLIO RETURN	-0.0019995	0.0043397	0.0110703	-0.0080429	-0.008116	-0.0082623
PORTFOLIO VARIANCE	0.0275098	0.0322039	0.0421188	0.0342506	0.0342795	0.0344225

1. Weights are presented in decimal form.

2. Units of returns are percent per day.

3. Ex ante optimum weights are the realized ex post optimum weights of the prior period. Optimum weights are obtained from quadratic programming with non-negativity constraints for all weights. The Markowitz-Sharpe formulation is implemented and the problems are solved using Wolfe's modification of the simplex algorithm. h represents the degree of risk-aversion or the willingness to trade higher expected returns for a reduction in the variance.

4. Due to risk-return structure of the currencies in the second prior period, only two currencies are in the optimum solution. In terms of Markowitz-Sharpe methodology, the problem contains only two corner portfolios with Canadian dollars entering first into the basis.

TABLE 24 Prior Period Results on the Best Alexander Filter Rules for the Index Approach, To Be Used as Ex Ante Rule for Portfolio Simulations in the Corresponding Subperiods.

| | PRIOR PERIOD 1 | | | | PRIOR PERIOD 2 | | | |
| | WEIGHTED ACCORDING TO h | | | EQUALLY WEIGHTED | WEIGHTED ACCORDING TO h | | | EQUALLY WEIGHTED |
	h = 0.414	h = 1.0	h = 2.414		h = 0.414	h = 1.0	h = 2.414	
Percent of Filter Up	0.80	0.80	0.60	3.40	0.40	0.40	0.40	1.00
Percent of Filter Down	0.80	0.80	0.60	3.40	0.40	0.40	0.40	1.00
X-statistics	0.0046810	0.0056270	0.0075230	0.0089130	0.0129900	0.0130400	0.0134100	0.0322900
	(1.7123)	(1.9591)	(2.2109)	(2.0445)	(4.2228)	(4.2368)	(4.354)	(3.9601)
Adjusted X-statistics	0.0034070	0.0041820	0.0051120	0.0086200	0.0089050	0.0089540	0.0093180	0.0280600
	(1.2464)	(1.4562)	(1.5023)	(1.9774)	(2.8946)	(2.9093)	(3.0255)	(3.4413)
Standard Deviation of X	0.0027340	0.0028720	0.0034030	0.0043590	0.0030760	0.0030780	0.0030800	0.0081540
Percent of Day Out of Market	0.4277778	0.3600000	0.444444	0.6722222	0.5344444	0.5344444	0.5433333	0.6144444
Profit from Filter	3.46280	8.09130	13.35070	9.08410	8.73250	8.74590	9.11140	21.50130
Adjusted Profit	2.31660	6.79151	11.18063	8.82095	5.05488	5.06891	5.42906	17.69471
Number of Transactions	9.	10.	16.	2.	28.	28.	28.	27.

1. The rules chosen as best were those which yielded the highest X-statistics, adjusted for transaction costs, in each prior period. The filter size ranged from 0.1 percent to 10.0 percent with step increments of 0.1 percent.

2. Units of X-statistics and average returns are percent per day.

3. Profits are based on $100 initial investment. Adjusted profits are profits net of total transaction costs. Transactions costs of one-eighth of 1 percent per round trip are assumed.

4. Adjusted X-statistics were computed by deducting the average transaction cost per day from the corresponding X-statistics.

5. Figures in the parentheses are the t-values of the corresponding estimated X-statistics.

156

TABLE 25 Prior Period Results on the Best Double Moving Average Rules for the Index Approach, To Be Used as Ex Ante Rule for Portfolio Simulations in the Corresponding Subperiods.

| | PRIOR PERIOD 1 | | | | PRIOR PERIOD 2 | | | |
| | WEIGHTED ACCORDING TO h | | | EQUALLY WEIGHTED | WEIGHTED ACCORDING TO h | | | EQUALLY WEIGHTED |
	h = 0.414	h = 1.0	h = 2.414		h = 0.414	h = 1.0	h = 2.414	
Short Moving Average	7.00	11.00	3.00	8.00	3.00	3.00	2.00	6.00
Long Moving Average	22.00	20.00	24.00	21.00	26.00	26.00	20.00	26.00
X-statistics	0.005075	0.005655	0.008604	0.01431	0.009904	0.009883	0.01185	0.02457
	(1.8376)	(1.9120)	(2.5672)	(3.1015)	(3.2279)	(3.2237)	(3.8578)	(3.0122)
Adjusted X-statistics	0.001967	0.002762	0.005079	0.01143	0.007176	0.007297	0.007563	0.02251
	(1.5156)	(0.9341)	(1.5156)	(2.4790)	(2.3387)	(2.3800)	(2.4610)	(2.7597)
Standard Deviation of X	0.002762	0.002957	0.003351	0.004612	0.003068	0.003066	0.003073	0.008158
Percent of Day Out of Mar!	0.3977777	0.424444	0.3977777	0.4422222	0.5500000	0.5555556	0.5544444	0.6133333
Profit from Filter	3.9098	7.8161	14.9966	15.1987	5.8725	5.863	7.6847	13.3007
Adjusted Profit	1.11253	5.2132	11.82464	12.61455	3.41714	3.5351	3.82172	11.44634
Number of Transactions	22.	20.	24.	19.	19.	18.	30.	14.

1. The rules chosen as best were those which yielded the highest X-statistics, adjusted for transaction costs, in each prior period. Degrees of moving averages ranged from 2 days to 30 days for the short moving average and 20 days to 50 days for the long moving average, both with step increments of 1 day. Intermediate cases, where the degrees of the long moving average were less than the degrees of the short moving average, were ruled out.

2. Units of X-statistics and average returns are percent per day.

3. Profits are based on $100 initial investment. Adjusted profits are profits net of total transaction costs. Transactions costs of one-eighth of 1 percent per round trip are assumed.

4. Adjusted X-statistics were computed by deducting the average transaction cost per day from the corresponding X-statistics.

5. Figures in the parentheses are the t-values of the corresponding estimated X-statistics.

TABLE 26 Prior Period Results on the Best Single Moving Average Rules for the Index Approach To Be Used as Ex Ante Rule for Portfolio Simulations in the Corresponding Subperiods.

	PRIOR PERIOD 1				PRIOR PERIOD 2			
	WEIGHTED ACCORDING TO h			EQUALLY WEIGHTED	WEIGHTED ACCORDING TO h			EQUALLY WEIGHTED
	$h = 0.414$	$h = 1.0$	$h = 2.414$		$h = 0.414$	$h = 1.0$	$h = 2.414$	
Degree of Moving Average	9.00	29.00	23.00	28.00	23.00	25.00	24.00	23.00
X-statistics	0.005826	0.004447	0.007628	0.01337	0.01091	0.01026	0.011	0.02804
	(2.1088)	(1.5117)	(2.2699)	(2.8941)	3.5549	(3.3421)	(3.5760)	(3.4087)
Adjusted X-statistics	-0.0047400	-0.0008895	0.0029480	0.0090060	0.0063590	0.0058600	0.0067300	0.0238900
	(-1.7158)	(-0.3024)	(0.8771)	(1.9487)	(2.0718)	(1.9082)	(2.1886)	(2.9039)
Standard Deviation of X	0.0027630	0.0029420	0.0033610	0.0046210	0.0030700	0.0030710	0.0030750	0.0082250
Percent of Day Out of Market	0.500000	0.408889	0.404444	0.451111	0.547778	0.547778	0.551111	0.594444
Profit from Filter	4.63960	6.72470	13.91310	14.21390	6.82040	6.16540	6.83050	16.35110
Adjusted Profit	-4.86975	1.92193	9.70043	10.28197	2.72321	2.20235	2.99065	12.61422
Number of transactions	74	37	32	29	32	31	30	28

1. The rules chosen as best were those which yielded the highest X-statistics, adjusted for transaction costs, in each prior period. Degrees of moving average ranged from 2 days to 50 days with step increments of 1 day.

2. Units of X-statistics and average returns are percent per day.

3. Profits are based on $100 initial investment. Adjusted profits are profits net of total transaction costs. Transactions costs of one-eighth of 1 percent per round trip are assumed.

4. Adjusted X-statistics were computed by deducting the average transaction cost per day from the corresponding X-statistics.

5. Figures in the parentheses are the t-values of the corresponding estimated X-statistics.

TABLE 27 Sensitivity Ranges of Transactions Costs on Ex Ante Optimum Rules for the Index Approach Using Various Rules.

TRADING RULE / WEIGHTING PROCEDURE	PRIOR PERIOD 1		PRIOR PERIOD 2	
	LOWER BOUND	UPPER BOUND	LOWER BOUND	UPPER BOUND
Alexander Filter				
h = 0.41	-0.0265963	0.5160914	-0.0149092	0.2760630
h = 1.00	-0.0335095	0.1625559	-0.0068370	0.2806789
h = 2.41	-0.0329955	0.1631539	-0.0115584	0.2660722
Equally Weighted	0.0967100	0.1641165	0.1132827	0.1893723
Double Moving Average				
h = 0.41	-0.0123545	0.1398095	-0.5795615	0.1262156
h = 1.00	0.0692916	1.1398549	-0.0321234	0.1288917
h = 2.41	0.0922934	1.3938770	0.0792014	0.1301440
Equally Weighted	0.0885950	0.3033882	0.0773975	0.5776739
Single Moving Average				
h = 0.41	0.1241107	0.4741213	-0.0809057	0.5417048
h = 1.00	0.1084547	0.6951771	0.1038456	0.3737655
h = 2.41	0.0371107	32.7841880	0.0356408	1.8075170
Equally Weighted	0.0241567	0.1371794	-0.0177060	1.8889815

1. Sensitivity range is defined as the range of transactions costs that can be varied without changing the ex post optimum rule in the prior period.

2. The base case of transactions costs used in the simulation is one-eighth of 1 percent per round trip.

3. Ranges of transactions costs are presented in terms of percent per round trip.

TABLE 28 Trading Rule and Statistical Results of the Index Approach for the Alexander Filter Rule in Both Subperiods.

	SUBPERIOD 1				SUBPERIOD 2			
	WEIGHTED ACCORDING TO h			EQUALLY	WEIGHTED ACCORDING TO h			EQUALLY
	$h = 0.414$	$h = 1.0$	$h = 2.414$	WEIGHTED	$h = 0.414$	$h = 1.0$	$h = 2.414$	WEIGHTED
TRADING RULE RESULTS								
Average Return on Trading Rule	0.010437	0.013275	0.017487	-0.001275	0.002707	0.004891	0.003752	0.019738
Average Return on Rebalancing Buy & Hold	-0.004496	-0.003607	-0.003069	-0.007780	-0.012222	-0.012406	-0.012694	-0.001806
Average Return on No Rebalancing Buy & Hold	-0.004648	-0.003858	-0.003482	-0.007887	-0.011627	-0.011799	-0.012067	-0.002152
Profits from Trading Rule	10.7255	13.8495	18.6084	-1.8861	2.3951	4.6305	3.4328	20.7750
Adjusted Profits from Trading Rule	7.0826	9.7235	10.7953	-3.3238	-7.1185	-4.9476	-6.5074	14.7433
Total Transactions Costs	3.6429	4.126	7.8131	1.4377	9.5136	9.5782	9.9402	6.0317
Average Transaction Costs per Day	0.003647	0.004130	0.007821	0.001439	0.009523	0.009588	0.009950	0.06038
STATISTICAL RESULTS								
CASE WITH REBALANCING								
X-statistics	0.0149326	0.0168826	0.0205558	0.0065050	0.0149291	0.0172965	0.0164461	0.0215445
	(2.9750)	(3.1195)	(3.1684)	(0.8485)	(2.0380)	(2.3216)	(2.1362)	(2.3418)
Adjusted X-statistics	0.0112861	0.0127525	0.0127349	0.0050658	0.0054060	0.0077088	0.0064960	0.0155067
	(2.2485)	(2.3564)	(1.9629)	(0.6608)	(0.7380)	(1.0347)	(0.8438)	(1.6855)
Standard Deviation of X	0.0050194	0.0054119	0.0064877	0.0076662	0.0073253	0.0074501	0.0076987	0.0092000
Wilcoxon Z-score	-2.6959843	-2.7710816	-2.6089196	-0.8563185	-0.9576560	-1.2578259	-0.7264352	-2.3154471

(Continues)

Table 28 (CONTINUED)

| | SUBPERIOD 1 | | | | SUBPERIOD 2 | | | |
| | WEIGHTED ACCORDING TO h | | | EQUALLY WEIGHTED | WEIGHTED ACCORDING TO h | | | EQUALLY WEIGHTED |
	h = 0.414	h = 1.0	h = 2.414		h = 0.414	h = 1.0	h = 2.414	
CASE WITH NO REBALANCING								
X-statistics	0.0152132	0.0172057	0.0210463	0.0068216	0.0157556	0.0181372	0.0173107	0.0226165
	(3.0386)	(3.1844)	(3.2613)	(0.9099)	(2.1436)	(2.4245)	(2.2368)	(2.4708)
Adjusted X-statistics	0.0115667	0.0130756	0.0132253	0.0053824	0.0062324	0.0085495	0.0073605	0.0165788
	(2.3102)	(2.4200)	(2.0494)	(0.7180)	(0.8480)	(1.1429)	(0.9511)	(1.8112)
Standard Deviation of X	0.0050067	0.0054031	0.0064534	0.0074969	0.0073499	0.0074808	0.0077391	0.0091535
Wilcoxon Z-score	-2.6959843	-2.7710816	-2.6089196	-0.8563185	-0.9576560	-1.2578259	-0.7264352	-2.3154471

1. Average returns are presented as percent per day.

2. Profits are based on $100 initial investment. Adjusted profits are profits net of total transaction costs. Transactions costs of one-eighth of 1 percent per round trip are assumed.

3. Rebalancing cases are those where the weights of the buy-and-hold benchmark portfolios are held constant through rebalancing. No rebalancing Buy & Hold are the cases with strict buy-and-hold, where the weights of the buy-and-hold benchmark portfolios change through time as the prices of currencies evolve.

4. Units of X-statistics and average returns are percent per day.

5. Adjusted X-statistics were computed by deducting average transactions costs per day from the corresponding X-statistics. Transactions costs of one-eighth of 1 percent per round trip are assumed.

6. Figures in the parentheses are the t-values of the corresponding estimated X-statistics.

TABLE 29 Trading Rule and Statistical Results of the Index Approach for the Double Moving Average Rule in Both Subperiods.

| | SUBPERIOD 1 | | | | SUBPERIOD 2 | | | |
| | WEIGHTED ACCORDING TO h | | | EQUALLY WEIGHTED | WEIGHTED ACCORDING TO h | | | EQUALLY WEIGHTED |
	h = 0.414	h = 1.0	h = 2.414		h = 0.414	h = 1.0	h = 2.414	
TRADING RULE RESULTS								
Average Return on Trading Rule	0.010412	0.009794	0.015379	0.012877	-0.003388	-0.003325	-0.00306	0.011485
Average Return on Rebalancing Buy & Hold	-0.004402	-0.003785	-0.002934	-0.005791	-0.01041	-0.010519	-0.011298	-0.001656
Average Return on No Rebalancing Buy & Hold	-0.004551	-0.004047	-0.003338	-0.005888	-0.009838	-0.009938	-0.010686	-0.001998
Trading Rule Profit	10.716	9.9691	16.1428	13.0482	-3.5964	-3.5435	-3.3251	11.2689
Adjusted Trading Rule Profit	7.7465	6.9444	12.6218	10.419	-6.9331	-6.88	-7.935	8.994
Total Transactions Costs	2.9695	3.0247	3.521	2.6292	3.3367	3.3365	4.6098	2.2749
Average Transaction Costs per Day	0.002972	0.003028	0.003525	0.002632	0.00334	0.00334	0.004614	0.002277
STATISTICAL RESULTS								
CASE WITH REBALANCING								
X-statistics	0.0148141	0.0135792	0.0183136	0.0186688	0.0070227	0.0071949	0.0082378	0.0131413
	(2.9560)	(2.4921)	(2.8197)	(2.3957)	(0.9689)	(0.9764)	(1.0758)	(1.4321)
Adjusted X-statistics	0.0118417	0.0105514	0.0147890	0.0160370	0.0036827	0.0038550	0.0036234	0.0108642
	(2.3629)	(1.9364)	(2.2770)	(2.0580)	(0.5081)	(0.5232)	(0.4732)	(1.1839)
Standard Deviation of X	0.0050115	0.0054489	0.0064948	0.0077925	0.0072485	0.0073688	0.0076573	0.0091763
Wilcoxon Z-score	-3.2189210	-2.6174834	-3.1527168	-2.9691454	-1.0110147	-1.0128812	-1.3621278	-2.2859132

(Continues)

TABLE 29 (CONTINUED)

| | SUBPERIOD 1 | | | | SUBPERIOD 2 | | | |
| | WEIGHTED ACCORDING TO h | | | EQUALLY WEIGHTED | WEIGHTED ACCORDING TO h | | | EQUALLY WEIGHTED |
	$h = 0.414$	$h = 1.0$	$h = 2.414$		$h = 0.414$	$h = 1.0$	$h = 2.414$	
CASE WITH NO REBALANCING								
X-statistics	0.0150895	0.0139167	0.0187910	0.0188877	0.0077556	0.0079385	0.0090327	0.0141774
	(3.0257)	(2.5704)	(2.9100)	(2.4473)	1.0655)	(1.0726)	(1.1757)	(1.5509)
Adjusted X-statistics	0.0121171	0.0108889	0.0152664	0.0162559	0.0044155	0.0045987	0.0044183	0.0119003
	(2.4300)	(2.0112)	(2.3642)	(2.1063)	(0.6066)	(0.6214)	(0.5751)	(1.3018)
Standard Deviation of X	0.0049872	0.0054141	0.0064574	0.0077176	0.0072789	0.0074010	0.0076827	0.091415
Wilcoxon Z-score	-3.2189210	-2.6174834	-3.1527168	-2.9691454	-1.0110147	-1.0128812	-1.3621278	-2.2859132

1. Average returns are presented as percent per day.

2. Profits are based on $100 initial investment. Adjusted profits are profits net of total transaction costs. Transactions costs of one-eighth of 1 percent per round trip are assumed.

3. Rebalancing cases are those where the weights of the buy-and-hold benchmark portfolios are held constant through rebalancing. No rebalancing Buy & Hold are the cases with strict buy-and-hold, where the weights of the buy-and-hold benchmark portfolios change through time as the prices of currencies evolve.

4. Units of X-statistics and average returns are percent per day.

5. Adjusted X-statistics were computed by deducting average transactions costs per day from the corresponding X-statistics. Transactions costs of one-eighth of 1 percent per round trip are assumed.

6. Figures in the parentheses are the t-values of the corresponding estimated X-statistics.

TABLE 30 Trading Rule and Statistical Results of the Index Approach for the Single Moving Average Rule in Both Subperiods.

| | SUBPERIOD 1 | | | | SUBPERIOD 2 | | | |
| | WEIGHTED ACCORDING TO h | | | EQUALLY WEIGHTED | WEIGHTED ACCORDING TO h | | | EQUALLY WEIGHTED |
	$h = 0.414$	$h = 1.0$	$h = 2.414$		$h = 0.414$	$h = 1.0$	$h = 2.414$	
TRADING RULE RESULTS								
Average Return on Trading Rule	0.013176	0.011462	0.017680	0.016813	-0.001039	0.002521	0.001926	0.027018
Average Return on Rebalancing Buy & Hold	-0.004686	-0.003727	-0.002899	-0.005727	-0.010704	-0.010621	-0.011017	-0.001697
Average Return on No Rebalancing Buy & Hold	-0.004841	-0.003986	-0.003299	-0.005823	-0.010127	-0.010037	-0.010410	-0.002043
Trading Rule Profit	13.7836	11.8286	18.8286	17.6138	-1.3087	2.2651	1.6377	29.8242
Adjusted Trading Rule Profit	4.0609	7.616	13.2224	13.1966	-6.7669	-2.7853	-3.5259	24.9867
Total Transactions Costs	9.7227	4.2126	5.6062	4.4173	5.4582	5.0505	5.1636	4.8375
Average Transaction Costs per Day	0.009732	0.004217	0.005612	0.004422	0.005464	0.005056	0.005169	0.004842
STATISTICAL RESULTS								
CASE WITH REBALANCING								
X-statistics	0.0178611	0.0151891	0.0205783	0.0225405	0.0096658	0.0131424	0.0129432	0.0287149
	(3.5628)	(2.7887)	(3.1717)	(2.8956)	(1.3292)	(1.7809)	(1.695)	(3.1169)
Adjusted X-statistics	0.0081287	0.0109723	0.0149665	0.0181188	0.0042021	0.0080869	0.0077744	0.0238725
	(1.6215)	(2.0145)	(2.3068)	(2.3276)	(0.5779)	(1.0959)	(1.0181)	(2.5913)
Standard Deviation of X	0.0050132	0.0054466	0.0064881	0.0077843	0.0072720	0.0073795	0.0076363	0.0092127
Wilcoxon Z-score	-2.9887981	-2.8607813	-3.2962142	-3.8036703	-1.5092483	-2.1327541	-2.1127720	-3.525294

(Continues)

TABLE 30 (CONTINUED)

| | SUBPERIOD 1 | | | | SUBPERIOD 2 | | | |
| | WEIGHTED ACCORDING TO h | | | EQUALLY WEIGHTED | WEIGHTED ACCORDING TO h | | | EQUALLY WEIGHTED |
	h = 0.414	h = 1.0	h = 2.414		h = 0.414	h = 1.0	h = 2.414	
CASE WITH NO REBALANCING								
X-statistics	0.0181494	0.0155230	0.0210514	0.0227565	0.0104146	0.0138917	0.0137231	0.0297725
	(3.6337)	(2.8652)	(3.2594)	(2.9569)	(1.4258)	(1.8724)	(1.7885)	(3.246)
Adjusted X-statistics	0.0084170	0.0113063	0.0154396	0.0183348	0.0049510	0.0088362	0.0085544	0.0249302
	(1.6851)	(2.0869)	(2.3905)	(2.3823)	(0.6778)	(1.191)	(1.1149)	(2.7181)
Standard Deviation of X	0.0049948	0.0054178	0.0064588	0.0076961	0.0073045	0.0074193	0.0076731	0.0091719
Wilcoxon Z-score	-2.9887981	-2.8607813	-3.2962142	-3.8036703	-1.5092483	-2.1327541	-2.112772	-3.5251294

1. Average returns are presented as percent per day.

2. Profits are based on $100 initial investment. Adjusted profits are profits net of total transaction costs. Transactions costs of one-eighth of 1 percent per round trip are assumed.

3. Rebalancing cases are those where the weights of the buy-and-hold benchmark portfolios are held constant through rebalancing. No rebalancing Buy & Hold are the cases with strict buy-and-hold, where the weights of the buy-and-hold benchmark portfolios change through time as the prices of currencies evolve.

4. Units of X-statistics and average returns are percent per day.

5. Adjusted X-statistics were computed by deducting average transactions costs per day from the corresponding X-statistics. Transactions costs of one-eighth of 1 percent per round trip are assumed.

6. Figures in the parentheses are the t-values of the corresponding estimated X-statistics.

TABLE 31 Trading Rule and Statistical Results of the Index Approach for the Mixed Rule in Both Subperiods.

	SUBPERIOD 1				SUBPERIOD 2			
	WEIGHTED ACCORDING TO h			EQUALLY WEIGHTED	WEIGHTED ACCORDING TO h			EQUALLY WEIGHTED
	$h = 0.414$	$h = 1.0$	$h = 2.414$		$h = 0.414$	$h = 1.0$	$h = 2.414$	
RULE IMPLEMENTED	ALEX	ALEX	DMOV	DMOV	ALEX	ALEX	ALEX	ALEX
TRADING RULE RESULTS								
Average Return on Trading Rule	0.010437	0.013275	0.015379	0.012877	0.002707	0.004891	0.003752	0.019738
Average Return on Rebalancing Buy & Hold	-0.004496	-0.003607	-0.002934	-0.005791	-0.012222	-0.012406	-0.012694	-0.001806
Average Return on No Rebalancing Buy & Hold	-0.004648	-0.003858	-0.003338	-0.005888	-0.011627	-0.011799	-0.012067	-0.002152
Trading Rule Profits	10.7255	13.8495	16.1428	13.0482	2.3951	4.6305	3.4328	20.7750
Adjusted Trading Rule Profits	7.0826	9.7235	12.6218	10.4190	-7.1185	-4.9476	-6.5074	14.7433
Total Transactions Costs	3.6429	4.1260	3.5210	2.6292	9.5136	9.5782	9.9402	6.0317
Average Transaction Costs per Day	0.003647	0.004130	0.003525	0.002632	0.009523	0.009588	0.009950	0.006038
STATISTICAL RESULTS								
CASE WITH REBALANCING								
X-statistics	0.0149326	0.0168826	0.0183136	0.0186688	0.0149291	0.0172965	0.0164461	0.0215445
	(2.9750)	(3.1195)	(2.8197)	(2.3957)	(2.0380)	(2.3216)	(2.1362)	(2.3418)
Adjusted X-statistics	0.0112861	0.0127525	0.0147890	0.0160370	0.0054060	0.0077088	0.0064960	0.0155067
	(2.2485)	(2.3564)	(2.2770)	(2.0580)	(0.7380)	(1.0347)	(0.8438)	(1.6855)
Standard Deviation of X	0.0050194	0.0054119	0.0064948	0.0077925	0.0073253	0.0074501	0.0076987	0.0092000
Wilcoxon Z-score	-2.6959843	-2.7710816	-3.1527168	-2.9691454	-0.9576560	-1.2578259	-0.7264352	-2.3154471

(Continues)

TABLE 31 (CONTINUED)

| | SUBPERIOD 1 | | | | SUBPERIOD 2 | | | |
| | WEIGHTED ACCORDING TO h | | | EQUALLY | WEIGHTED ACCORDING TO h | | | EQUALLY |
	h = 0.414	h = 1.0	h = 2.414	WEIGHTED	h = 0.414	h = 1.0	h = 2.414	WEIGHTED
CASE WITH NO REBALANCING								
X-statistics	0.0152132	0.0172057	0.0187910	0.0188877	0.0157556	0.0181372	0.0173107	0.0226165
	(3.0386)	(3.1844)	(2.9100)	(2.4473)	(2.1436)	(2.4245)	(2.2368)	(2.4708)
Adjusted X-statistics	0.0115667	0.0130756	0.0152664	0.0162559	0.0062324	0.0085495	0.0073605	0.0165788
	(2.3102)	(2.4200)	(2.3642)	(2.1063)	(0.8480)	(1.1429)	(0.9511)	(1.8112)
Standard Deviation of X	0.0050067	0.0054031	0.0064574	0.0077176	0.0073499	0.0074808	0.0077391	0.0091535
Wilcoxon Z-score	-2.6959843	-2.7710816	-3.1527168	-2.9691454	-0.9576560	-1.2578259	-0.7264352	-2.3154471

1. Average returns are presented as percent per day.

2. Profits are based on $100 initial investment. Adjusted profits are profits net of total transaction costs. Transactions costs of one-eighth of 1 percent per round trip are assumed.

3. Rebalancing cases are those where the weights of the buy-and-hold benchmark portfolios are held constant through rebalancing. No rebalancing Buy & Hold are the cases with strict buy-and-hold, where the weights of the buy-and-hold benchmark portfolios change through time as the prices of currencies evolve.

4. Units of X-statistics and average returns are percent per day.

5. Adjusted X-statistics were computed by deducting average transactions costs per day from the corresponding X-statistics. Transactions costs of one-eighth of 1 percent per round trip are assumed.

6. Figures in the parentheses are the t-values of the corresponding estimated X-statistics.

7. The mixed rule strategy exploits the best of all types of trading rules found in the corresponding prior period.

TABLE 32 Results of Simulations Using the Index Approach and
Alexander Filter Rule for the Whole Period.

	WEIGHTED ACCORDING TO h			EQUALLY WEIGHTED
	$h = 0.414$	$h = 1.0$	$h = 2.414$	
TRADING RULE RESULTS				
Average Return on				
Trading Rule	0.006572	0.009083	0.010620	0.009232
Average Return on				
Rebalancing Buy & Hold	-0.008359	-0.008007	-0.007881	-0.004793
Average Return on No				
Rebalancing Buy & Hold	-0.008137	-0.007829	-0.007774	-0.005020
Profits from Trading				
Rule Speculation	13.1207	18.4800	22.0413	18.8889
Adjusted Trading Rule				
Profits	-.0358	4.7759	4.2880	11.4195
Total Transactions Costs	13.1565	13.7042	17.7533	7.4694
Average Transaction				
Costs per Day	0.006586	0.006589	0.008886	0.003739
STATISTICAL RESULTS				
CASE WITH REBALANCING				
X-statistics	0.0149309	0.0170896	0.0185010	0.0140247
	(3.3628)	(3.7118)	(3.6753)	(2.3422)
Adjusted X-statistics	0.0083460	0.0102306	0.0096154	0.0102863
	(1.8797)	(2.2220)	(1.9101)	(1.7179)
Standard Deviation of X	0.0044400	0.0046042	0.0050339	0.0059877
CASE WITH NO REBALANCING				
X-statistics	0.0154844	0.0176715	0.0191785	0.0147191
	(3.4823)	(3.8300)	(3.8065)	(2.4881)
Adjusted X-statistics	0.0088996	0.0108125	0.0102929	0.0109806
	(2.0014)	(2.3434)	(2.0429)	(1.8561)
Standard Deviation of X	0.0044466	0.0046140	0.0050383	0.0059159

1. Average returns are presented in percent per day.

2. Profits are based on $100 initial investment. Adjusted profits are profits net of total transactions costs. Transactions costs of one-eighth of 1 percent per round trip are assumed.

3. Rebalancing cases are those cases where the weights of the buy-and-hold benchmark portfolios are held constant through rebalancing. No rebalancing Buy & Hold are the cases with strict buy-and-hold, where the weights of buy-and-hold benchmark portfolios change through time as the prices of currencies evolve.

4. X-statistics are presented in percent per day.

5. Adjusted X-statistics were computed by deducting average transactions costs per day from the corresponding X-statistics. Transactions costs of one-eighth of 1 percent per round trip are assumed.

6. Figures in the parentheses are the associated t-values of the estimated X-statistics.

TABLE 33 Results of Simulations Using the Index Approach and
Double Moving Average Rule for the Whole Period.

| | WEIGHTED ACCORDING TO h | | | EQUALLY WEIGHTED |
	h = 0.414	h = 1.0	h = 2.414	
TRADING RULE RESULTS				
Average Return on				
Trading Rule	0.003512	0.003235	0.00616	0.012181
Average Return on				
Rebalancing Buy & Hold	-0.007406	-0.007152	-0.007116	-0.003724
Average Return on No				
Rebalancing Buy & Hold	-0.007195	-0.006993	-0.007012	-0.003943
Profits from Trading				
Rule Speculation	7.1196	6.4256	12.8177	24.3170
Adjusted Trading Rule				
Profits	0.8134	0.0644	4.6869	19.413
Total Transactions Costs	6.3062	6.3612	8.1308	4.904
Average Transaction				
Costs per Day	0.003156	0.003184	0.004070	0.002445
STATISTICAL RESULTS				
CASE WITH REBALANCING				
X-statistics	0.0109184	0.0103871	0.0132757	0.0159051
	(2.4780)	(2.2668)	(2.6444)	(2.6424)
Adjusted X-statistics	0.0077622	0.0073032	0.0092006	0.0134506
	(1.7617)	(1.5720)	(1.8338)	(2.2346)
Standard Deviation of X	0.0044061	0.0045823	0.0050204	0.0060193
CASE WITH NO REBALANCING				
X-statistics	0.0114226	0.0109276	0.0134119	0.0165326
	(2.5891)	(2.3834)	(2.6727)	(2.7638)
Adjusted X-statistics	0.0082663	0.0077438	0.0081913	0.0140781
	(1.8737)	(1.689)	(1.9614)	(2.3535)
Standard Deviation of X	0.0044118	0.0045850	0.0050180	0.0059818

1. Average returns are presented in percent per day.

2. Profits are based on $100 initial investment. Adjusted profits are profits net of
total transactions costs. Transactions costs of one-eighth of 1 percent per round trip
are assumed.

3. Rebalancing cases are those cases where the weights of the buy-and-hold
benchmark portfolios are held constant through rebalancing. No rebalancing Buy &
Hold are the cases with strict buy-and-hold, where the weights of buy-and-hold
benchmark portfolios change through time as the prices of currencies evolve.

4. X-statistics are presented in percent per day.

5. Adjusted X-statistics were computed by deducting average transactions costs per
day from the corresponding X-statistics. Transactions costs of one-eighth of 1
percent per round trip are assumed.

6. Figures in the parentheses are the associated t-values of the estimated
X-statistics.

TABLE 34 Results of Simulations Using the Index Approach and
Single Moving Average Rule for the Whole Period.

	WEIGHTED ACCORDING TO h			EQUALLY WEIGHTED
	h = 0.414	h = 1.0	h = 2.414	
TRADING RULE RESULTS				
Average Return on				
Trading Rule	0.006068	0.006992	0.009803	0.021916
Average Return on				
Rebalancing Buy & Hold	-0.007695	-0.007174	-0.006958	-0.003712
Average Return on No				
Rebalancing Buy & Hold	-0.007484	-0.007012	-0.006855	-0.003933
Profits from Trading				
Rule Speculation	12.4749	14.0937	20.4663	47.4381
Adjusted Trading Rule				
Profits	-2.706	4.8307	9.6965	38.1833
Total Transactions Costs	15.1809	9.263	10.7698	9.2548
Average Transaction				
Costs per Day	0.007589	0.004636	0.005391	0.004632
STATISTICAL RESULTS				
CASE WITH REBALANCING				
X-statistics	0.0137634	0.0141658	0.0167607	0.0256277
	(3.1165)	(3.0890)	(3.3453)	(4.2496)
Adjusted X-statistics	0.0061654	0.0095296	0.0113704	0.0209957
	(1.3961)	(2.0780)	(2.2695)	(3.4816)
Standard Deviation of X	0.0044163	0.0045859	0.0050102	0.0060305
CASE WITH NO REBALANCING				
X-statistics	0.014282	0.0147074	0.0173873	0.0262645
	(3.2280)	(3.2018)	(3.4672)	(4.3873)
Adjusted X-statistics	0.006684	0.0100712	0.011997	0.0216325
	(1.5107)	(2.1925)	(2.3923)	(3.6135)
Standard Deviation of X	0.0044245	0.0045934	0.0050148	0.0059865

  1. Average returns are presented in percent per day.

  2. Profits are based on $100 initial investment. Adjusted profits are profits net of
total transactions costs. Transactions costs of one-eighth of 1 percent per round trip
are assumed.

  3. Rebalancing cases are those cases where the weights of the buy-and-hold
benchmark portfolios are held constant through rebalancing. No rebalancing Buy &
Hold are the cases with strict buy-and-hold, where the weights of buy-and-hold
benchmark portfolios change through time as the prices of currencies evolve.

  4. X-statistics are presented in percent per day.

  5. Adjusted X-statistics were computed by deducting average transactions costs per
day from the corresponding X-statistics. Transactions costs of one-eighth of 1
percent per round trip are assumed.

  6. Figures in the parentheses are the associated t-values of the estimated
X-statistics.

TABLE 35 Results of Simulations Using the Index Approach and Mixed Rule for the Whole Period.

	WEIGHTED ACCORDING TO h			EQUALLY WEIGHTED
	$h = 0.414$	$h = 1.0$	$h = 2.414$	
TRADING RULE RESULTS				
Average Return on				
Trading Rule	0.006572	0.009083	0.009566	0.016308
Average Return on				
Rebalancing Buy & Hold	-0.008359	-0.008007	-0.007814	-0.003799
Average Return on No				
Rebalancing Buy & Hold	-0.008137	-0.007829	-0.007703	-0.004020
Profits from Trading				
Rule Speculation	13.1207	18.4800	19.5756	33.8232
Adjusted Trading Rule				
Profits	-0.0358	4.7759	6.1144	25.1623
Total Transactions Costs	13.1565	13.7042	13.4612	8.6609
Average Transaction				
Costs per Day	0.006585	0.006589	0.006738	0.004335
STATISTICAL RESULTS				
CASE WITH REBALANCING				
X-statistics	0.149309	0.0170896	0.0173799	0.0201067
	(3.3628)	(3.7118)	(3.4510)	(3.3654)
Adjusted X-statistics	0.0083460	0.0102306	0.0106425	0.0157719
	(1.8797)	(2.2220)	(2.1132)	(2.6163)
Standard Deviation of X	0.0044400	0.0046042	0.0050362	0.0060283
CASE WITH NO REBALANCING				
X-statistics	0.154844	0.176715	0.180509	0.0207521
	(3.4823)	(3.8300)	(3.5818)	(3.4665)
Adjusted X-statistics	0.0088996	0.0108125	0.0113135	0.0164174
	(2.0014)	(2.3434)	(2.2449)	(2.7424)
Standard Deviation of X	0.0044466	0.0046140	0.0050396	0.0059864

1. Average returns are presented in percent per day.

2. Profits are based on $100 initial investment. Adjusted profits are profits net of total transactions costs. Transactions costs of one-eighth of 1 percent per round trip are assumed.

3. Rebalancing cases are those cases where the weights of the buy-and-hold benchmark portfolios are held constant through rebalancing. No rebalancing Buy & Hold are the cases with strict buy-and-hold, where the weights of buy-and-hold benchmark portfolios change through time as the prices of currencies evolve.

4. X-statistics are presented in percent per day.

5. Adjusted X-statistics were computed by deducting average transactions costs per day from the corresponding X-statistics. Transactions costs of one-eighth of 1 percent per round trip are assumed.

6. Figures in the parentheses are the associated t-values of the estimated X-statistics.

7. The mixed rule strategy exploits the best rules of all types of trading rules found in the corresponding prior period.

TABLE 36 Sensitivity Analysis Results on the Maximum Transactions Costs Allowable for Statistical Significance of the Adjusted X-statistics under the Index Approach Using Various Rules.

WEIGHTING METHOD/ & SUBPERIOD	ALEXANDER FILTER	DOUBLE MOVING AVERAGE	SINGLE MOVING AVERAGE	MIXED RULE
Subperiod 1				
h = 0.414	0.1851113*	0.2234973*	0.1073681	0.1851113*
h = 1.000	0.2002259*	0.1364542*	0.1453777*	0.2002259*
h = 2.414	0.1342162*	0.2175600*	0.1869309*	0.2175600*
Equally Weighted	-0.6837413	0.1786422*	0.216889*	0.1786422*
Subperiod 2				
h = 0.414	0.0177172	-0.2436695	-0.0892777	0.0177172
h = 1.000	0.0452743	-0.2458029	-0.0160748	0.0452743
h = 2.414	0.0269098	-0.1632225	-0.0318304	0.0269098
Equally Weighted	0.0969404	-0.2053017	0.3044931*	0.0969404
Whole Period				
h = 0.414	0.1284979*	0.1099179	0.0922937	0.1284979*
h = 1.000	0.1572398*	0.0762061	0.1537988*	0.1572398*
h = 2.414	0.1308779*	0.0856372	0.1752753*	0.1564017*
Equally Weighted	0.1044515	0.2448702*	0.3921352*	0.2390892*

1. Allowable Maximum Transactions Costs (MTC) are computed from

$$MTC = \frac{X - 1.96\,SDX}{8T}$$

where X is the X-statistic (unadjusted for transactions costs), SDX is the standard deviation of X, and T is the estimated average transactions costs per 100 dollars of investment per day evaluated using transactions costs of one-eighth of one percent per round trip. Thus, MTC is the maximum transaction costs per round trip that will make the adjusted X-statistics significant at the 95 percent confidence level. Any per-round-trip transactions costs higher than MTC will make the trading rule return insignificantly better than buy-and-hold.

2. Figures with an asterisk are the cases where the adjusted X-statistics are significant at the 95 percent level when transactions costs of one-eighth of 1 percent are used.

8

Speculating with a
Portfolio Upgrade Approach

So far, we have examined two classes of technical analysis. In one class, the equally and variably weighted portfolio approaches rely on tailoring technical rules, for example, the double moving average rule, for each currency by finding optimal parameters in prior periods. These two portfolio approaches differ only in how the speculations are combined into portfolios. The second general class of technical analysis considered above looks at speculation on indexes, whether optimally weighted or simple equally weighted indexes; the technical rules are then applied to the index as a whole with rule parameters optimally chosen for the particular index rather than for each currency in the index. The third general class that this book considers is the "portfolio upgrade" approach.

A popular type of technical analysis, the portfolio upgrade approach concentrates on each asset's relative performance rather than fully exploiting price trends in individual assets.[1] Thus, it does not exploit any of the three trading rules described in Section 4A and used in speculation in the equally weighted and variably weighted portfolio approaches or in the index approach in Chapters 5 to 7. There are two rule parameters involved in the portfolio upgrade approach. First is the top chosen rank, R. This parameter is used to select the assets to be held in the portfolio. Only the assets that are in the top R rank are initially bought. The second parameter is the maximum rank tolerance, K. This is the maximum rank allowed for any of the assets to be retained in the portfolio, with K > R. Any asset held in the portfolio that shows a decline in performance such that its rank falls below K is sold, with the funds generated used equally to buy shares in the current top R assets.

The portfolio upgrade approach is significantly profitable in the first subperiod but not in the second subperiod. The poor performance of this approach in the second subperiod leads to insignificant results for the whole period despite the strong performance in the first subperiod. The variability in performance across the subperiods is perhaps to be expected because in both subperiods the approach has the investor holding a poorly diversified portfolio of only two currencies at any time.

8A. Using the Portfolio Upgrade Approach

Asset ranks are based on "relative strength indices" in descending order. A relative strength index is defined as the relative price of an asset compared to its past average price; the currency that is highest relative to its average gets the rank "1." Typically, the average price of the past six months is used. Because the data used in this study are daily, average prices from the past 125 trading days are used, as this is a good approximation for six months.

Figure 7 illustrates the portfolio upgrade approach. Ex ante optimum parameters, K and R, are selected from ex post optimum parameters found using data from prior periods with K ranging from 3 to 12 and R ranging from 2 to 6. The cases where K is less than R are ruled out. Speculation in the following subperiod uses these optimum parameters. In the initial period, funds are equally invested in the top R ranked currencies. Then in the periods that follow, if the rank of any asset held in the portfolio falls below K, that asset is sold. Proceeds from sales of these poorly performing assets are equally divided to buy the top R ranked assets. The process goes on until the end of the subperiod, when new optimum parameters are selected from data in the new prior period, and speculation in the next subperiod begins.

By following this process, the portfolio of currencies held by the investor is updated so that it contains mainly currencies that the relative strength indices predict will have high performance. The key issue is whether these relative strength indices give signals that point to profits in the future.

8B. Best Rules in the Prior Periods

Table 37 shows the ex ante best parameters R and K used for speculation under the portfolio upgrade approach in both subperiods, obtained from the best results from the prior periods. Best results are defined as the rule parameters that yield the highest adjusted X-statistic. We used the X-statistics in the case with no rebalancing of the buy-and-hold benchmark portfolio. In both prior periods, R = 2 and K = 5. Surprisingly, the prior-period best rules, even though they are the results of search on an ex post basis, do not give performances that are significantly superior to that of buy-and-hold. The adjusted X-statistics in prior periods 1 and 2 are, respectively, 0.0126445 percent and 0.0205220 percent per day, or 3.16 percent and 5.13 percent per year, which are reasonably high. Both of these adjusted X-statistics, however, also have such high standard errors that they are not significant at the 95 percent level. These large standard errors relative to some in past chapters are perhaps to be expected, because with R = 2, only 13.33 percent of the currencies are held in any period, thus limiting diversification relative to say an equally weighted index. Further, the weight of any one currency that always has a strong relative strength index and is thus always in the portfolio can become large as other currencies go in and out of the portfolio but the one always in receives 1/R of any proceeds from sold currencies.

There is one point to be noted here. The ex post best rules in both prior periods have exactly the same parameters, i.e., they are the same rule. This implies that the portfolio upgrade strategy here effectively assumes that the relative strength structures of these currencies are roughly the same in both prior periods.

The prior-period best parameters under the portfolio upgrade approach are generally not sensitive to the level of transactions costs. As Table 38 shows, the lower bounds of the sensitivity ranges of transactions costs are negative in both prior periods, which implies that the results are totally insensitive to reductions in transactions costs. Similarly, the high level of the upper bounds in both prior periods indicates the insensitivity of the results to an increase in transactions costs. Transactions costs have to rise to a level higher than 2.54 percent in order to change the best rule in the first prior period. For the second prior period, transactions costs have to increase to a level higher than 10.77 percent. Because these levels of transactions costs are unrealistically high, the best rule results in Table 37 are extremely insensitive to the level of transactions costs.

8C. Results of Speculation

The ex post best rule in the first prior period perform remarkably well when used ex ante in the first subperiod. This should be expected, however, on the basis of what we know about the results in the two prior periods and the fact that both prior periods give the same best rule to use in the subperiods—a substantial portion of data in the first subperiod overlaps with the second prior period's data. As Table 39 shows, the dollar profit from speculation, net of transactions costs, is $21.04 on an initial investment of $100. Although the returns on both buy-and-hold portfolios are negative, the trading rule yields a positive return of 0.02069 percent per day, which is 0.023133 percent per day or approximately 5.78 percent per year higher than the average return on buy-and-hold. The adjusted X-statistics in both the rebalancing case and the no-rebalancing case are statistically significant at the 95 percent level. This is confirmed by the Wilcoxon Z-score, which is significant even at the 99 percent confidence level.

Unlike the first subperiod results, portfolio performance under the portfolio upgrade approach is not significantly superior to buy-and-hold in the second subperiod, as indicated by the t-value of the unadjusted X-statistic as well as the value of Wilcoxon Z-score. The average returns on both (rebalancing and no-rebalancing) buy-and-hold portfolios are positive in this subperiod and are only slightly less than the return on the trading rule. After adjusting for transactions costs, the adjusted no-rebalancing X-statistic turns out to be only 0.0037796 percent per day or 0.9449 percent per year, which is not statistically different from zero at the 95 percent confidence level. Taking the results in the first subperiod as a good estimate of the adjusted X-statistic to be expected in the second subperiod, the high standard errors are a warning that there may easily be a bad realization. Perhaps this is what happened in the second subperiod. Alternative explanations are that the first period's risk-adjusted profits are really spurious or that there was a substantial shift in process between the second prior period and the second subperiod.

The poor performance of the portfolio upgrade approach in the second subperiod results in small X-statistics for the whole period. The whole-period unadjusted X-statistic is significant at the 95 percent level. After adjusting for transactions costs, however, the whole-period adjusted X-statistic turns out to be statistically insignificant, even though the speculation still yields a total net profit of $20.4198 on a $100 initial investment. The excess return, net of transactions costs, on speculating for the whole period is 0.0161113 percent per day or 3.36 percent per year higher than the average return on no-rebalancing buy-and-hold. The standard error is so large, however, that the X-statistic is insignificant. As discussed above, this large standard error is perhaps to be expected.

8D. Sensitivity of the Statistical Results to the Level of Transactions Costs

The statistical results under the portfolio upgrade approach are generally not sensitive to changes in transactions costs, as the maximum transactions costs (MTC) in Table 38 show. In the first subperiod, where the speculative profits are statistically significant, the MTC is 0.3268566, which implies that transactions costs can be as high as 0.3268556 percent and the adjusted X-statistic is still significant at the 95 percent level. Hence, doubling the transactions costs from one eighth to one fourth, or even going to one third, of 1 percent will not change the significance of the results. The negative MTC in the second subperiod implies that the second subperiod results are not significant for any level of non-negative transactions costs. An MTC of 0.074719 in the whole period means that the adjusted X-statistic for the whole period will be significant if transactions costs are no higher than 0.074719 percent. This implies that transactions costs would have to decrease from one eighth to approximately one fourteenth of 1 percent in order to make the whole-period results significant.

Notes

1. For a detailed explanation and discussion of the implications of this approach, see Levy (1967a, 1967b, 1967c).

FIGURE 7

Flow Chart for the
Portfolio Upgrade Approach

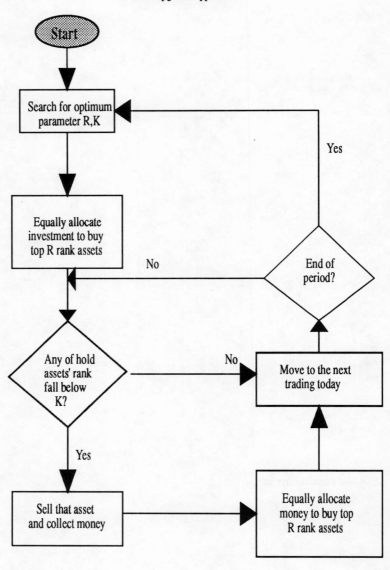

TABLE 37 Best Rules Under the Portfolio Upgrade
Approach in Both Prior Periods, to be Used as the
Ex Ante Rules in the Corresponding Subperiods.

	Prior Period 1	Prior Period 2
Number of Asset in Portfolio (R)	2	2
Degree of ranking (K)	5	5
X-Statistics	0.0162568	0.0222694
	(1.5646)	(2.1330)
Adjusted X-Statistics	0.0126445	0.0205220
	(1.2170)	(1.8830)
Standard Deviation of X	0.0103903	0.0108988
Trading Rule Profit	41.9949	19.4358
Adjusted Trading Rule Profit	39.0427	16.9860

1. The rules chosen as best were those which yielded the highest
adjusted X-statistic in each prior period. The search for the best rule is
performed by ranging the values of K from 3 to 12 and the values of A
from 2 to 6.

2. The unit of the X-statistics is percent per day.

3. Adjusted X-statistics were computed by deducting the average
transactions costs per day from the X-statistics.

4. Profits are based on $100 initial investment. Adjusted profits are
profits net of total transactions costs; transactions costs of one-eighth
of 1 percent per round trip are assumed.

TABLE 38 Sensitivity Analyses of the Effect of Transactions Costs on the Ex Ante Optimum Rule and the Statistical Significance of their X-statistics under the Portfolio Upgrade Approach.

	SUBPERIOD 1	SUBPERIOD 2	THE WHOLE PERIOD
SENSITIVITY RANGES			
Lower Bound	-4.022359	-3.396129	N/A
Upper Bound	2.543591	10.774048	N/A
MAXIMUM TRANSACTIONS COSTS	0.326857	-0.834278	0.0747194

1. Sensitivity range is defined as the range of transactions costs that can be varied without changing the ex post optimum rule in the prior period.

2. The base case of transactions costs used in the simulation is one-eighth of 1 percent per round trip.

3. Ranges of transactions costs are presented in terms of percent per round trip.

4. Maximum Transactions Costs (MTC) are computed from

$$MTC = \frac{X - 1.96\,SDX}{8\,T}$$

where X is the X-statistic (unadjusted for transactions cost), SDX is the standard deviation of X, and T is the estimated average transaction cost per 100 dollars of investment per day evaluated using transactions costs of one-eighth of one percent per round trip. Thus, MTC is the maximum transaction costs per round trip that will make the adjusted X-statistics significant at the 95 percent confidence level. Any per-round-trip transactions costs higher than MTC will make the trading rule return insignificantly better than buy-and-hold.

TABLE 39 Results of Simulations Using the Portfolio Upgrade Approach.

	SUBPERIOD 1	*SUBPERIOD 2*	*THE WHOLE PERIOD*
TRADING RULE RESULTS			
Average Return on Filter Rule	0.0206907	0.0154564	0.0160449
Average Return on Rebalancing Buy-and-Hold	-0.0046039	0.0095727	0.0024844
Average Return on No Rebalancing Buy-and-Hold	-0.0052092	0.0115868	0.0031888
Filter Rule Profit	21.0421	14.3820	35.4241
Adjusted Filter Rule Profit	18.0177	12.3050	30.3227
Total Transactions Costs	3.0244	2.0770	5.1014
Average Transactions Cost per Day	0.003027	0.002077	0.002552
STATISTICAL RESULTS			
CASE WITH REBALANCING			
X-statistics	0.0252946	0.0058837	0.0155891
	(2.3853)	(0.5398)	(2.0503)
Adjusted X-statistics	0.0222671	0.003599	0.0129331
	(2.1001)	(0.3302)	(1.7010)
Standard Deviation of X	0.0106042	0.0108989	0.0076032
Wilcoxon Z-score	-3.528533	-1.567328	
CASE WITH NO REBALANCING			
X-statistics	0.0261604	0.0060623	0.0161113
	(2.5003)	(0.5579)	(2.1361)
Adjusted X-statistics	0.023133	0.0037796	0.0134563
	(2.2107)	(0.3478)	(1.7841)
Standard Deviation of X	0.0104628	0.0108661	0.0075423
Wilcoxon Z-score	-3.582533	-1.567328	
PARAMETER RULE USED			
Number of Assets in Portfolio	2	2	
Tolerance Level of Ranking	5	5	

1. Average returns are reported in term of percent per day.

2. Profits are based on $100 initial investment.

3. Adjusted profits are profits net of total transactionscosts. Transactions costs of one-eighth of 1 percent per round trip are assumed.

4. Rebalancing cases are those where the weights of the buy-and-hold benchmark portfolios are kept constant through rebalancing. No rebalancing cases are those with strict buy-and-hold, where the weights of buy-and-hold benchmark portfolios change through time as the prices of currencies evolve. The initial weights used for buy-and-hold benchmark portfolios are the average weights of speculations.

5. Unit of X-statistics is percent per day.

6. Adjusted X-statistics were computed by deducting average transactions costs per day from the X-statistics.

7. Whole period results were computed using the averages or the sums of the subperiod results, depending upon each result entry. Standard deviations were computed from the sample moment formula, assuming no serial-correlation between the X-statistics in the two subperiods. The value of the Wilcoxon Z-scores is not computable since combining the results in the two subperiods implies changes in the ranking order.

8. Figures in the parentheses are t-statistics.

9

Comparing the Performances of Technical Trading Strategies

In Chapters 5 through 8 we examined the performance of four technical trading rules and also the performance of four approaches to combining speculative positions across currencies into portfolios. This chapter marshals the evidence on comparative performances of trading rules and portfolio approaches.

Section 9A is a comparison of the performances of different technical trading techniques—the Alexander filter, double moving average, single moving average, and mixed rules. Performances of these techniques for speculation on equally weighted portfolios, variably weighted portfolios and indexes are compared. Direct comparison of the adjusted X-statistics shows that the Alexander filter rule gives the worst performance. Under the variably weighted portfolio and index approaches, the single moving average technique yields the highest adjusted X-statistics, and the Alexander filter has the lowest. Matched-pair nonparametric tests find significant differences in the performances within the pair of the single moving average and the Alexander filter, but not in the other matched pairs.

Another issue is the relative performance of the alternative approaches to forming portfolios. These issues are addressed in Sections 9B and 9C. In Section 9B we compare the variably weighted portfolio, the index and the portfolio upgrade approaches to each other. The variably weighted portfolio approach significantly outperforms both the index and portfolio upgrade approaches for every technical trading rule save the Alexander filter rule. The index approach for the single moving average rule beats the portfolio upgrade approach.

Section 9C is a systematic comparison of the equally weighted portfolio approach to the other approaches. The variably weighted significantly outperforms the equally weighted portfolio approach for every rule save the Alexander filter rule. There is only one significant difference among the performances of the equally weighted portfolio approach under the four rules as compared to the performances of either the index approach or the

183

portfolio upgrade approach—the index approach gives significantly better results for the single moving average rule.

Looking at subperiod results somewhat blurs conclusions, as seen in Section 9D. In particular, there are some signs of instability in performance over time—in Chapter 10 we discuss in some detail various issues of stability of speculative profits. Nevertheless, subperiod results generally confirm the impression that the Alexander filter rule is not attractive relative to other trading rules and that the variably weighted portfolio approach is attractive relative to other approaches for forming diversified portfolios under technical trading.

In Section 9E we offer a summary and some conclusions.

9A. Comparing the Performances of the Technical Trading Rules

In Table 40 we present the whole-period adjusted X-statistics, in terms of percent per year, across the four technical trading techniques as well as across the four approaches to diversification—the equally weighted and variably weighted approaches to forming portfolios, the index approach, and the portfolio upgrade approach. Because there are four cases of weight vectors used in the index approach, the equally weighted index case is presented as representative of the index approach. This is perhaps the most suitable case, because it contains all 15 currencies in the index in both subperiods and the optimally weighted indexes contain only two currencies in the second subperiod. Because the portfolio upgrade approach does not use any of the four technical trading techniques, this approach's results are compared in Table 40 only to the averages across rules of the results under the three other approaches.

For all three of the variably weighted, equally weighted and index approaches, the Alexander filter technique gives the worst performance of all four technical rules in terms of the adjusted X-statistic.

In both the index and variably weighted portfolio approaches, the single moving average yields the highest adjusted X-statistics among all four of the technical trading techniques considered, with the double moving average and the mixed rule lying between the two extremes. The test results in Table 41 show, however, that the differences among the performances of these four technical trading techniques are statistically significant only for the matched pair of the two extremes, the Alexander filter versus the single moving average rule.

For each technical trading technique, Table 41 shows the results of nonparametric tests of the difference between the adjusted X-statistics for both the variably weighted portfolio and index approaches. For these two portfolio approaches, Wilcoxon signed-rank tests were performed on all matched pairs of the time series of the adjusted X-statistics under each of the four technical trading techniques. (A negative sign indicates that the first technique performed less well than the second in the comparison.) In addition, a Friedman ANOVA was used to test the joint hypothesis of the differences in these matched pairs. The tests use the whole period data, in other words, the data in subperiods 1 and 2 combined. In Table 41 the two-tailed p-values are reported in parentheses.

For both the index and variably weighted approaches, the only matched pair that shows a significant difference between the adjusted X-statistics is that of the single moving average and the Alexander filter. As mentioned above, these are the techniques that yield, respectively, the highest and the lowest adjusted X-statistics. The Wilcoxon Z-scores of the differences in the adjusted X-statistics within these matched pairs are significant at the 95 percent level. For the other matched pairs, however, the results indicate no significant difference in performance within the pair (though the single moving average mixed–rule comparison is borderline significant). The differences in the adjusted X-statistics within these pairs are quite small, so that the Friedman Chi-squares are not significant, though the statistic is borderline significant for the variably weighted portfolio approach.[1]

9B. Comparing the Performances of the Variably Weighted Portfolio, Index, and Portfolio Upgrade Approaches

This section's comparison of these three approaches shows that the variably weighted portfolio approach seems to be the most profitable approach. In particular, nonparametric tests show some significant differences in the performances of these three approaches.

As Table 40 shows, for all four technical rules the variably weighted portfolio approach yields higher adjusted X-statistics than the index or portfolio upgrade approaches. For the average across the four technical rules, the index approach yields higher adjusted X-statistics than the portfolio upgrade approach, and the average across techniques for the variably weighted portfolio approach gives a higher adjusted X-statistic than either of the index or portfolio upgrade approaches. These results suggest that the variably weighted portfolio approach is the best, in terms of having the highest X-statistics, with the index approach the second and the portfolio upgrade approach the third best. An important issue is whether the differences among the adjusted X-statistics obtained from the three approaches are statistically significant.

Time series of the adjusted X-statistics under the three types of specula-

186 Comparing the Performances of Technical Trading Strategies

tions were collected. The X-statistics for the case of no rebalancing in the buy-and-hold portfolio were used. Following equation (3.4) in Chapter 3, the value of the X-statistic at time t is computed from

$$X_t = \Sigma\, u_{jt}\, R_{jt} - \Sigma\, u'_{jt}\, R_{jt}.$$

In the case of the index approach, where four weight types (h = 0.414, 1, 2.414, and equally weighted) are studied, the equally weighted case is chosen as the representative—recall that it is the only index that includes more than two currencies in the second subperiod and is hence the most relevant case for comparison to the variably weighted portfolio and portfolio upgrade approaches, which in principle include all currencies.[2] Wilcoxon matched-pair signed-rank tests are applied to each combination of pairs of these adjusted X-statistics time series. Friedman Chi-square ANOVA is also used to test if there is, at least, a significant difference between the time series of these pairs.

Table 42 shows the results. The figures in the parentheses are the corresponding two-tailed p-values of the Wilcoxon Z-score and Friedman statistics. The "average" row in Table 42 shows the results of the difference in the average adjusted X-statistics across technical trading techniques. Because the portfolio upgrade approach does not involve any kind of technical trading technique, it has only one time series of adjusted X-statistics; this time series of the adjusted X-statistics under the portfolio upgrade approach is compared to all cases of technical trading techniques under the index and variably weighted portfolio approaches.

Average performance across rules is useful as a summary of the relative profitability of the three portfolio approaches. The results in the "average" row indicate that the variably weighted portfolio approach is significantly superior to the index and portfolio upgrade approaches. The performance of the index approach, on the average, is not significantly different from that of the portfolio upgrade approach at the 95 percent confidence level, though the difference is borderline significant. The Wilcoxon Z-score between the matched pairs of the variably weighted portfolio and portfolio upgrade approaches is significant at the 99 percent level. The differences between the adjusted X-statistics under the index and portfolio upgrade approaches are not significant at the 95 percent level, though they are at the 92 percent level.

Turn now to the performances of the three approaches under each of the individual technical trading techniques. The performances of the variably weighted portfolio approach are significantly better than those of the index approach when double moving average and single moving average techniques are used—the Wilcoxon Z-scores are significant at the 99 percent and 95 percent levels. The variably weighted portfolio approach also yields adjusted X-statistics that are significantly higher than those of the portfolio upgrade approach for all technical trading techniques except the Alexander filter.

The adjusted X-statistics from using the index and portfolio upgrade approaches are only slightly different. Only for the single moving average case does the index approach show significantly higher adjusted X-statistics. The Friedman Chi-square test supports the Wilcoxon signed-rank test results. There are significant differences among the three approaches for the double moving average, single moving average, and mixed rules. The differences among the adjusted X-statistics of the three approaches are not significant, however, for the Alexander filter rule.

9C. The Equally Weighted versus the Variably Weighted, Index, and Portfolio Upgrade Approaches

Nonparametric tests results below show that the variably weighted portfolio approach yields adjusted X-statistics that are significantly higher than the equally weighted portfolio approach, and the performances of the index and portfolio upgrade approaches are not statistically different from those of the equally weighted portfolio approach.

Table 43 shows the results of applying the Wilcoxon matched-pair signed-rank tests to the matched pairs between the time series of the adjusted X-statistics for the equally weighted portfolio for the various technical trading rules and the time series of the adjusted X-statistics for the variably weighted portfolio, index, and portfolio upgrade approaches. The columns give the speculation approaches and the rows the technical trading techniques. There are three rows of results for each technical trading rule. The first row reports the differences between the whole-period average of the adjusted X-statistics of the equally weighted portfolio less the whole-period average of the adjusted X-statistics for the alternative approaches in the corresponding columns, with figures from Table 40. Thus, the difference is positive if the average adjusted X-statistic of the equally weighted portfolio approach is higher than the average adjusted X-statistic of the alternative approach. These differences in the adjusted X-statistics are in percent per year. The second row reports the Wilcoxon Z-scores for the matched pairs between the time series of the adjusted X-statistics of the equally weighted portfolio approach and the time series of the adjusted X-statistics of the alternative approaches in the corresponding columns. The third row reports the p-values of these Wilcoxon Z-scores.

For the four technical trading techniques, there are two cases (the Alexander filter and the double moving average rule) where the equally weighted portfolio approach yields slightly higher adjusted X-statistics than the index approach. These differences in the adjusted X-statistics, however, are small (0.3244 percent per year under the Alexander filter and 0.0833 percent per year under the double moving average) and are, according to their Wilcoxon Z-score, insignificant at the 95 percent confidence level. Under the single moving average and mixed rules, however, the index seems to perform better than the equally weighted portfolio approach. The adjusted X-statistics of the index approach for the single moving average and mixed rules are 2.1294 percent per year and 0.4193 percent per year higher than the adjusted X-statistics of the equally weighted portfolio approach. Wilcoxon Z-scores indicate that the index approach is significantly superior when the single moving average is used, but not when the mixed rule is used. On average, as indicated by the "average" results across these technical trading techniques, the performance of the index approach is better, but not significantly, than that of the equally weighted portfolio approach. The average adjusted X-statistic of the index approach is 0.5350 percent per year higher than that of the equally-weighted portfolio approach; but the difference between these adjusted X-statistics, according to the Wilcoxon Z-score, is not statistically different from zero at the 95 percent level.

The variably weighted portfolio approach seems to perform better than the equally weighted portfolio approach. For all four technical rules, the variably weighted portfolio approach yields higher adjusted X-statistics; and in three out of these four cases, the differences between the adjusted X-statistics of the two approaches are significantly nonzero at the 95 percent level. These three cases are the double moving average, the single moving average, and the mixed rule, with adjusted X-statistics that are 1.8122 percent, 2.9898 percent, and 1.1547 percent per year higher than the adjusted X-statistics of the corresponding equally weighted portfolio speculations. Averaging across the four technical trading techniques, the variably weighted is still superior to the equally weighted portfolio approach. The average adjusted X-statistic across the technical trading techniques under the variably weighted is 1.5832 percent per year higher than that of the equally weighted portfolio approach. The Wilcoxon Z-score for the average case is significant at the 95 percent level.

Comparisons between the performance of the portfolio upgrade and equally weighted portfolio approaches show that the two, on average, are neither inferior nor superior to each other. Because the portfolio upgrade approach does not use any of the four technical trading rules, only one time series of adjusted X-statistics can be obtained under this approach. This time series is compared with the four time series (given by four technical trading rules) of the adjusted X-statistics of equally weighted portfolio speculations. The performance of the portfolio upgrade approach is only slightly better than that of the equally weighted portfolio approach under the Alexander filter and single moving average and slightly worse than when the double moving average and mixed rule are used. Wilcoxon Z-scores indicate no significant difference between the adjusted X-statistics of the two approaches at the 95 percent level. On average, the portfolio upgrade approach yields an adjusted X-statistic that is only 0.1044 percent per year less than those from the equally weighted portfolio approach, and this difference in the adjusted X-statistics is statistically insignificant.

9D. Subperiod Results

The adjusted X-statistics for the two subperiods show a lack of stability in Table 44 that is perhaps disturbing; in Chapter 10 we address issues of stability in some detail. Among the welter of numbers in Table 44, three points stand out.

First, the whole-period results above showed that the Alexander filter rule seems to be the least attractive of the four trading rules considered. This view is reinforced by the instability of the results across subperiods under this rule. An example is the variably weighted portfolio approach where profits under the Alexander rule fall from 6.20 percent in the first subperiod to only 0.69 percent in the second subperiod. Contrast this to any of the other three trading rules, where the stability of profits seems much greater.

Second, for both subperiods the single moving average rule produces very attractive results for both the variably weighted portfolio and index approaches, reinforcing the impression from whole-period results.

Third, whole-period results showed that the variably weighted portfolio approach outperformed the other approaches. Examining subperiod results makes this superiority less clear. The Alexander filter rule is a bit of a disaster for this approach, as noted above. Neglecting the Alexander rule, the approach performs well relative to the other approaches save in a few cases. In subperiod 2, the index approach does marginally better than the variably weighted portfolio approach under the single moving average rule. In subperiod 1, the variably weighted portfolio's performance under the mixed rule is less than that of the portfolio upgrade approach. Nevertheless, the subperiod results still make the variably weighted portfolio approach seem attractive relative to the others, especially when the poorly performing Alexander filter rule is not used.

Perhaps a useful way of cutting through the large number of bi- and multi–lateral comparisons that can be made is to look at the average results across technical trading rules in Table 45. In this table, the entry 5.74 percent for the variably weighted portfolio approach, for example, shows the average adjusted X-statistic the approach got in the first subperiod across all four of the technical rules. The portfolio upgrade approach outperforms all the others in the first subperiod but fades very badly in the second subperiod, both in absolute and relative terms; further, the portfolio upgrade beats the variably weighted portfolio approach in the first subperiod by only a very small amount. In the second subperiod, the index approach on average outperforms the others but beats the variably weighted portfolio approach by only a small amount. Taken as a whole, the variably weighted portfolio approach remains relatively attractive on the basis of these results.

Tables 44 and 45 not only show some signs of instability, they also show some tendency for speculative profits to fall between the two subperiods. For example, the performance of the approaches averaged across rules shows an improvement in Table 45 only for the index approach, and the declines for the other approaches are all larger than the improvement for the index approach. In Chapter 10 we provide an extensive discussion of issues of stability of profits overtime and whether profits are declining over time.

9E. Conclusions

The above results make it clear that portfolio approaches to speculation, i.e., speculating in more than one currency at a time, are generally more profitable than the naive buy-and-hold strategy. Trading rules perform extraordinarily well in the first subperiod. On average, the performance of trading rules persists in the second subperiod but to a smaller degree than in the first subperiod.

Further, it is clear that the choice of technical trading technique may have significant effects on performance. For the overall period, the single moving average technique is significantly superior to the Alexander filter technique in both the index and the variably weighted portfolio approaches. The performances of the double moving average and the mixed rule, however, are not statistically different, not only from each other but also from the Alexander filter and the single moving average techniques.

Approaches to diversification also make a difference. This chapter analyzes the performance of four approaches to speculation: the equally weighted and variably weighted portfolio approach, the index approach, and the portfolio upgrade approach.

The variably weighted portfolio approach uses the buy or sell signals of each individual currency to speculate simultaneously in all currencies according to the availability of funds. Under this approach, the Alexander filter, double moving average, and single moving average techniques perform remarkably well in the first subperiod and give statistically significant profits; the mixed rule gives substantial though insignificant profits. The single moving average and mixed-rule techniques beat the market significantly in the second subperiod; the double moving average rule gives large but statistically insignificant profits. For the average of these two subperiods, as indicated by the whole-period results, all four technical trading rules yield impressive profits that are significantly superior to buy-and-hold.

With the exception of the case where the Alexander filter technique is used, the speculative performances under the variably weighted portfolio approach are *significantly* better for the overall period than the performances under the equally weighted portfolio approach; in all cases, the variably weighted portfolio approach yields higher adjusted X-statistics than the equally weighted portfolio approach. The performances of the index and portfolio upgrade approaches are generally the same statistically as those of the equally weighted portfolio approaches; in the case where the single moving average technique is used, the index approach yields an adjusted X-statistic that is significantly higher than that of the equally weighted portfolio approach.

Broadly speaking, speculation using the variably weighted portfolio approach is, on average, either as good as or better than speculation using the equally weighted portfolio approach. The intuitive reasons for this are as follows. First, the variably weighted portfolio approach allows the funds to be invested intensively and, hence, increases the chance of making profits. Under the variably weighted portfolio approach, in the periods where the trading rules keep the investor out of the market in some assets, they are likely to keep the investor in the market for other assets rather than in the risk-free Euro-dollar asset that has no profit potential. As a result, if the underlying rules are profitable, intensive use of the invested funds will enhance the profit opportunities. Second, as seen with the case of the single moving average rule, the variably weighted portfolio approach can raise profits by cutting down on transactions and hence transactions costs. Some buy signals result in no purchases because all funds are already fully invested. The cost of this is an increase in risk, as shown by larger standard errors relative to the equally weighted portfolio approach. The investor can never have more than approximately one fifteenth of total funds in a single foreign currency under the equally weighted portfolio approach; it is possible to be much less diversified under the variably weighted portfolio approach. The instability noticed in adjusted X-statistics for the variably weighted portfolio approach may be due not to changing profitability but simply to randomness to be expected in the presence of substantial risk. It should be noted that much of the increased risk from the variably weighted approach relative to the equally weighted approach may be diversifiable in a larger portfolio that holds assets other than currency positions, as discussed in Chapter 6.

The index approach speculates on a basket of currencies; that is, the whole portfolio, with a predetermined weight vector, is purchased at a buy signal and is sold at a sell signal derived from movements in the index with the same weights. Speculation under the optimally weighted index approach works very well in the first subperiod, not so well in the second. The main reason is that the ex ante optimum weight vectors used in the second subperiod force the investor to speculate in only the Australian dollar and the Canadian dollar; the single-currency speculation results reported in Chapter 5 suggest that profit opportunities in these two currencies were small in both subperiods.

For the equally weighted index approach, the single moving average technique is significantly profitable in both subperiods. The double moving average and mixed rule techniques also perform well in the first subperiod, but less well in the second. The Alexander filter seems to perform poorly in the equally weighted index case.

The portfolio upgrade approach works very well in the first subperiod but not very well at all in the second subperiod. The poor performance in the second subperiod reduces the average performance across both periods so that the whole period results are not statistically significant. It may be that the portfolio upgrade approach is not attractive for currency speculation, because in both subperiods it used only two of the 15 currencies at any one time. This drastically reduces diversification, increases risk, and suggests the type of instability actually observed in adjusted X-statistics.

For the overall period, the variably weighted portfolio approach seems to be the best in terms of having the highest average return in excess of buy-and-hold. The index approach is slightly better than the portfolio upgrade approach. Two points can be made regarding these comparative results. First, because the portfolio upgrade approach does not directly use any of the four technical trading rules, the fact that it has the worst performance among the three alternative approaches lends some support to the view that direct use of technical trading techniques is better than relying on the other properties of past prices such as the relative strength of the currencies (though we noted above that relative strength indices are related to the moving average rule). Second, using individual signals from each currency may be better than using the overall signal triggered by index movements. Even though using an index to trigger signals for portfolio changes has the advantage that these indexes contain less noise (because of diversification) and hence are less erratic, this advantage is evidently offset by the fact that buying and selling currencies as a basket constrains some currencies to be purchased or sold against their individual signals. Further, it may be the case that a substantial portion of the nonidiosyncratic price movements of individual currencies, too, were canceled out in the process of portfolio formation. As a result, what is expected to be low-noise price patterns may turn out to be too smooth, so that trading rules cannot trigger the signal correctly.

The subperiod results show some potentially disturbing signs of instability. Further, for three of the four approaches, save only the index approach, profits averaged across technical trading techniques fell from the first to the second subperiod. In Chapter 10 are extensive discussions of issues of stability and declining profits over time.

Notes

1. The slight conflict between the Wilcoxon signed-rank test and the Friedman ANOVA test is not uncommon. It is well known from the theory of statistical inference that this type of conflict can happen when the observed sample point lies within the ellipsoid of the acceptance region of the joint hypothesis, and at the same time lies outside one of the confidence intervals of the single hypothesis. This is analogous to the conflict that can happen between the parametric t-test and the F-test.

2. In circumstances where more than one currency triggers a buy signal, the variably weighted portfolio and the portfolio upgrade approaches always allocate the funds in an equally weighted fashion. Hence the equally weighted case under the index approach should perhaps be considered as the most relevant case for comparison with the variably weighted portfolio and the portfolio upgrade approaches. However, the portfolio upgrade approach holds only two currencies in both subperiods (R=2), and one might feel uncomfortable with the sample results for this approach as with the optimally weighted indexes in the second subperiod.

TABLE 40 Whole-Period Adjusted X-statistics for Alternative Portfolio Approaches and Technical Rules.

TRADING TECHNIQUE	EQUALLY WEIGHTED	INDEX	VARIABLY WEIGHTED	PORTFOLIO UPGRADE
Alexander Filter	3.06950	2.74515	3.44660	
Double Moving Average	3.60275	3.51953	5.41497	
Single Moving Average	3.27875	5.40812	6.26857	
Mixed Rule	3.68500	4.10435	4.83975	
Portfolio Upgrade				3.36408
AVERAGE	3.40225	3.94428	4.99247	3.36408

1. Adjusted X-statistics are presented as percent per year.
2. Only one adjusted X-statistic is computed for the portfolio upgrade approach, because this approach does not use any of the four technical trading techniques.

Source: Computed from Tables 13 to 16, 29 to 32, 35, and 38.

TABLE 41 Nonparametric Results on the Difference in the Adjusted X-statistics from Various Technical Trading Rules.

STATISTICAL TESTS AND PAIRS OF TRADING TECHNIQUES	PORTFOLIO FORMATION TECHNIQUES	
	INDEX	VARIABLY-WEIGHTED
WILCOXON MATCHED-PAIR SIGNED-RANK Z-SCORE		
ALEX-DMOV	-0.4390	-1.3987
	-(0.6607)	-(0.1619)
ALEX-SMOV	-1.9854	-2.5191
	-(0.0471)	-(0.0118)
ALEX-MIX	-0.6988	-0.4688
	-(0.4847)	-(0.6392)
DMOV-SMOV	-1.4077	-0.8252
	-(0.1592)	-(0.4093)
DMOV-MIX	-0.1347	-0.9684
	-(0.8928)	-(0.3328)
SMOV-MIX	-0.6530	-1.8912
	-(0.5158)	-(0.0586)
FRIEDMAN ANOVA CHI-SQUARE	5.6668	7.6658
	-(0.1290)	-(0.0534)

1. The figures in the parentheses are the corresponding two-tailed p-values.

TABLE 42 Nonparametric Tests on the Difference in the Adjusted X-statistics of the Variably Weighted Portfolio, Index, and Portfolio Upgrade Approaches.

TRADING TECHNIQUE	WILCOXON Z-SCORE			FRIEDMAN CHI-SQUARE ANOVA TEST
	INDEX-VW	INDEX-PU	VW-PU	
Alexander Filter	-1.3016	-0.6217	0.9156	2.5892
	(0.1931)	(0.5342)	(0.3599)	(0.2740)
Double Moving	-2.6748	1.0507	2.2200	9.5162
Average	(0.0075)	(0.2934)	(0.0264)	(0.0103)
Single Moving	-2.3740	2.6886	2.7005	12.7924
Average	(0.0176)	(0.0072)	(0.0069)	(0.0017)
Mixed Rule	-1.9268	1.8662	2.1886	9.1568
	(0.0540)	(0.0620)	(0.0286)	(0.0103)
Average	-2.3679	1.8086	2.6447	11.5238
	(0.0179)	(0.0705)	(0.0082)	(0.0092)

1. The figures in the parentheses are the corresponding two-tailed p-values.

2. Average is the arithmetic average of the adjusted X-statistics of the four technical trading techniques.

TABLE 43 Wilcoxon Matched-Pair Test Results on the Difference between the Adjusted X-statistics from the Equally Weighted Portfolio Approach as Compared to the Index, Variably Weighted Portfolio, and Portfolio Upgrade Approaches.

TRADING TECHNIQUE	INDEX	VW	PU
ALEXANDER FILTER			
Difference (Xe - Xa)	0.3244	-0.3771	-0.2353
Wilcoxon Z-score	-0.7663	-1.2203	-0.2707
Two-tailed p-value	(0.4435)	(0.2224)	(0.7866)
DOUBLE MOVING AVERAGE			
Difference (Xe - Xa)	0.0833	-1.8122	0.2979
Wilcoxon Z-score	-0.5860	-2.4284	-0.7177
Two-tailed p-value	(0.5578)	(0.0152)	(0.4729)
SINGLE MOVING AVERAGE			
Difference (Xe - Xa)	-2.1294	-2.9898	-0.0261
Wilcoxon Z-score	-2.6886	-2.8931	-0.5283
Two-tailed p-value	(0.0072)	(0.0038)	(0.5973)
MIXED RULE			
Difference (Xe - Xa)	-0.4193	-1.1547	0.3803
Wilcoxon Z-score	-0.4660	-2.2694	-0.6191
Two-tailed p-value	(0.6412)	(0.0232)	(0.5359)
AVERAGE			
Difference (Xe - Xa)	-0.5350	-1.5832	0.1044
Wilcoxon Z-score	-0.6273	-2.3679	-0.3510
Two-tailed p-value	(0.5304)	(0.0179)	(0.7256)

1. Difference (Xe - Xa) represents the difference between the adjusted X-statistics of the equally weighted portfolio (Xe) and the adjusted X-statistics of the alternative speculations (Xa). The unit measured is in terms of percent per year.

2. Average is the arithmetic average of the adjusted X-statistics of the four technical trading techniques.

198

TABLE 44 Average Annual Excess Returns on Speculation Under Various Rules and Portfolio Approaches.

TRADING RULE/ PERIOD	EQUALLY WEIGHTED PORTFOLIO	INDEX	VARIABLY WEIGHTED PORTFOLIO
ALEXANDER FILTER			
Subperiod 1	3.57825**	1.34560	6. 19900**
	(2.93480)	(0.71800)	(3.02970)
Subperiod 2	2.56050	4.14470	0.69420
	(1.46550)	(1.81120)	(0.24420)
Whole Period	3.06950**	2.74515	3.44660**
	(2.88130)	(1.71790)	(1.96820)
DOUBLE MOVING AVERAGE			
Subperiod 1	4.49425**	4.06397*	5.81383*
	(2.96430)	(2.10630)	(2.21810)
Subperiod 2	2.71125	2.97508	3.01612
	(1.42690)	(1.30180)	(1.77820)
Whole Period	3.00275**	3.51953*	5.41497**
	(2.96420)	(2.35350)	(2.81250)
SINGLE MOVING AVERAGE			
Subperiod 1	3.46675*	4.58370**	6.56937*
	(2.18830)	(2.95690)	(2.45260)
Subperiod 2	3.09075	6.23255**	5.96758*
	(1.67160)	(2.71810)	(2.19360)
Whole Period	3.27875**	5.40812**	6.26857**
	(2.69320)	(3.61350)	(3.28380)
MIXED RULE			
Subperiod 1	4.65275**	4.06397*	4.36732
	(3.27710)	(2.10630)	(1.63740)
Subperiod 2	2.66350	4.14470	5.31215*
	(1.54390)	(1.81120)	(1.97730)
Whole Period	3.68500**	4. 10435**	4.83975*
	(3.27450)	(2.74240)	(2.55680)

1. The figures in the parentheses are the t-values of the corresponding X-statistics.
2. * = significant at the 95 percent level; * * = significant at the 99 percent level.

TABLE 45: Performance of Speculative Approaches Averaged Across Technical Trading Rules.

TRADING RULE/ PERIOD	EQUALLY WEIGHTED PORTFOLIO	INDEX	VARIABLY WEIGHTED PORTFOLIO	PORTFOLIO UPGRADE
AVERAGE				
Subperiod 1	4.04800**	3.51431*	5.73743**	5.78325*
	(3.2650)	(2.3633)	(2.9864)	(2.2107)
Subperiod 2	2.75650	4.37326*	4.24751*	0.94490
	(1.7020)	(2.3115)	(2.0342)	(0.3478)
Whole Period	3.40225**	3.94428**	4.99247**	3.36408
	(3.3361)	(3.2777)	(4.8954)	(1.7841)

1. The figures in the parentheses are the t-values of the corresponding X-statistics.
2. * = significant at the 95 percent level; ** = significant at the 99 percent level.
3. The Portfolio Upgrade Approach results are not averaged across the technical trading rules, because this approach does not use them.

PART 4

Stability of Speculative Profits

10

The Stability of Speculative Profits

Preceding chapters focused on which technical trading rules and which portfolio formation approaches are most profitable. This chapter turns to the related issue of the stability of speculative profits.

10A. Importance of the Stability of Speculative Profits

A number of papers in the 1970s asked whether technical trading rules could make speculative profits in the foreign exchange market. The results were somewhat inconclusive (Dooley and Shafer 1976; Logue, Sweeney, and Willett 1978; Cornell and Dietrich 1978). In part, it was not clear how to measure performance, in particular, how to take account of risk; in part, there were real issues of the stability of the measured profits.[1] Later, however, Dooley and Shafer (1983) presented evidence of continued profitability, and Sweeney (1986a) proposed a risk-adjusted performance measure and argued that statistically significant speculative profits could be made in the late 1970s and into the very early 1980s on the basis of patterns detectable in previous data. Preceding chapters, however, give some evidence of declining profitability from the first to second subperiod of the technical rules studied in this book, raising the issue of whether speculative profits are stable over time. In particular, are speculative profits showing a secular decline that will ultimately see them vanish?

In another meaning of stability, it is important to know whether speculative profits are stable, or insensitive, with regard to the amount of data one uses to select trading strategies and the frequency with which one revises strategies.

Stability of profits is clearly an issue of great interest to anyone who intends to use technical analysis to beat the market. For efficient markets advocates, the measured profits detected in some technical studies can be reconciled with market efficiency by assuming time-varying risk premia, so that the measured profits are not economic profits but simply a reward for bearing risk. Nevertheless, it helps preserve the concept of efficiency if the measured profits of the past seem no longer available. Hence, the stability of profits is of substantial interest both to practitioners and to academic researchers.

Sweeney (1986a) used 1,830 observations, from mid-1973 until early 1980. He used the first 610 observations to look for profitable technical rules of the sort used by Alexander (1961, 1964) and then applied the most promising of them on the remaining 1,220 observations as a test of whether profits could be earned by using patterns previously detected in the data. Although the measured profits were on average lower in the test period than in the period where the rules were generated, the profits seemed large and statistically significant. Still, even assuming that these measured profits were economic profits, these results might have been a fluke. Further, there is always the very real possibility that the market will catch on and eliminate any genuine speculative opportunities. Thus, the issue arises as to whether these measured profits show some degree of stability over time after the period Sweeney examined.

The results in Chapters 5 through 9 cast some doubt on the stability of speculative profits. In these chapters we look at four technical rules and four different portfolio approaches on 2,000 out-of-sample observations, from mid-1978 to mid-1986, thus overlapping to some extent with Sweeney's 1,220-observation test period but including about five years' or 1,250 observations' worth of fresh data. The Alexander rules worked well on individual currencies in the first 1,000 out-of-sample observations (overlapping substantially with Sweeney's (1986a) test period), but not nearly as well in the final 1,000, roughly mid-1982 to mid-1986. This was so even though we changed the sizes of our filters between the two 1,000-observation samples, the changes based always on prior data, in order to catch any changes in whatever underlying process is allowing measured speculative profits.

The issue is complicated, however, by our rather more successful results on alternative speculative techniques. A major purpose in Chapters 5 through 9 is, in fact, to assess the relative performance of various technical approaches rather than to address the stability of speculative profits. These chapters use not only Alexander filter rules but also double moving average and single moving average rules. For each of these rules, we consider a number of different approaches to combining speculations on individual currencies into a portfolio. The equally weighted portfolio approach of Chapter 5 focuses on finding a separate rule for each currency, as in Sweeney (1986a); here, speculation on each currency is treated as a separate mutual fund, with overall results being judged as an equally weighted portfolio of such funds. Another approach uses more integrated speculation, where in effect these mutual funds can borrow from one another, with the final results depending on the performance of a portfolio with *variable* rather than equal weights over time. If the currency speculation is indeed profitable, it turns out that this variable-weight approach should tend to give higher profits than the equal-weight approach, though at the cost of greater variability in terms of standard errors, as discussed in Chapters 6 and 9.

In Tables 46 and 47 the issue of the stability of speculative profits is raised. Both show results using Alexander filter rules. The first (based on Sweeney 1986a) looks at equally weighted portfolios and shows some fall-off in performance in the mid-1975 to mid-1980 period of the 1 percent and particularly the 2 percent filters, both of which looked very promising in the prior period from April 1973 to mid-1975.[2] Table 47 (based on results reported above) does not show prior-period results but instead shows test results for "best" rules for each currency in two separate test periods, or "subperiods," where the "best" rules were chosen based on prior-period performance. The first column in Table 47 is comparable to the approach in Table 46 in using an equally weighted portfolio of independent mutual funds and shows a fall-off in performance in the later period. This fall-off in performance in the later period raises the suspicion that technical trading rules may be losing their effectiveness. The second column in Table 47 shows an even more alarming fall-off for speculation under the variable-weight, integrated multi-currency speculation described in Chapter 6. This fall-off in the second approach is particularly striking, since this variably weighted portfolio approach should tend to give larger profits if indeed there are profits there to be made from the rules used. The average of the two portfolio approaches shows a fall-off of more than two thirds (column (3), from 4.89 percent to 1.63 percent), with the results from the second subperiod more than a percentage point lower than the average for the test sample in Table 46.

Chapter 9 shows, however, that the Alexander rule is the worst approach that we consider over the whole 2,000-observation period. Hence, the finding that the Alexander results in the second 1,000-observation period are not nearly as impressive as in the first may not be important.

Further, the question arises as to the source of the instability in preceding chapters' results, because we changed trigger values between the two test periods for virtually every currency. On the one hand, well-chosen changes in rules can lead to enhanced profits. On the other, unwise changes can reduce profits. We can get some insights from Table 48 by looking at how the 1 percent and 2 percent Alexander filters—which Table 46 shows looked promising in Sweeney (1986a)—perform after Sweeney's test period for an equally weighted portfolio of currencies. For the following six years, the two together average 2.06 percent, not too much below the average of 2.65 percent in Sweeney's test period (see Table 46) and better than the 1.63

percent found for the second subperiod in Table 47. This suggests that these simple rules give persistent profits and that efforts to improve on them by switching rules carry some genuine risk of actually reducing performance. Plainly, there are many issues worth considering about the stability of speculative profits in the foreign exchanges. That is the purpose of this chapter. Although we do not use new data beyond those used above, we make special efforts to avoid data mining that might be viewed as trying to get around the instability of Alexander-type results as revealed in Table 47.

In Section 10B we briefly review some issues in the measurement of trading rule profits, and Section 10C reviews some issues in choosing rule parameters and forming portfolios.

In Sections 10D and 10E we discuss the stability of speculative profits. We use the final 1,500 of the 2,000 observations used above, dividing them into two 750-observation periods, and also into six 250-observation periods (or "years"). The main stability issues considered are these. First, does there seem to be an optimum amount of prior data to use in selecting filters and lag lengths to use in speculating in a test period? The results are somewhat inconclusive. Second, does there seem to be an optimum period after which the trigger values in a particular rule should be altered? Again the answer is somewhat inconclusive, though there is little support for mechanically altering triggers on a yearly basis as opposed to sticking with the same triggers for the entire test period. Third, do measured profits persist? The answer is a strong yes. Fourth, does there seem to be an approach that gives stability of speculative profits across periods? Not surprisingly, it turns out that simultaneously employing a basket of approaches gives fairly stable results.

In Section 10F we explicitly return to the issues that started this chapter: Has there been a decline in profits over time? and Are speculative profits vanishing? It seems clear that profits are not vanishing. The results in earlier chapters may through randomness, however, overstate the average level of profits one can expect over time.

In Section 10G we offer a summary of results and some conclusions.

10B. The Measurement of Performance

As discussed in Chapter 3, the X-statistic profit measure used here is based on Sweeney (1990c) and is a generalization of the one used in Sweeney (1986a). The profits reported here are risk-adjusted economic profits on the assumption that all assets' risk premia are conditionally constant through time and the EMH (Efficient Markets Hypothesis) condition that expected excess returns equal these risk premia. This joint assumption implies that there is no serial correlation in assets' returns and no lead-lag cross correlations across assets' returns. Given conditionally constant risk premia, any significant measured profits are inconsistent with the EMH. Alternatively, measured profits and the EMH are consistent only if there are time-varying risk premia.

In principle, the returns on foreign assets are measured as the appreciation of the foreign currency plus the foreign risk-free rate, less the home-country risk-free rate. Because overnight risk-free rates are difficult to collect, in practice this interest-rate differential is omitted, as discussed in Chapter 4. Sweeney (1986a) shows that this omission makes no difference to measured performance if the differential is on average the same on the days the investor is in the foreign asset as it is for the overall period; further, he shows for the dollar-DM rate for his sample that the empirical impact of neglecting the differential is small.

The X-statistic has the dimension of profits per day (though the tables below report them as profits per year by multiplying by 250). These profits are risk adjusted in the sense that risk premia are reflected in the return on buy-and-hold.

10C. Approaches to Technical Trading

In this chapter we use the same four trading rules investigated above-the Alexander filter, double moving average, single moving average, and mixed rule. We also use two approaches to combining speculations in different currencies—the equally weighted portfolio of separate mutual funds (as used in Sweeney (1986a) and Chapter 5) and the variably weighted portfolio of mutual funds that in effect borrow and lend to each other (as in Chapter 6).

Choosing Trigger Values and Lag Lengths

In all cases, trigger values for the Alexander rules and lag lengths for the moving averages for any period are chosen by examining, for each individual currency, the performance of various triggers and lengths in prior periods, using as a criterion the highest transactions-costs adjusted rate of profit in the prior period, as outlined in Chapter 4. For each 750-observation test period in this chapter, we use from 250 to 1,400 preceding observations to search for the "best" triggers and lengths.

Estimated Standard Errors

As discussed in Chapter 3, it is unclear how much weight to put on the covariance terms in finding the standard error of measured rates of profit. These terms are of the form

$$u_{it} \, u_{ht} \, \text{cov}(R_i \, R_h),$$

where the standard error formulas take the u's as given. Patterns of u's that show positive cross correlation lead to higher standard errors. The variance σ_x^2 is calculated conditional on the u's. There may well be a difference, however, in the pattern of the u's expected under efficiency and the pattern actually observed. To the extent that positive cross correlations of the u's are due to inefficiencies (positive cross correlations of divergences between expected returns and the conditionally constant risk premia) and are higher than would be expected under efficiency (no divergences and hence no cross correlations from this source), the standard error is artificially high. In this way, it makes sense to view the estimate from these standard error formulas as an upper bound. A truncated version that ignores the covariance terms may serve as a lower bound; indeed, to the extent that the u's would get completely out of sync under efficiency, the contribution of the covariance terms to the standard error is negative.[3]

For these reasons, it is unclear exactly how to report standard errors and t-statistics. In Sweeney (1988), the t-statistics for results for U.S. equities are relatively insensitive to whether the covariance terms are included. For foreign exchange markets, the difference can be substantial. A feel for this difference is given by the two sets of t-statistics reported in Table 48, where the t-statistics neglecting the correlation terms are over twice as large. To conserve on space, t-statistics are generally omitted in the tables below. Table 49, based on results in preceding chapters, gives a good feel, however, for what the t-statistics are when the upper bound standard error is used or lower bound t-statistics are reported.[4]

10D. Choosing Filter Sizes and Lag Lengths, and the Stability of Profits Over Time

A number of possibilities are consistent with the fall-off that the preceding chapters observe in the profitability of the Alexander rule. First, any nonzero measured profits may be wholly spurious or fluky, with the fall-off meaning nothing. For the sake of discussion, assume that the results are not merely spurious or accidental. Second, the market may be catching on over the sample and acting in ways that reduce, and perhaps eventually eliminate, the measured profits. This interpretation would assume that the measured profits were economic profits that learning behavior was eliminating. The time over which the profits persisted would be impressive even if they were being reduced and ultimately eliminated. Third, the process generating profits may change over time, and the trigger values and lag lengths used may not be suitable for the changed process. One way that inappropriate triggers and lengths can be chosen is by using inappropriate amounts of data in prior periods to select rules to use for speculation in the test periods. For example, using 900 days worth of data to select the size of an Alexander filter, as done in preceding chapters, may be too much when the process is shifting substantially, say, each 300 days. Fourth, the process may be changing rapidly enough that the 1,000 observation test samples used in previous chapters are inappropriately long, as might have been the case in Sweeney's (1986a) 1,220 observation test period. Fifth, the process may be changing in such a way that the best class of rules (for example, Alexander versus double moving average) varies over time. Sixth, in a world in which the unknown best rule may come from changing classes of rules and changing amounts of prior data, the best ex ante approach may be to stick with one class and one amount of data. For example, using 500 days and a double moving average may not be best in any period, but may give the best average over time. This chapter casts some light on the third through sixth points.

Stability of Profits for Differing Prior Periods

Table 50 shows results for the four classes of rules (Alexander, double moving average, single moving average, and mixed) and two portfolio approaches (equally weighted portfolio of individual funds versus variably weighted portfolio of interdependent funds that can in effect borrow and lend to each other) for various amounts of data used in the prior period to select the rules to use in the test sample of 1,500 days. The length of the prior period ranges from 500 to 1,400 observations. This range was chosen arbitrarily before any empirical work for this chapter was done. This test sample runs from mid-1980 to mid-1986 and thus takes up approximately where Sweeney's (1986a) sample leaves off. Several results seem clear.

First, looking at the "average" row, the Alexander rules seem to have dropped off in performance from what Sweeney found with an equally weighted portfolio (an average of 2.62 percent), whether we use the equally weighted (2.30 percent) or variably weighted (1.20 percent) portfolio approach.

Second, comparing column (1) for the Alexander rule in Table 50 with the average in Table 48 for the 1 percent and 2 percent rules, the tailored trigger values in Table 50 give a superior performance, 2.30 percent versus 2.06 percent, as opposed to sticking with the 1 percent and 2 percent trigger values that might have been picked based on Sweeney (1986a). This difference in profitability is not, however, significant.

Third, neglecting the Alexander rule, it is clear from the "average" row in Table 50 that the variably weighted beats the equally weighted portfolio approach for the average of the columns for each rule. Even including the Alexander rule, the averages of the averages in Table 50 show that the variably weighted beats the equally weighted approach by almost half a percentage point (0.4888 percent), though this is not statistically significant.

Fourth, for most sizes of the prior period, say 500, profits to the variably weighted approach are on average (and sometimes substantially) larger than to the equally weighted approach, as shown by comparing the "average" columns. Exceptions are the 700- and 900-observation prior periods. Recall that in Chapters 5 through 8 we arbitrarily used a 900-observation prior period chosen in advance of any empirical work. (The effectiveness of a 900-observation prior period arises again in the discussion in Section 10F of whether profits are falling over time.)

Fifth, based on the "average" row, the single moving average variably weighted portfolio approach dominates by far. Of course, this may be highly sample dependent. There are good, intuitive reasons, however, why this approach works. The equally weighted approach works for the single moving average in this table, and thus the variably weighted approach that keeps money busier on average should do even better. Further, as pointed out in earlier chapters, the single moving average runs up sizable transactions costs with the equally weighted approach, costs that the variably weighted approach ends up reducing, because sometimes a transaction is signaled but there are no funds available and hence it is not carried out.

Sixth, in comparing average results in Tables 49 and 50, it is clear that a major reason for the lower average profits in the 1,500-observation period is the fall–off in performance of the double moving average and Alexander filter rules. In turn, the superior performance of these rules seems to have come in the first 500 observations of the 2,000-observation period. One possibility is that these were a particularly fortunate 500 observations. Another is that there is a trend to decreasing profits over time. We can check on this by splitting the 1,500-observation period, as we do below.

Seventh, it is hard to see a clear advantage to any particular sample size used in the prior period to select rules for the test sample in Table 50. The "average" columns show no very clear pattern for the equally weighted portfolio. The "average" columns show that the short prior periods (500 or 600) and the long prior periods (1,300 or 1,400) seem to work better than intermediate lengths for the variably weighted portfolio approach; both of these possible patterns suggested by averages suffer at least some contradiction from results for specific rules. For example, for variably weighted portfolios, the double moving average does roughly better with short prior periods, the single moving average with long.

Eighth, the "average" row and columns show the advantages of diversification across the 15 currencies, four rules, and ten lengths of prior periods. For the variably weighted portfolio, the average return is 3.23 percent per year, with a deviation of 3.78 percent above and 2.73 percent below. For the equally weighted portfolio, the average return is 2.67 percent per year, with a deviation of 2.89 percent above and 2.45 percent below. Clearly, this is yet another case where diversification seems to work.

The Temporal Stability of Profits

Turn now to two subperiods of the 1,500-observation period.

The Equally Weighted Portfolio Approach. Table 51 sheds some light on the stability of profits by looking at two subperiods of 750 observations each for equally weighted portfolios. The general picture, supported by the "average" row, is very clear. There is a substantial *increase* in profits from the first subperiod to the second. This is in contrast to earlier chapters' results where the first subperiod had substantially larger profits than the second; the fall-off in earlier chapters was especially pronounced for the Alexander rules as Table 47 shows, but also occurred for the double moving average and single moving average rules as Table 49 shows. Because the test period here is the last 1,500 observations of earlier chapters' 2,000-observation test period, there is clearly something of a puzzle here, to which we return below. At this point, we merely want to stress the obvious, that for the three years up to mid-1986, there seems to be little difference from the results Sweeney (1986a) found for the average of the 1 percent and 2 percent triggers (2.65 percent—see Table 46 above) and the results in Table 51 (2.73 percent for the Alexander rule on average, 2.93 percent for the average of all the rules' averages).

The Variably Weighted Portfolio Approach. Results are much more mixed for the variably weighted than for the equally weighted portfolio approach. Table 52 shows that there is substantial instability over the two halves of the 1,500-observation test period. For the Alexander rule, the second period gives much better results than the first, and for the single moving average rule the second gives somewhat better results. This is notably different from the results in earlier chapters where the performance falls off from the first to the second period, especially for the Alexander rule.

The results are complicated, however, by the fact that the double moving average and mixed rules give stronger performances in the second subperiod, as shown by the "average" row.

Further, the subperiod results seem quite sensitive to the number of observations used in the prior periods, especially the second subperiod's results.

Switching Rule Parameters Between 750-Observation Subperiods

Table 53 reveals an important point about measuring the performance of the rules. For example, the Alexander rule, equally weighted portfolio, in Table 50 gives an average of 2.30 percent for the whole period of 1,500 observations. The average of the two 750-observation subperiods in Table 51 (1.46 percent and 2.73 percent) is only 2.09 percent for the Alexander rule. Table 53 summarizes Tables 50 and 51 and shows that there are major, consistent difference across the two ways of measuring performance. The averages of averages show a difference of 0.45 percent.

There are two reasons for the divergence. First, in Table 50 the same rule parameters are used throughout, but in Table 51 the rule parameters are switched after the first 750 observations. Second, whenever any rule starts, the program begins with the investor in the foreign currency, and when the period ends, the program forces the investor to sell out. Thus, breaking the 1,500 observations into two periods may force the investor at the end of the first 750 and start of the next 750 to make transactions s/he would not otherwise make. If the investor is in the DM, say, and would like to stay there, forcing him/her to sell out on day 750 and buy back in on day 751 should have trivial impact. But if the investor is out of the DM, forcing the investor to buy in on day 751 and to hold until receiving a sell signal can be quite costly if the rule being used has some genuine predictive power.

It is of some interest to see how much difference these forced sales and purchases make. In Table 54 we provide information on this question by assuming that the same filters and lengths are used in each 750-observation period as in the overall period but that the investor is forced to make a fresh start after 750 observations. By comparing the averages of averages, it is clear that the fresh-start approach (2.37 percent) relative to the constant approach (2.74 percent) costs the investor 0.38 percent. The difference between Tables 50 and 51, as shown in Table 53, is the net of the impacts of the changes in filters and lengths and of the forced sales and purchases due to the fresh-start approach. Because this net difference is 0.45 percent, and the impact of the forced sales is 0.38 percent, it appears that the forced sales and purchases are the only important cause of the difference in performance between pursuing the same filters and lengths over the entire 1,500 observations versus switching filters and lengths halfway through. This is bad news, however, for those who believe that mechanically switching filters and lengths can produce superior performance.

Speculation using the variably weighted portfolio approach gives similar bad news about switching rule parameters. Table 55 compares the average of the results in Table 50 to the results from using the same filters and lengths throughout the 1,500-observation test period. The raw results in Table 55, for the averages of the averages, show superiority for using the same rule throughout rather than switching rules (though the results for the Alexander and Double Moving Average rules show some advantage to switching triggers and lengths). Recalling the above discussion of the cost to the investor of being forced to start over in the middle of the sample, it seems that a reasonable conclusion is that there is no clear cut superiority of sticking to filters and lengths or mechanically switching them after 750 observations (three years).

10E. When to Change Filter Sizes and Lag Lengths?

The results so far apply to using long test periods (from three to six years in this chapter and up to eight years in earlier chapters) and to using long prior periods to form guesses about promising strategies (from 500 to 1,400 observations here, and 900 observations in earlier chapters). It is not at all clear that such long periods are at all optimal, either in applying rules or searching for them. For example, in using a one half of 1 percent filter rule on U.S. equities, Sweeney (1990f) reports that changing stocks on a trading list every year gives superior performance compared to changing stocks every two years, though the list maintained for two years gives positive measured profits. Of course, changing the composition of a trading list while maintaining the same filter is not the same as holding constant the list of currencies traded but changing the rule parameters used, as in this book. The next step, however, is to consider shorter holding periods, in particular 250 trading days (approximately one trading year).

Changing Rule Parameters Every Year

Table 56 gives the results for changing the filters and lengths every year for equally weighted portfolios of independent funds. The results are extremely discouraging for the prospect of mechanically changing rule parameters every year, with the Alexander rule giving average profits of only 0.13 percent per year and the rules averaging only 0.09 percent per year overall. These results are particularly discouraging in comparison to holding the filters and lengths constant throughout the six-year period, with the Alexander rule giving 2.30 percent per year and the rules averaging 2.74 percent per year. Recall from Section 10D, though, that we should expect some fall-off in performance from columns (2) to (1) because the program for column (1) forces the investor to sell off at the end of each year and to buy at the beginning of the next year. In particular, the program may be forcing the investor to buy at a time when the rule would otherwise be strongly signaling that he should be out of the currency, and the program also forces the buyer to hold the currency until a sell signal.

Table 57 sheds light on this issue. In this table we show the results of using the same filters and lag lengths from the initial prior period if we force the investor to start over at the beginning of each period in column (1) versus simply keeping on with the same rule for the entire period as in column (2). In particular, the only difference between columns (1) and (2) is that the investor is forced to sell at the end of each year and buy at the beginning of the next year in column (1) but not in column (2). The average of results for all prior periods and all four rules is 0.5153 percent per year when the investor is forced to start over each year versus 2.7393 percent when exactly the same filters and lag lengths are used but the investor is not forced to make a fresh start each year. Table 56 shows that forcing the investor not only to make a fresh start each year but also use a new set of triggers pays 0.0925 percent per year. In other words, the results in Table 57 show that the fresh start approach reduces profits by 2.224 percent (= 2.7393 percent - 0.5153 percent), but Table 56's results show that the combined impact of switching filters or lag lengths and the fresh start approach is to reduce profits by 2.6468 percent (= 2.7393 percent - 0.0925 percent). Thus, the effect of changing filters and lag lengths each year is to reduce profits by 0.4228 percent per year (= 2.6468 percent - 2.2240 percent).

Two points should be made. First, Table 57 shows that forcing the investor to make a fresh start every year reduces profits by 2.224 percent per year, or since there are five fresh starts, by 0.4448 percent per year per fresh start. Earlier estimates in this chapter of the costs of one fresh start after 750 observations was that it cost the investor 0.38 percent per year per one fresh start. These two estimates of the costs of always starting "in" the foreign currency—plunging in on investments without considering market timing—are remarkably consistent. If the average rate of profit in the whole period is taken as 2.8 percent per year and the cost of one fresh start as 0.4 percent, then the fresh start reduces the profit rate by 14.3 percent (= [0.4 percent/2.8 percent] 100). Put another way, in looking at aggregates of subperiods, the profit rate should be grossed up by almost 16.7 percent (= [2.8 percent/2.4 percent] 100 - 1) for each fresh start and so should the t-statistic. In terms of Table 49, for example, the whole-period "average" results across rules for the equally weighted and variably weighted portfolio approaches, 3.40 percent (3.34) and 4.99 percent (4.90), can be grossed up by 16.7 percent to 3.97 percent (3.90) and 5.82 percent (5.72) to take account of the mechanical switch after the first period. The same logic argues that the returns in both subperiods are also reduced because the investor plunges right into each currency rather than looking at past data for buy or sell signals. This argues that the results should be grossed up by 16.7 percent for the subperiod results and by 33.3 percent for the whole period, giving whole-period results of 4.53 percent (4.45) and 6.65 (6.53).

Second, comparison of Tables 56 and 57 shows that mechanically switching filters and lag lengths each year reduces profits by more than 0.4 percent per year relative to simply sticking with initial parameter values. This reduction is not statistically significant. Nevertheless, this result is a warning that switching filters and lengths relatively frequently, in this case on a yearly basis, may have very low value. This conclusion holds, though, only for relatively long prior periods, in this case periods of from 500 to 1,400 observations.

Using Shorter Prior Periods

Table 58 shows the dismal results in columns (1) from using shorter prior periods, of from 250 to 450 observations, along with changing filters and lag lengths each year. The average across these prior-period lengths and the rules is -0.364 percent per year. It is clear by now that some major part of these poor results is due to forcing the investor to sell at the end of each year and to buy at the start of the next and then hold until a sell signal. These results, however, are poor relative to switching rules every year but using longer prior periods; for example, Table 56 shows an average profit of 0.0925 percent per year for prior periods of from 500 to 1,400 observations even though the filters and lag lengths are changed each year in both cases and both cases require a fresh start. Thus, the shorter prior periods cost the investor an average of 0.4565 percent per year as a best guess as compared to longer prior periods (though the difference is not significant). Further, compare the averages in Table 58 for the columns (1) and (2). This shows that the effect of changing the filters and lag lengths every period is to reduce profits by 0.8806 percent per year, from 0.5166 percent to - 0.3640 percent.

10F. Have Speculative Profits Declined Over Time?

This chapter began by noting results in earlier chapters that found declining profits for the Alexander filter rule for the four years ending in mid-1986 as compared to the preceding four years. One interpretation is that speculative profits are vanishing over time. For the equally weighted portfolio approach, as seen in Table 51, there were larger average profits, however, for every technical trading rule for the three years ending in mid-1986 than for the three preceding years. Table 52, for the variably weighted portfolio approach, shows very similar average profits over the two 750-observation subperiods, with two rules showing larger profits and two smaller profits in the second subperiod. On this evidence, then, profits do not seem to show a downward trend as time goes on.

The results in Tables 51 and 52 raise another problem, however, because they show a decline in average profits for the 1,500-observation test period in comparison to average profits in Table 49 for the 2,000-observation period. The equally weighted portfolio approach gives 2.67 percent versus 3.40 percent. Similarly, comparisons for the variably weighted portfolio approach show that average profits are 4.99 percent in the 2,000-observation period and only 3.23 percent in the 1,500-observation period.

How do we interpret these results? Start by noting that the profit rates are not strictly comparable, because previous chapters used only a 900-observation prior period; the averages quoted in this chapter are across not only rules but also prior periods ranging from 500 to 1,400 observations. Table 59 gives a stricter comparison by looking at results from this chapter for 900-observation prior periods. For 900-observation prior periods, there is an even more substantial fall in moving from 2,000 to 1,500 test observations, from an average of 4.99 percent to 2.46 percent for the variably weighted and from 3.40 percent to 2.31 percent for the equally weighted portfolio approach. (Note that 900-observation prior periods do not perform very well in the 1,500-observation test period as compared to different-sized prior periods.)

Clearly, the 500-observation difference in the two test periods matters substantially. Its importance might arise for three reasons. First, the 500 observations gone from the sample might be particularly profitable. Second, the deletion of these observations changes both prior periods and the rules they generate for use in the subperiods. Third, the new first subperiod overlaps only for 500 observations with the old first subperiod and overlaps for the first 250 observations of the old second subperiod, while the new second subperiod is simply the last 750 observations of the old second subperiod. Simple redivision of periods may introduce random fluctuations in profits.

Table 60 sheds some light on these possibilities by showing the results from running earlier chapters' filters and lag lengths on the periods used here as compared with the results of the 900-observation prior periods used in this chapter. The difference, then, is due simply to the subperiod rules being chosen from prior periods that are 500 observations apart.

From Table 60, there is no clear superiority of one set of filters and lag lengths over the other when both the equally weighted and variably weighted portfolio approaches are considered. Looking at the approaches separately, however, does show some interesting differences.

For the equally weighted portfolio approach, the filters and lag lengths from Chapter 5 work better on average in each subperiod (though only by a very small amount in the second subperiod) and hence overall than the new filters and lag lengths. However, the new parameters show increasing profits in the second subperiod relative to the first, but Chapter 5's parameters show decreasing profits between the two subperiods. The old parameters give better results than the new in the first subperiod for every rule; the new outperform the old for two of the four rules in the second subperiod. The results for the second subperiod are so close, however, that the big superiority of the old parameters in the first subperiod makes it appear that it was a mistake not to stick with the old parameters overall. For the equally weighted portfolio approach, then, one may want to ascribe the decline in whole-period profits to a bad but random change in rule parameters.

For the variably weighted approach, the new parameters give better average performance for the whole period than do those in Chapter 6 (2.46 percent versus 1.73 percent). The average performance of the new parameters is about constant over subperiods (2.55 percent versus 2.48 percent); the performance of parameters from Chapter 6 shows substantial decline across subperiods (3.45 percent versus 0.12 percent). The profits from the new parameters rise between the two subperiods for all of the rules save the double moving average rule, where the fall between subperiods is large—but smaller than the fall under the rule parameters from Chapter 6.

It is worthwhile to compare the results of the old parameters for the new subperiods (in Table 60) and for the old subperiods (in Table 49) to show the effect of altering the subperiods—see Table 61. The equally weighted portfolio's excellent performance in the shorter whole period is even better than in the longer whole period. It is tempting to put this improvement down to sheer randomness. By the same token, one might want to view both the seeming fall-off in performance between subperiods (of both 750 and 1,000 observations) in Table 61 and the seeming improvement across subperiods in Table 60 for the new parameters as simply due to randomness. Looked at in this way, one might view the difference in whole-period results for the 2,000- and 1,500-observation periods when different 900-observation prior periods are used, 3.40 percent and 2.31 percent, as essentially random.

For the variably weighted portfolio approach, Table 61 shows that changing the length of subperiods while keeping the same parameters is very costly—the whole-period average falls from 4.99 percent to 1.73 percent. Further, the fall-off in profits between subperiods is accentuated by the shift to the shorter subperiods. Recall that Table 60 shows essentially no fall-off in profits between subperiods for the new parameters. One reasonable view is that there is no ongoing tendency for profits to fall between subperiods but that the 500-observation difference in the two different whole periods considered has a big though random effect on profits under the variably weighted portfolio approach. How can there be so much randomness with the variably weighted portfolio approach? Recall that the standard errors from this approach tend to be large relative to those from the equally weighted portfolio approach, as can be seen from Table 49 for the first subperiod, where the implied ratio of standard errors is 1.5496 (=1.9212/1.2398). This is so even though both approaches use exactly the same rule parameters and hence get exactly the same buy and sell signals for the individual currencies. Intuitively, the variably weighted portfolio approach is subject to more randomness because it allows the possibility of more extreme positions. The equally weighted portfolio approach never lets the fraction of total wealth invested in any one currency rise above roughly one fifteenth, because each currency is treated essentially as an independent mutual fund. Under the variably weighted portfolio approach, however, the funds can be thought of as borrowing and lending to each other. Suppose, for example, that all currencies get a sell signal—the funds realized from the sales are all put in Euro-dollar accounts and the investor is completely out of foreign currencies. Several days later, there is a buy signal for one currency and no others. All of the funds are then put in this one currency—the weight on this currency is unity. If things go well, they go really well—and if they go badly, they go really badly. The variably weighted portfolio approach allows the possibility of the investor getting into an ill-diversified position.

If one is willing to ascribe to randomness the different average performances of rules in the 2,000- and 1,500-observation periods, the question arises of the best estimate of true underlying performance. The longer period seems to say 3.40 percent and 4.99 percent for the equally weighted and variably weighted portfolio approaches (Table 49), while the shorter seems to say 2.67 percent and 3.23 percent (Table 50). A major message of this chapter seems to be that although there is not a clear change in the level of profits over subperiods, it is unclear what level of profits to expect.

10G. Conclusions

Speculative profits in the foreign exchanges show a degree of stability across periods that is perhaps somewhat surprising in light of the volatility of these markets. This chapter began with the observation that profits seem to have fallen off for the Alexander filter rule from levels found earlier, leading to the possibility that the speculative potential of these markets was drying up and might ultimately vanish. Instead, the profitability of speculation could be argued to be roughly the same over, say, 12 years, based on the results in Sweeney (1986a) and this chapter. It seems, however, that the first 500 observations in the 2,000-observation sample we use in Chapters 5 through 9 give particularly favorable results for the Alexander filter and double moving average rules, enhancing the impression that later profits fall off. Whether one wants to estimate average profits for the future on the basis of the more favorable average results found in Chapters 5-9 or the more conservative results found in this chapter is unclear.

The Alexander rule does not appear to be either the most profitable or to give the most stable results. Moving average rules appear to be superior, with some evidence that the single moving average rule gives best performance. The double moving average rule shows substantially more instability than does the single moving average rule, though this is particularly true for the variably weighted portfolio approach that is inherently subject to more randomness than the equally weighted portfolio approach.

Further, the variably weighted portfolio approach, treating speculations across different currencies as part of an interdependent set of funds that borrow and lend to each other, rather than wholly independent funds, seems to raise profits. This appears especially true for the single moving average rules. The increase in average profits seems to be bought at the cost of greater variability.

Changing filters or lag lengths on a yearly basis does not seem to improve profits. Indeed, point estimates say this reduces profits.

There does not seem to be a clear advantage across all rules to using larger or smaller amounts of data to select filters or lag lengths. The point estimates seem to indicate clearly, however, that one is better off using from 500 to 1,400 observations to select filters or lag lengths rather than using smaller amounts of data, say from 250 to 500 observations.

Finally, it seems impossible to look across the tables of results without concluding that diversification pays—diversification across rules and across amounts of data used to select filters and lag lengths.

Notes

1. Praetz (1976) argues that the filter rule test of Fama and Blume (1966) was substantially biased against filter rules. Levich (1982), in a comment on Sweeney (1982), argues that risk may be different on average in the periods a technical rule has the speculator in the asset as opposed tp out of the asset.

2. Profits are measured in percent per year, using one or another version of the X-statistic. All profits discussed here are reported net of transactions costs. Trans-

actions costs of one eighth of 1 percent per round trip are assumed; see Sweeney (1986a) and Chapter 4 for discussions of transactions costs.

3. Suppose that there are 14 currencies, and that for every period seven have positive u's and seven have negative u's. Let u_{1t} be negative. Then, u_{it} for all i not equal to 1 shows six negative values and five positive values. If the covariances across currencies are roughly the same or is there is no systematic pattern of u-products and covariances, then the net impact of the covariance terms on the standard error will be negative.

4. In interpreting the tables below, it is useful to recall that ceteris paribus t-statistics vary proportionately both within the X-statistic and with the inverse of the square root of the number of observations in the period. A change that reduces the X-statistic from 6 percent to 3 percent cuts the t-statistic in half. A given realization of X in a 750-observation period has a t-statistic that is only 86.6 percent as large as if from a 1000-observation period.

TABLE 46 Alexander Filter Rules, Equally Weighted Portfolios;
Profits in Percent per Year

	1%	2%	Average of 1%,2%
April 1973 to Mid-1975 (Prior Period)	3.69%	4.41%	4.05%
	(4.31)	(5.31)	
Mid-1975 to Mid-1980 (Test Sample)	3.36%	1.99%	2.65%
	(6.35)	(3.48)	

1. Based on Sweeney (1986a). These are results for an equally weighted portfolio
of currencies. Profits are net of transaction costs. The t-statistics in parentheses
assume that the profit measures across currencies are uncorrelated; this may overstate
the t-statistics. For comparison of t-statistics across the two subperiods, multiply
the t-statistics of the shorter period by 1.414 (= the square root of 2), since the longer
period has twice as many observations.

TABLE 47 Alexander Filter Rules, Equall and Variably Weighted Portfolios; Profits in Percent per Year

	(1) Equally Weighted Portfolio	(2) Variably Weighted Portfolio	(3) Average of (1) and (2)
Mid-1978 to Mid-1982 (Test Sample)	3.58%	6.20%	4.89%
	(2.94)	(3.03)	
Mid1982 to Mid-1986 (Test Sample)	2.56%	0.69%	1.63%
	(1.47)	(0.24)	
Whole period (average of the two subperiods)	3.07%	3.45%	3.26%
	(2.88)	(1.97)	

1. Based on results in Chapters 5-9. Profits are net of transaction costs. The t-statistics in parentheses assume the population covariances of the profit measures across currencies are equal to the sample covariances; this may understate the t-statistic.

TABLE 48 Alexander Filter Rules, Equally Weighted Portfolios;
Profits in Percent per Year

	1%	2%	Average of 1% and 2%
Mid-1980 to Mid-1983 (Test Sample)	0.84%	1.43%	1.14%
	(1.04)	(1.82)	
	[0.46]	[0.78]	
Mid-1983 to Mid-1986 (Test Sample)	2.38%	3.59%	2.99%
	(2.47)	(3.75)	
	[1.05]	[1.58]	
Whole Period (average of two subperiods)	1.6196	2.5196	2.06%
	(2.56)	(4.05)	
	[1.11]	[1.72]	

1. These are the results for equally weighted portfolios of currencies. Profits are net of transactions costs. The t-statistics in parentheses assume that the profit measures across currencies are uncorrelated; this may overstate the t-statistics. The t-statistics in brackets assume that the population covariances of the profit measures across currencies are equal to the sample covariances; this may understate the t-statistics.

TABLE 49 Profits in Percent per Year of (1) Equally Weighted Portfolio of Individual Funds and (2) Variably Weighted Portfolio of Independent Funds

TEST PERIODS	ALEXANDER		DOUBLE MOVING AVERAGE		SINGLE MOVING AVERAGE		MIXED		AVERAGE	
	(1)	(2)	(1)	(2)	(1)	(2)	(1)	(2)	(1)	(2)
Mid-1978 to Mid-1982	3.5783% (2.9348)	6.1990%** (3.0297)	4.4943%** (2.9643)	5.8138%** (2.2181)	3.4668%** (2.1883)	6.5696%** (2.4526)	4.6528%** (3.2771)	4.3673% (1.6374)	4.0480%** (3.2650)	5.7374%** (2.9864)
Mid-1982 to Mid-1986	2.5605% (1.4655)	0.6942%** (0.2242)	2.7113% (1.4269)	5.0161% (1.7782)	3.0908%** (1.6716)	5.9676%** (2.1936)	2.6635% (1.5439)	5.3122%** (1.9773)	2.7565% (1.7020)	4.2475%** (2.0342)
Whole period (average of the two subperiods)	3.0695%** (2.8813)	3.4466%** (1.9682)	3.6028%** (2.9642)	5.4150%** (2.8125)	3.2788%** (2.6932)	6.2686%** (3.2838)	3.6250%** (3.2745)	4.8398%** (2.5568)	3.4023%** (3.3361)	4.9925%** (4.8954)

1. Drawn from earlier chapters. To compare t-statistics for the subperiods with those of the whole period, multiply by 1.414. X-statistics are computed for a benchmark portfolio with no rebalancing.

2. **Significant at the 95% confidence level.

TABLE 50 Adjusted X-Statistics: Profits in Percent per Year
(1) Equally Weighted Portfolio of Individual Funds, 1500 OBS
(2) Variably Weighted Portfolio of Interdependent Funds, 1500 OBS
Mid-1980 to Mid-1986

PRIOR PERIOD*	ALEXANDER		DOUBLE MOVING AVERAGE		SINGLE MOVING AVERAGE		MIXED		AVERAGE	
	(1)	(2)	(1)	(2)	(1)	(2)	(1)	(2)	(1)	(2)
500	2.2950	3.0940	2.6600	4.4445	2.5225	3.0573	2.3275	2.1677	2.4513	3.1909
600	2.3200	2.9776	2.9225	3.0802	3.0650	5.9354	2.4900	3.1444	2.6994	3.7844
700	2.1875	-1.7301	2.9825	3.4492	3.1775	5.4112	2.9275	3.7814	2.8188	2.7281
800	2.3000	-1.3460	2.8300	3.9657	3.0650	4.7606	3.0775	4.2382	2.8871	2.9045
900	2.0975	-0.6384	2.7300	2.2551	3.4025	5.2982	3.1950	4.0987	2.8563	2.7534
1,000	2.0300	1.5331	2.6775	2.1206	3.1600	4.3573	2.8950	4.1755	2.7331	3.0466
1,100	1.9675	1.4147	2.4550	1.7284	3.3250	5.4854	2.6875	3.6667	2.6088	3.0730
1,200	2.5650	2.4018	2.5575	1.7524	3.2450	6.2080	2.9450	3.7669	2.8281	3.5323
1,300	2.5775	1.9939	2.5775	2.5587	3.1775	6.3340	2.9250	3.1411	2.8144	3.5070
1,400	2.6875	2.3305	2.4475	2.3900	3.1925	6.7408	2.9250	3.6030	2.8131	3.7661
Average	2.3028	1.2031	2.6840	2.7745	3.1333	5.3588	2.8395	3.5794	2.7399	3.2287

* Number of observations used to choose filters and lag lengths ranges from 500 to 1400. These results are not the average of two 750-observation sub-periods.

TABLE 51 Adjusted X-Statistics: Profits in Percent per Year
(1) Equally Weighted Portfolio of Individual Funds, First 750 OBS
(2) Equally Weighted Portfolio of Individual Funds, Second 750 OBS

PRIOR PERIOD	ALEXANDER		DOUBLE MOVING AVERAGE		SINGLE MOVING AVERAGE		MIXED		AVERAGE	
	(1)	(2)	(1)	(2)	(1)	(2)	(1)	(2)	(1)	(2)
500	1.6500	3.0775	1.6075	2.8200	1.7150	3.4300	1.4075	3.0875	1.5950	3.1038
600	1.7475	2.7525	1.7200	2.4475	1.6525	3.2000	1.3775	2.8250	1.6244	2.8063
700	1.2175	2.6775	1.7875	2.3300	1.7100	3.8150	2.0800	2.2773	1.3944	2.7750
800	1.2475	2.7800	1.8475	2.9425	1.6225	3.6675	2.5900	2.5375	1.8269	2.9819
900	0.9900	3.0200	1.6275	2.7975	1.5550	3.6625	2.2575	2.5500	1.6075	3.0075
1,000	1.0175	2.6725	1.6125	2.8400	1.5625	3.3375	1.9300	2.8100	1.5306	2.9150
1,100	1.2125	2.4275	1.4225	2.5475	1.5200	3.4825	1.3675	2.5725	1.3806	2.7575
1,200	1.7725	2.8400	1.6100	3.1225	1.7075	3.2450	2.0225	3.1400	1.7781	3.0869
1,300	1.7675	2.5275	1.2700	3.1625	1.7325	3.2850	1.9200	2.4575	1.6725	2.8581
1,400	1.9425	2.4900	1.2800	3.2350	1.0650	3.3425	2.0175	3.0375	1.5763	3.0263
Average	1.4565	2.7265	1.5285	2.8245	1.5843	3.4468	1.8970	2.7295	1.6291	2.9318

TABLE 52 Adjusted X-Statistics: Profits in Percent per Year
Variably Weighted Portfolios of Interdependent Funds
(1) First 750 OBS (2) Second 750 OBS

PRIOR PERIOD	ALEXANDER		DOUBLE MOVING AVERAGE		SINGLE MOVING AVERAGE		MIXED		AVERAGE	
	(1)	(2)	(1)	(2)	(1)	(2)	(1)	(2)	(1)	(2)
500	2.7769	3.9045	6.8768	5.1526	4.7365	4.4030	5.0512	3.8526	4.8604	4.3282
600	2.4419	3.0270	7.3475	0.7179	4.5632	3.2004	0.9281	0.1666	3.8202	1.7405
700	-4.9096	6.3768	7.4739	-0.0053	4.1369	4.3329	0.5609	3.2878	1.8155	3.4981
800	-5.2962	4.4145	6.5714	-1.3408	3.4942	4.5321	1.3844	-3.5735	1.5385	1.0081
900	-0.2969	1.7236	6.1946	-0.4446	2.7164	5.8868	1.5650	2.3660	2.5448	2.3830
1000	0.7137	2.5489	6.1897	-1.7902	3.5233	2.8253	3.3447	-1.9577	3.4439	0.4066
1100	1.1050	2.0248	5.6963	-1.6976	3.5758	5.5694	2.7957	-0.0016	3.2932	1.4738
1200	0.7934	3.7824	5.5059	-0.8716	3.6938	3.9510	2.1286	2.0449	3.0304	2.2267
1300	0.2874	3.3038	3.8256	-0.2358	4.8850	4.4493	3.2522	2.6103	3.0626	2.5319
1400	0.7491	2.7226	2.6155	-0.1225	5.6049	5.2408	3.2388	0.3797	3.0521	2.0552
Average	-0.1635	3.3602	5.8297	0.0047	4.0930	4.4391	2.2930	0.9175	2.2998	2.1804

TABLE 53 Adjusted X-Statistics: Profits in Percent per Year
Equally Weighted Portfolios of Independent Funds, 1500 OBS
(1) Same Rule for Total 1500 OBS
(2) Rule Changed for Each 750 OBS, Average of Halves

PRIOR PERIOD	ALEXANDER		DOUBLE MOVING AVERAGE		SINGLE MOVING AVERAGE		MIXED		AVERAGE	
	(1)	(2)	(1)	(2)	(1)	(2)	(1)	(2)	(1)	(2)
500	2.2950	2.3650	2.6600	2.2150	2.5225	2.5725	2.3275	2.2475	2.4513	2.3500
600	2.3200	2.2500	2.9225	2.0850	3.0650	2.4275	2.4900	2.1025	2.6994	2.2163
700	2.1875	1.9475	2.9825	2.0600	3.1775	2.7625	2.9275	2.4250	2.8188	2.2988
800	2.3000	2.0125	2.8300	2.3950	3.0650	2.6450	3.0775	2.5625	2.8871	2.3550
900	2.0975	2.0050	2.7300	2.2125	3.4025	2.6075	3.1950	2.4025	2.8563	2.3181
1000	2.0300	1.8450	2.6775	2.2250	3.1600	2.4500	2.8950	2.3700	2.7331	2.2225
1100	1.9675	1.8200	2.4550	1.9850	3.3250	2.5000	2.6875	1.9700	2.6088	2.0688
1200	2.5650	2.3075	2.5575	2.3650	3.2450	2.4775	2.9450	2.5825	2.8281	2.4331
1300	2.5775	2.1475	2.5775	2.2175	3.1775	2.5100	2.9250	2.1875	2.8144	2.2656
1400	2.6875	2.2150	2.4475	2.2575	3.1925	2.2025	2.9250	2.5275	2.8131	2.3086
Average	2.3028	2.0915	2.6840	2.2018	3.1333	2.5155	2.8395	2.3378	2.7399	2.2867

1. The (1) columns here are from the (1) columns in Table 50, while the (2) columns here are the averages of columns (1) and (2) in Table 51.

TABLE 54 Adjusted X-Statistics: Profits in Percent per Year
Equally Weighted Portfolios of Independent Funds, 1500 OBS
(1) Same Rule, but Fresh Start for each 750 OBS, Average
(2) Same Rule for All 1500 OBS, No Fresh Start

PRIOR PERIOD	ALEXANDER		DOUBLE MOVING AVERAGE		SINGLE MOVING AVERAGE		MIXED		AVERAGE	
	(1)	(2)	(1)	(2)	(1)	(2)	(1)	(2)	(1)	(2)
500	1.9525	2.2950	2.2500	2.6600	2.2075	2.5225	1.9700	2.3275	2.0950	2.4513
600	2.0125	2.3200	2.4900	2.9225	2.7275	3.0650	2.1600	2.4900	2.3475	2.6994
700	1.8325	2.1875	2.5650	2.9825	2.8050	3.1775	2.5775	2.9275	2.4450	2.8188
800	2.0100	2.3000	2.4075	2.8300	2.7100	3.0650	2.7300	3.0775	2.4644	2.8871
900	1.7450	2.0975	2.3000	2.7300	3.0325	3.4025	2.8575	3.1950	2.4838	2.8563
1000	1.6425	2.0300	2.2475	2.6775	2.7825	3.1600	2.5225	2.8950	2.2988	2.7331
1100	1.6250	1.9675	2.0300	2.4550	2.9450	3.3250	2.3000	2.6875	2.2250	2.6088
1200	2.2200	2.5650	2.1375	2.5575	2.8700	3.2450	2.5975	2.9450	2.4563	2.8281
1300	2.2150	2.5775	2.1575	2.5775	2.8050	3.1775	2.5525	2.9250	2.4325	2.8144
1400	2.3325	2.6875	2.0225	2.4475	2.7050	3.1925	2.5500	2.9250	2.4025	2.8131
Average	1.9588	2.3028	2.2608	2.6840	2.7590	3.1333	2.4818	2.8395	2.3651	2.7399

1. The (2) columns here are from the (1) columns in Tables 50 and 53 above.

TABLE 55 Adjusted X-Statistics: Profits in Percent per Year
Variably Weighted Portfolio of Interdependent Funds, 1500 OBS
(1) Rules Switched After First 750 OBS, Average of Halves
(2) Rules Unchanged Over Total 1500 OBS

PRIOR PERIOD	ALEXANDER		DOUBLE MOVING AVERAGE		SINGLE MOVING AVERAGE		MIXED		AVERAGE	
	(1)	(2)	(1)	(2)	(1)	(2)	(1)	(2)	(1)	(2)
500	3.3407	3.0940	6.0102	4.4445	4.5698	3.0573	4.4519	2.1677	4.5932	3.1909
600	2.7344	2.9776	4.0331	3.0802	3.8818	5.9354	0.5474	3.1444	2.7992	3.7844
700	0.7336	-1.7301	3.7343	3.4492	4.2349	5.4112	1.9243	3.7814	2.6568	2.7281
800	-0.4328	-1.3460	2.6153	3.9657	4.0131	4.7606	-1.0946	4.2382	1.2828	2.9045
900	0.7134	-0.6384	2.8750	2.2551	4.3016	5.2982	1.9655	4.0987	2.4639	2.7534
1000	1.6312	1.5331	2.1998	2.1206	3.1743	4.3573	0.6935	4.1755	1.9247	3.0466
1100	1.5740	1.4147	1.9993	1.7284	4.5726	5.4854	1.1953	3.6667	2.3353	3.0730
1200	2.2880	2.4018	2.3172	1.7524	3.8220	6.2080	2.0868	3.7669	2.6285	3.5323
1300	1.7956	1.9939	1.7949	2.5587	4.6671	6.3340	2.9313	3.1411	2.7972	3.5070
1400	1.7359	2.3305	1.2465	2.3900	5.4228	6.7408	1.0816	3.6030	2.3717	3.7661
Average	1.6114	1.2031	2.8826	2.7745	4.2660	5.3588	1.4666	3.5784	2.5567	3.2287

1. The (1) columns here are the averages of the (1) and (2) columns in Table 52. The (2) columns here are the same as the (2) columns in Table 50.

TABLE 56 Adjusted X-Statistics: Profits in Percent per Year
Equally Weighted Portfolios of Independent Funds, 1500 OBS
(1) Rules Changed Each Year; Results Are Average of Six Years
(2) Same Rule for All 1500 OBS, No Fresh Start

PRIOR PERIOD	ALEXANDER		DOUBLE MOVING AVERAGE		SINGLE MOVING AVERAGE		MIXED		AVERAGE	
	(1)	(2)	(1)	(2)	(1)	(2)	(1)	(2)	(1)	(2)
500	0.1300	2.2950	-0.3975	2.6600	-0.2150	2.5225	-0.6775	2.3275	-0.2900	2.4513
600	-0.1400	2.3200	-0.0250	2.9225	0.3800	3.0650	0.0700	2.4900	0.0713	2.6994
700	0.3750	2.1875	-0.1850	2.9825	0.2675	3.1775	0.2425	2.9275	0.1750	2.8818
800	0.4725	2.3000	0.4600	2.8300	0.3550	3.0650	0.4200	3.0775	0.4269	2.8871
900	0.4150	2.0975	-0.2400	2.7300	0.7525	3.4025	0.3350	3.1950	0.3156	2.8563
1000	0.2250	2.0300	-0.3550	2.6775	0.9600	3.1600	0.3525	2.8950	0.2956	2.7331
1100	0.0450	1.9675	-0.3375	2.4550	0.2375	3.3250	-0.1525	2.6875	-0.0519	2.6088
1200	-0.2750	2.5650	-0.3700	2.5575	0.4450	3.2450	-0.0825	2.9450	-0.0706	2.8281
1300	-0.2500	2.5775	-0.3200	2.5775	0.3625	3.1775	-0.4725	2.9250	-0.1700	2.8144
1400	0.3400	2.6875	0.2025	2.4475	0.2325	3.1925	0.1175	2.9250	0.2231	2.8131
Average	0.1338	2.3028	-0.1568	2.6840	0.3778	3.1333	0.0153	2.8395	0.0925	2.7399

1. Columns (2) are also columns (2) in Table 54.

TABLE 57 Adjusted X-Statistics: Profits in Percent per Year
Equally Weighted Portfolios of Independent Funds, 1500 OBS
(1) Rules Are Not Changed, But Funds Start Over Each Year
(2) Same Rule for All 1500 OBS, No Fresh Start

PRIOR PERIOD	ALEXANDER		DOUBLE MOVING AVERAGE		SINGLE MOVING AVERAGE		MIXED		AVERAGE	
	(1)	(2)	(1)	(2)	(1)	(2)	(1)	(2)	(1)	(2)
500	0.8700	2.2950	0.0350	2.6600	0.6275	2.5225	0.7025	2.3275	0.5588	2.4513
600	0.9175	2.3200	0.2175	2.9225	0.8975	3.0650	0.5575	2.4900	0.6475	2.6994
700	-0.0050	2.1875	0.3150	2.9825	0.8375	3.1775	0.5875	2.9275	0.4338	2.8188
800	0.4200	2.3000	0.1800	2.8300	0.7900	3.0650	0.7700	3.0775	0.5400	2.8871
900	0.3825	2.0975	0.0300	2.7300	1.0525	3.4025	0.9600	3.1950	0.6063	2.8563
1000	0.3325	2.0300	-0.0075	2.6775	0.8575	3.1600	0.5075	2.8950	0.4225	2.7331
1100	0.3600	1.9675	-0.2400	2.4550	0.9425	3.3250	0.4075	2.6875	0.3675	2.6088
1200	0.9100	2.5650	-0.1025	2.5575	0.8750	3.2450	0.8200	2.9450	0.6256	2.8281
1300	0.8925	2.5775	-0.0625	2.5575	0.7725	3.1775	0.5300	2.9250	0.5331	2.8144
1400	1.0025	2.6875	-0.2350	2.4475	0.3775	3.1925	0.5250	2.9250	0.4175	2.8131
Average	0.6083	2.3028	0.0130	2.6840	0.8030	3.1333	0.6368	2.8395	0.5153	2.7399

1. Columns (2) are also columns (2) in Table 54.

TABLE 58 Adjusted X-Statistics: Profits in Percent per Year
Equally Weighted Portfolios of Independent Funds
(1) Filters and Lag Lengths Are Changed Each 250 OBS
(2) Same Filters and Lag Lengths Throughout, Fresh Start Each 250 OBS

PRIOR PERIOD	ALEXANDER		DOUBLE MOVING AVERAGE		SINGLE MOVING AVERAGE		MIXED		AVERAGE	
	(1)	(2)	(1)	(2)	(1)	(2)	(1)	(2)	(1)	(2)
250	-0.1025	0.5625	-0.2700	0.3150	-0.4150	0.5800	-0.3975	0.3300	-0.2963	0.4469
300	-0.4750	0.5300	-0.9450	0.2815	-0.3700	0.7550	-0.9425	0.3375	-0.6631	0.4760
400	0.3575	0.1575	-0.8850	0.4050	-0.0550	0.6950	-0.5000	0.6475	-0.2706	0.4763
450	-0.2675	0.6300	-0.4525	0.2125	-0.0500	0.5375	-0.6775	0.9450	-0.3619	0.5813
500	-0.1025	0.7825	-0.3625	0.2325	-0.1775	0.3550	-0.1900	1.0400	-0.2081	0.6025
Average	-0.1180	0.5325	-0.5830	0.2893	-0.2135	0.5845	-0.5415	0.6600	-0.3640	0.5166

TABLE 59 Adjusted X-Statistics: Profits in Percent per Year
Comparing the 1500- and 2000-Observation Test Periods, with 900-Observation Prior Periods
(1) Results from Chapters 5 and 6, with 2000-Observations
(2) Results Using 1500-Observations

	ALEX		DMA		SMA		MIXED		AVERAGE	
	(1)	(2)	(1)	(2)	(1)	(2)	(1)	(2)	(1)	(2)
Variably-Weighted Portfolio Approach										
Subperiod 1	6.1990	-0.2969	5.8138	6.1946	6.5690	2.7164	4.3673	1.5650	5.7373	2.5448
Subperiod 2	0.6942	1.7236	5.0161	-0.4446	5.9676	5.8868	5.3122	2.3660	4.2475	2.4830
Whole Period	3.4466	0.7134	5.4150	2.8750	6.2686	4.3016	4.8398	1.9655	4.9924	2.4639
Equally-Weighted Portfolio Approach										
Subperiod 1	3.5783	0.9900	4.4943	1.6275	3.4668	1.5550	4.6528	2.2575	4.0480	1.6075
Subperiod2	2.5605	3.0200	2.7113	2.7975	3.0908	3.6625	2.6635	2.5500	2.7565	3.0075
Whole Period	3.0695	2.0050	3.6028	2.2125	3.2788	2.6088	3.6850	2.4038	3.4023	2.3075

TABLE 60 Adjusted X-Statistics: Profits in Percent per Year
1500 OBS, Divided into Two Subperiods
(1) Filters and Lag Lengths Used in Chapters 5 and 6
(2) Filters and Lag Lengths Developed Here

	ALEXANDER		DOUBLE MOVING AVERAGE		SINGLE MOVING AVERAGE		MIXED		AVERAGE	
	(1)	(2)	(1)	(2)	(1)	(2)	(1)	(2)	(1)	(2)
Variably Weighted Interdependent Mutual Funds										
Subperiod 1	3.2762	-0.2969	4.0517	6.1946	1.8512	2.7164	4.6114	1.5650	3.4476	2.5448
Subperiod 2	-1.1192	1.7236	-4.0516	-0.4446	3.7735	5.8868	1.4451	2.3660	0.1195	2.4830
Whole Period	1.0785	0.7134	0.0001	2.8750	2.8123	4.3016	3.0282	1.9655	1.7297	2.4639
Equally Weighted Independent Mutual Funds										
Subperiod 1	5.2600	0.9900	5.7550	1.6275	4.3975	1.5550	6.0150	2.2575	5.3794	1.6075
Subperiod 2	2.7300	3.0200	2.8250	2.7975	3.5125	3.6625	2.9950	2.5500	3.0156	3.0075
Whole Period	3.9950	2.0050	4.2900	2.2125	3.9550	2.6088	4.5050	2.4038	4.1863	2.3075

1. All rule parameters are from 900-observation prior periods.

TABLE 61 Adjusted X-Statistics – Profits in Percent per Year; Averages Across Rules Based on Filters and Lag Lengths from Chapters 5 and 6 (1) 1000-Observation Subperiods; (2) 750-Observation Subperiods

| | Equally Weighted | | Variably Weighted | |
	(1)	(2)	(1)	(2)
Subperiod 1	4.05%	5.38%	5.74%	3.4476
Subperiod 2	2.76%	3.02%	4.25%	0.12%
Whole Period (average)	3.40%	4.19%	4.99%	1.73%

1. Filters and lag lengths are those chosen from the 900-observation prior periods and used in Chapters 5 and 6. Results in (1) columns are from Table 49, and results in (2) columns are from Table 60.

PART 5

Implications for Policymakers

11

Implications for the Theory and Practice of Financial Economics

The empirical results in Chapters 5 through 10 document substantial, fairly consistent, statistically significant measured profits from using technical trading rules in spot foreign exchange markets. As they stand, these profits are a serious challenge to the view that the foreign exchange markets are efficient and to the widespread view that financial markets in general are efficient. Because much policy advice to both private and public decisionmakers assumes efficient foreign exchange markets, these results are a serious challenge to much conventional wisdom in policy circles. Our view is that the Efficient Markets Hypothesis (EMH) is a powerful tool and a useful description of financial forces and markets. We view markets as efficient at some level, and our results simply question at what level markets are efficient. The EMH is so fundamental to finance, however, that it is not to be abandoned lightly at any level. In this chapter we evaluate how serious a challenge this book's results really are to the view of foreign exchange market efficiency and the implications for private policymakers. In the following chapter we draw the implications of these results for key issues of public policy.

Section 11A briefly reviews the empirical results in Chapters 5–10. In Section 11B we discuss whether the measured profits we report from computer simulations can actually be earned in real time or might instead be due to data problems, underestimation of transactions costs, programming errors, or inability to make the transactions without unduly moving the markets. In this discussion, the issue is whether the measured profits could actually be made. In Section 11C we assume the profits could be made and discusses whether the measured profits found above might be explained by time-varying risk premia and hence might not be economic profits. It simply is not clear whether time-varying risk premia can explain the profits; the measured profits remain as a serious challenge to the view that financial markets are generally efficient. In Section 11D we offer brief conclusions.

11A. Summary of Results on Speculation

The overwhelming message of Chapters 5–10 is that portfolio approaches to speculation (speculating in more than one currency at a time) are generally profitable compared to a naive buy-and-hold strategy. Averaged across trading rules, whole-period results (and t–statistics) for the equally and variably weighted portfolio approaches are 3.4 percent per year (with a t–statistic of 3.34) and 3.94 percent per year (with a t–statistic of 3.28), as Table 45 in Chapter 9 shows. Trading rules perform extraordinarily well in the first subperiod. On average, trading rule profits persist in the second subperiod but are smaller than in the first subperiod.

The choice of technical trading technique may substantially affect performance. For the overall period, the single moving average technique is significantly superior to the Alexander filter technique in both the index and the variably weighted portfolio approaches. The performances of the double moving average and the mixed rule are both between those of the single moving average and Alexander filter rules and are not statistically different from each other or from the Alexander filter and the single moving average techniques.

Further, approaches to diversification also make a difference. Chapter 9 examined the performance of four approaches to speculation: the equally weighted and variably weighted portfolio approach, the index approach, and the portfolio upgrade approach. The variably weighted portfolio approach uses the buy or sell signals of each individual currency to speculate simultaneously in all currencies according to the availability of funds. Under this approach, the Alexander filter, double moving average, and single moving average techniques yield substantial profits in the first subperiod that are also statistically significant; the mixed rule gives substantial though insignificant profits. The single moving average and mixed-rule techniques beat the market significantly in the second subperiod; the double moving average rule gives large but statistically insignificant profits. For the whole period, all four technical trading rules yield impressive profits that are significantly greater than buy-and-hold.

For every technique but the Alexander filter rule, the speculative performances under the variably weighted portfolio approach are *significantly* better for the overall period than the performances under the equally weighted portfolio approach; in all cases, the variably weighted portfolio approach yields higher adjusted X-statistics than the equally weighted portfolio approach. The performances of the index and portfolio upgrade approaches are generally the same statistically as those of the equally weighted portfolio approach; in the case where the single moving average technique is used, the index approach yields an adjusted X-statistic that is significantly higher than that of the equally weighted portfolio approach.

Broadly speaking, speculation using the variably weighted portfolio approach is, on average, either as good as or better than speculation using the equally weighted portfolio approach, for good, intuitive reasons. First, the variably weighted portfolio approach allows the funds to be invested intensively and hence increases the chance of making profits. Under the variably weighted portfolio approach, in the periods where the trading rules keep the investor out of the market in some assets, they are likely to keep the investor in the market for other assets rather than in the risk-free Euro-dollar asset that has no profit potential. As a result, if the underlying rules are profitable, intensive use of the invested funds will enhance the profit opportunities. Second, as seen with the case of the single moving average rule, the variably weighted portfolio approach can raise profits by cutting down on transactions and hence transactions costs. Some buy signals result in no purchases because all funds are already fully invested. The cost of this is an increase in risk, as shown by larger standard errors relative to the equally weighted portfolio approach. Although the investor can never have more than approximately one fifteenth of total funds in a single foreign currency under the equally weighted portfolio approach, it is possible to be much less diversified under the variably weighted portfolio approach. The instability noticed in adjusted X-statistics for the variably weighted portfolio approach may be due not to changing profitability but simply to randomness to be expected in the presence of substantial risk. It should be noted that much of the increased risk from the variably weighted approach relative to the equally weighted approach may be diversifiable in a larger portfolio that holds assets other than currency positions (this is discussed in Chapter 6).

The index approach speculates on a basket of currencies; that is, the whole portfolio, with a predetermined weight vector, is purchased at a buy signal and is sold at a sell signal derived from movements in the index with the same weights. This book examines two versions of the index approach, one using optimally weighted indexes, the other using an equally weighted index. Speculation under the optimally weighted index approach works very well in the first subperiod, not so well in the second. The main reason is that the ex ante optimum weight vectors used in the second subperiod force the investor to speculate in only the Australian dollar and the Canadian dollar; the single-currency speculation results reported in Chapter 5 suggest that profit opportunities in these two currencies were small in both subperiods.

For the equally weighted index approach, the single moving average technique is significantly profitable in both subperiods. The double moving average and mixed-rule techniques also perform well in the first subperiod, but less well in the second. The Alexander filter seems to perform poorly in the equally weighted index case.

The portfolio upgrade approach works very well in the first subperiod but not very well at all in the second subperiod. The poor performance in the second subperiod reduces the average performance across both periods so that the whole-period results are not statistically significant. It may be that the portfolio upgrade approach is not attractive for currency speculation, because in both subperiods it used only 2 of the 15 currencies at any one time. This drastically reduces diversification, increases risk, and suggests the type of instability actually observed in adjusted X-statistics.

For the overall period, the variably weighted portfolio approach seems to be the best in terms of having the highest average return in excess of buy-and-hold. The index approach is slightly better than the portfolio upgrade approach. This suggests two points. First, because the portfolio upgrade approach does not directly use any of the four technical trading rules, the fact that it has the worst performance among the three alternative approaches lends some support to the view that direct use of technical trading techniques is better than relying on the other properties of past prices such as the relative strength of the currencies (though we noted above that relative stren_th indices are related to the single moving average rule). Second, using individual signals from each currency may be better than using the overall signal triggered by index movements. Even though using an index to trigger signals for portfolio changes has the advantage that these indexes contain less noise (because of diversification) and hence are less erratic, this advantage is evidently offset by the fact that buying and selling currencies as a basket constrains some currencies to be purchased or sold against their individual signals. Further, it may be the case that a substantial portion of the nonidiosyncratic price movements of individual currencies, too, were canceled out in the process of portfolio formation. As a result, what is expected to be low-noise price patterns may turn out to be too smooth, so that trading rules cannot trigger the signal correctly.

In Chapters 5–9, the subperiod results show some potentially disturbing signs of instability. Further, for three of the four portfolio approaches, save only the index approach, profits averaged across technical trading techniques fell from the first to the second subperiod. After further investigation, we argue in Chapter 10 that, in fact, speculative profits in the foreign exchanges show a degree of stability across periods that is perhaps somewhat surprising in light of the volatility of these markets. The profitability of speculation seems to be roughly the same over the period since floating began in March 1973 until early 1986, based on the results in Sweeney (1986a) and this book. It seems, however, that the first 500 observations in the 2,000-observation sample we use in Chapters 5 through 9 give particularly favorable results for the Alexander filter and double moving average rules, enhancing the impression that later profits fall off. Whether one wants to estimate average profits for the future on the basis of the more favorable average results found in Chapters 5-9 or the more conservative results found in Chapter 10 is unclear.

In Chapters 5-9 we see that the Alexander rule does not appear to be the most profitable and in Chapter 10 that it also does not give the most stable results. Moving average rules appear to be superior, with some evidence that the single moving average rule gives the best performance. The double moving average rule shows substantially more instability than does the single moving average rule, though this is particularly true for the variably weighted portfolio approach that is inherently subject to more randomness than the equally weighted portfolio approach.

Further, the variably weighted portfolio approach, treating speculations across different currencies as part of an interdependent set of funds that borrow and lend to each other rather than as wholly independent funds, seems to raise profits. This appears especially true for the single moving average rules. The increase in average profits seems to be bought at the cost of greater variability.

Changing filters or lag lengths on a yearly basis does not seem to improve profits. Indeed, point estimates say this reduces profits.

There does not seem to be a clear advantage across all rules to using larger or smaller amounts of data to select filters or lag lengths. The point estimates seem to indicate clearly, however, that one is better off using from 500 to 1,400 observations to select filters or lag lengths rather than using smaller amounts of data, say from 250 to 500 observations.

A major conclusion of this study was predictable: diversification pays, diversification across rules and across amounts of data used to select filters and lag lengths. Diversification pays in terms of profits and in terms of stability of profits across time.

11B. Are These Measured Profits True Economic Profits?

One might be skeptical on a number of different grounds about the profits found in Chapters 5-10. At one level, the measured profits of the simulations might not actually be obtainable in real time. At another level, the measured profits may simply be compensation for bearing systematic risk, meaning that there are no true economic profits here. In this section we discuss whether the measured profits can actually be earned and in the next section whether any measured profits might in fact be due to risk, implying the measured profits are not economic profits.

For a number of different reasons turning mainly on the quality of our data and the level of transactions costs we use, the investor may not be able to earn in real time the measured profits found in the simulations reported above. There may be a wide variety of problems with the data—the data used may be too dirty for accurate conclusions to be drawn. The data were carefully cleaned, however, and in doubtful cases checked against alternative sources, as discussed in Chapter 4.

The Board of Governors of the Federal Reserve System collects these data as averages of noon quotes. By using averages, we may never get a true transactions price; the only way to avoid this problem is to work with actual transactions data, which are difficult to get. Further, because the individual quotes in the averages are collected at slightly different times around noon, there is spurious serial correlation built into the data along the lines of Working (1960); however, because the time between the individual quotes on one day is small relative to the 24 hours between reported data (with a longer gap of course for weekends and holidays), the bias should be trivial (as, for example, under a continuous time random walk process).

The banks queried may systematically report prices different from transactions prices. After all, the true prices are valuable information that they may want to protect. Banks are presumably loathe to get on the wrong side of the Fed, however, by knowingly reporting systematically misleading data. Further, a constant bias would have minimal effect on the results, for example always reporting a price higher—by say an eighth—than the actual price. For misreporting to make a major difference the banks would have to report a higher than obtainable price on days when the rule used says to sell and a lower price than obtainable on days when the rule says to buy. This becomes more problematic when one recalls the results in Chapter 5 about how a number of rules can be profitable for the same currency without the signals being at all the same for the alternative profitable rules.

As noted, real difficulties arise when the data systematically overstate the price on days when the rules say sell and understate the price on days when the rules say buy. Although we are skeptical of this arising from conscious misreporting by banks, this might arise in cases where the prices do not follow random walks but instead drift up and down with buying and selling pressure. The reported price on days with buying pressure may lag behind the actual price and the reverse on days with selling pressure. This story, however, holds the promise of exploitable inefficiency. If one can detect such pressures and get into or out of the market early, it is possible that even larger profits than those reported might be earned.

In a different type of data problem, it may be that the estimates of transactions costs on which we based our simulations are incorrect and transactions costs are larger than assumed. Large enough transactions costs will, of course, eliminate any measured profits. Note that for some rules and approaches to portfolio formation, we saw in Chapters 5 through 8 that rather substantial increases would be required to eliminate profits.

For these and many other possible difficulties, there are many plausible pro and con arguments (see, for example, Sweeney 1988). The only fully satisfactory conclusion is, You can't know until you try it in real time with real money on real currencies. For what it is worth, our judgment is that none of the caveats about the data raise serious doubts.

There is another possible problem: We may have made programming errors. Profits here are broadly consistent, though, with those of Sweeney (1986a) on earlier data from the same source and using a different program. Further, the programs used here and in Sweeney (1986a) were compared for data from equities markets with results from independently written programs, with only trivial differences. All of the programs used were extensively tested on rates of returns series derived from random number generators, with results showing essentially zero significant profits and no consistency in measured profits, as predicted. Further, other authors using their own programs have replicated with only minor differences the results in Sweeney (1986a).

Someone implementing the strategies discussed above might find profits dissipated either because his/her transactions move the market enough to eliminate profits or because others observe profits being made, catch onto the strategy, free ride on it, and thus eliminate profits. Because it costs a substantial amount of money to do the work reported on in this book, one who expected the type of evidence documented above might be reluctant to put up funds to develop knowledge that in effect cannot likely be used for private reward.[1] In this view there may be many market participants who are not surprised by the above results but who had no incentive to put up their own funds to develop these results. Note that an implicit prediction of this line of argument is that now that these results are available in this book, market participants will act and the speculative strategies investigated here will no longer work in the future. We shall see.

As for moving the market, evidence from the U.S. equities markets argues that large transactions do move the market. Berkowitz, Logue, and Noser (1988) argue that of the total estimated cost of .23 of 1 percent of asset value per one-way transaction on the New York and American Stock Exchanges, approximately .05 of 1 percent is due to moving the market (see also Beebower and Priest 1980). The markets for major currencies seem to be thicker, however, than those for most individual stocks in the United States

As for the danger of people catching on to one's exercise of a profitable strategy, this argument is both a confession that the market is inefficient and an explanation of why private activity, hindered by the strong likelihood of freeriding, does not eliminate the inefficiency. Would others catch on? In one view, this depends on how many have to be let in on the "secrets" of the strategy in order to implement it, on the propensity of the principals to gossip, and on the ability of the principals to compensate those in the know enough to prevent them from trying to go out on their own. It is probably not productive to speculate on these issues. You cannot know if these strategies will make money in real time until you try.

Perhaps it is worth noting that a number of market participants who claim to exploit inefficiencies have also claimed that these inefficiencies persist for substantial time periods even after they are fairly well known. These participants argue that the persistence is due to conservatism among even money managers, who are reluctant to go into new strategies that look good but have the danger of losses; managers who forego profits that their investors do not know about suffer opportunity losses, but managers who embark on new and dangerous strategies that lose, perhaps only for a time, can be in deep trouble.

11C. Are the Measured Profits Simply Compensation for Bearing Risk?

From discussion in Chapter 3 of the various forms of the X-statistic, it is clear that measured profits depend on the difference between the average rate of return on the currency on the days the rule has the investor in the currency versus the average rate of return on days over the whole period. A positive X-statistic means the investor is successful in getting in for days with above-average rates of return and at getting out for days with below-average rates of return. The difference in the average rates of return is a measure of economic profits, however, only to the extent that systematic risk premia are constant over all days, or more generally, to the extent that the average systematic risk premium is the same on days the investor is in the currency as on the total number of days. Suppose, on the contrary, that systematic risk is not constant and that the rule gets the investor in for days when risk is particularly high. Under a wide variety of asset pricing models, the expected return for being in on such days would be higher than average. Similarly, the rule may get the investor out for days with above-average risk, days on which the currency would be expected to pay a below-average rate of return.

Thus, in the face of the measured profits reported above, one can maintain that the risk premia in the rates of return are constant over time and reject the hypothesis of efficient spot foreign exchange markets, or one can maintain the hypothesis of efficiency and reject the view that risk premia are constant. Those on either side of the argument should feel pressure to investigate the existence of time-varying risk premia.

The existence of time-varying risk premia would not necessarily mean the measured profits are not economic profits, nor would it necessarily rescue efficiency. For example, suppose that risk premia are time varying but that the average risk premium on days in is the same as the average risk premium over the whole period. This means that while the premia are varying, none of the measured profits are due to this variation. Further, the risk premia may vary but to an extent that explains only a minor portion of the profits, leaving a statistically significant residual unexplained.

An examination of the results in Chapter 5 for the different rules on the individual currencies reveals that rules often give quite different average lengths of investment, defined as total number of days divided by the number of round-trip transactions. Nevertheless, different rules with differing average lengths of investment can give fairly similar measured profits for the same currency. To take an actual case in Chapter 5, one rule may seem to say that the periodicity of profits for the currency is every 35 days, while another argues for a periodicity of 16 days. At face value, this seems to indicate that the different rules are picking up different periodicities in risk premia if time-varying premia are what explain the profits found. Of course, the underlying variation in risk premia may be capable of explaining these seemingly contradictory patterns. The point is, the time-varying risk premia should be explicitly tested for, both to see whether the premia in fact vary and to see whether detectable variation can explain the measured profits.

The remainder of this section discusses briefly the evidence on time-varying risk premia, particularly as an explanation for measured speculative profits. This is a large topic, touching on a number of related literatures. Here we can provide only a brief discussion of how this topic fits with this book's results (for a survey of this topic, with references, see Sweeney 1990e). Not surprisingly, perhaps, the evidence is somewhat inconclusive. In the meantime, decisionmakers must act. Section 11D argues that wealth-maximizing money managers have the incentive to act on the belief that the measured profits reported above are true economic profits simply because we cannot yet discriminate between the possibilities that they are due to risk or are not. Inertia and conservatism in the face of possible losses in new activities, however, may well slow down money managers' reactions.

Time-varying risk premia are plausible to consider but may be hard to detect. Think of the risk premium on the DM as being the sum of the products of the DM's betas on risk factors times the premia on these risk factors; this is a natural interpretation in terms of a Ross (1976) arbitrage pricing model (APM), with the capital asset pricing model (CAPM) as a special case where the only priced factor is the market. Variation in the DM's risk premium can arise, then, through changes over time in either betas or in factor risk premia. Empirical work on the market model makes clear that market betas change over time. Often these shifts can be related to economic fundamentals. If a firm substantially changes its leverage, for example, beta is expected to reflect this. If a firm goes through a series of acquisitions and divestitures, or revises its capital structure, its beta should reflect this. Much of this detected instability of market betas arises in estimation on monthly data, however, and the detected instability seems to have fairly long periodicity; for both reasons, it is perhaps unwise to put too much weight on this analogy to daily movements in exchange rates where the periodicity seems to be on the order of, say, 16 to 35 trading days rather than many months.

Many studies have looked at the stochastic properties of market betas. This is not an easy task because of the noisiness of financial data (though exchange rates are less noisy than stocks' rates of return on average). For example, for betas estimated on monthly data with 60 observations under the assumption that beta is constant, a standard error of only 0.10 is quite low. It may be very hard to detect reliably any pattern of time variation in beta unless the pattern of variation is particularly simple and sharp.

Alternatively, the time-varying risk premium in the DM may arise from variations in factor risk premia. These premia are extremely difficult to measure with any precision; see, for example, Roll and Ross (1980), Chen, Roll and Ross (1985), Sweeney and Warga (1986). Thus, we can have little intuition from past work on how variable are these premia and what may be the periodicity in the time variation. Further, there is some reason for skepticism about our ability to detect and measure time variability in these factor premia.

This is not to say that we should not try to find, measure, and understand the time variability of risk premia in foreign exchange rates. Rather, we may well expect this to be a very long and arduous process, with no very clear results one way or the other in the near future. Explaining measured profits as due to time-varying risk premia seems not to be on the near-term horizon.

To our knowledge, Sweeney (1990a) is the only paper testing whether time-varying risk premia in daily spot exchange rates exist and can explain measured speculative profits; we briefly discuss this paper below. There has been some work on time-varying risk premia in 30-day and 90-day forward exchange rates. The spot and forward markets are of course related, but any time-varying risk premia found for 30-day forward rates need have no particular relationship with measured profits from day-to-day speculation in spot markets. Nevertheless, it is worthwhile asking what light forward market research can shed.

Sweeney (1990a) assumes that risk is measured by the currency's beta on the market. He argues that the betas must be larger on days with signals that have the speculator in the currencies than on average days and that the betas must be enough larger to explain measured profits. Using dummy variables based on buy and sell signals from technical rules, he finds that often the dummies are insignificant or have the wrong sign. Further, when the dummies have the correct positive sign, they are an order of magnitude too small to explain the measured profits. He concludes that his model of time-varying risk premia cannot explain profits. Of course, a different model might have more success.

Turn now to related forward market research. Fama (1984) provides very strong evidence of what he calls a time-varying risk premium in the forward exchange rate. (Hodrick and Srivastava 1986 and Sweeney 1990d confirm his results using different data and statistical techniques.) This "risk premium" is misnamed, however. It is nothing other than the difference between the forward premium and the rational expectation of the coming percentage change in the spot rate over the next 30 days. This difference is the so-called bias in the forward premium as a predictor of coming changes in the spot exchange rate, with Fama's work showing that this bias exists and is time varying. Whether this time-varying bias is a risk premium is the key issue, and thus it is not helpful of Fama simply to refer to it as a risk premium. Furthermore, Sweeney (1990d) argues that this risk premium must be due to systematic risk, not just overall or unsystematic risk, for time-varying premia to explain measured profits; any unsystematic risk can be diversified away, leaving any profits it causes as true economic profits. There are many models that allow for a bias in the forward rate, including a time-varying bias caused by systematic risk premia. Do these models adequately explain the data?

Past work modeling markets for forward foreign exchange contracts points up some of the difficulties and ambiguities of searching for time-varying risk premia. Take two examples (there are many others, including Frankel 1982 and 1984, Domowitz and Hakkio 1985, and Mark 1986; for a survey, see Sweeney 1990e). In the first approach, Hanson and Hodrick (1983) and Hodrick and Srivastava (1984) explore measured profits to forward market speculation in an intertemporal asset pricing model where betas on all currencies are constant and of the same sign, and the risk premium on a benchmark portfolio (playing a role similar to the risk premium on the market in a standard CAPM) varies over time. Variations in this risk premium are supposed to explain the systematic part of variations in the measured profits to speculation in the forward markets. In turn, Hodrick and Srivastava (1984) model the risk premium as a linear function of the forward premia on the set of currencies considered and decisively reject the model.

What does this failure mean? The risk premium may not be time varying, or not in any way that their test can detect. Or, the assumption of constant betas with all the same sign may be a critical misspecification; Sweeney and Lee (1990) report that in their simulations of speculation in the forward exchange markets the investor often took buy positions for some currencies and in the same period sell positions for others and that over time currencies often shifted from buy to sell signals, both of which are inconsistent with the assumption of constant betas all of the same sign and a positive expected return on the benchmark portfolio. The risk premium on the benchmark portfolio may vary with the forward premium in some way Hodrick and Srivastava did not try or may vary with some variables they omitted. Note that even had they found evidence of time-varying risk premia, this might not explain measured profits. To explain measured profits, the risk premia would have to be above average on days when the speculator is in the currency, below average on days out, and the variations in the risk premia would have to be of the right order of magnitude to justify the profits.

Sweeney (1990d) takes an opposite tack from Hanson, Hodrick, and Srivastava and models the risk premium on the benchmark portfolio as constant with time-varying betas on forward speculations. As compared to the work of Hanson, Hodrick and Srivastava where betas are constant and all have the same sign, Sweeney's approach allows for the investor to take buy positions in some currencies and sell positions in others in the same period and to switch from buy to sell positions for the same currency over time (with a positive risk premium on the benchmark portfolio). He proxies the benchmark portfolio with a market index. He finds that the slope coefficients on the test variable are generally not significant, and those significant are an order of magnitude smaller than the theory predicts.

But perhaps the market index used was a bad proxy. Or perhaps an APM should have been used with more factors than the market. In general, if a particular model of time-varying premia does not seem to work very well, one can always reject that model while maintaining that in a better model the hypothesis of time-varying premia will be seen to work just fine.

The wide variety of possible models of time-varying risk premia is an argument that we do not yet have a clear theory of how these premia should behave in a system of efficient markets. This is yet another reason for expecting no resolution in the near future of the issue of whether time-varying risk premia explain the measured profits we find.

11D. Implications for Private Policymakers

To start, consider a private money manager. His or her success will depend to some extent on performance, performance as judged by people who put up the money managed. Conventional wisdom in financial economics urges using risk-adjusted profit standards for judging performance. In practice, this very often comes down to adjusting measured performance for beta risk. The beta measure used virtually always assumes that the underlying beta is constant over the period being evaluated, though of course estimated betas change over time. In other words, in conventional, state-of-the-art performance evaluation, there is no provision made for time-varying risk premia within the period studied.[2] Furthermore, the preceding section's discussion made it clear that it will be difficult getting any very precise measures of time-varying premia, so the conventional approach is likely to stay in force for a considerable period of time.[3]

The wealth-maximizing money manager might reasonably then act on the assumption that risk premia are constant. Suppose s/he speculates in spot foreign exchange markets along the lines used above. This would have raised measured profits by, say, 3 percent to 5 percent per year over the period studied. All of this increase may be due to extra risk. There is, however, absolutely no evidence that this is so. Further, even if true, there is no way of detecting this under current evaluation procedures.

Alternatively, let the manager forego these profits. Then s/he looks bad by comparison to any competitors who reap the profits. The more cautious manager can assure the people who put up the money that those profits are illusory, arising only through extra risk, but the manager has no evidence of this. The people putting up the money can see only that competitors offer the same measured risk and higher returns. The implications are clear for those with money and those who manage money.

Nevertheless, money managers may be reluctant to rush into a new area, particularly because there is necessarily risk of loss. The standard errors on the percentage profit rates show the risk to a portfolio that holds only Euro-currency deposits, with lower risk available to portfolios diversified across other assets; because exchange rates show relatively low betas, the systematic risk to the foreign exchange strategies discussed in this book is quite low. The usual intuitive argument in support of the EMH is that patterns in prices or returns that offer net risk-adjusted profits on the margin will be exploited by so many eager investors with such large funds that the profit opportunities will quickly be destroyed. Conservatism on the part of money managers may allow the profit opportunities detailed in earlier chapters to persist. Such conservatism would be a blow to usual EMH arguments.

Financial managers of, say, multinational manufacturing firms may face much the same pressures, both to take advantage of the opportunities for measured profits and to go slow in the face of possible losses from a new strategy. These managers face exchange risk every day. For example, suppose they receive a large payment today in French francs. Often the advice they receive on how to manage exchange risk rests on the view that exchange markets are efficient. In this view, the francs may be sold or held to help hedge other positions or more generally to diversify the firm's portfolio of risks, but under the efficient markets hypothesis, the decision is independent of recent moves in the franc's exchange rate in the sense that these moves have no predictive power for future moves. The results reported above give quite a different implication. If the technical rule being used gives a sell signal when the payment is received, this argues the manager should hold fewer of the francs than otherwise. This does not mean that only the signals matter or that the manager should be organized to act instantly on any signal. Rather, it means that the signals as well as various hedging and portfolio considerations must all be balanced.

Of course, few firms are going to talk explicitly about foreign exchange speculation; this can cause grave troubles with host governments and with stockholders if things ever go awry and can even tangentially be related to the firm's foreign exchange policy. But every firm always has the option of leaving its foreign exposure more or less unhedged.

Arguments above were in terms of beta risk, and the firm may constrain the manager to be concerned with overall risk rather than just systematic risk. The point remains that technical analysis evidently has information content that will allow a manager to increase expected returns for any level of beta or overall risk being aimed at.[4]

Many nonfinancial companies already act on advice that assumes the foreign exchange markets are inefficient, but it is not clear that this is good advice. For example, there are many exchange rate forecasting services available that are simply processing publicly available information. Some of these services rely on purchasing power parity as a main component of their forecasts. Some rely on movements in the trade balance or in other international and macroeconomic indicators. Explicitly or implicitly, most of these services are selling the notion that their forecasts can be used to alter a subscriber's behavior and improve profits—beat the market. (Most of the services are not giving advice about risk-return trade-offs or risk management, both of which are valuable activities in an efficient market.) Are these services' forecasts consistent with what we found in earlier chapters? The evidence of inefficiency found in these earlier chapters is not the same thing as evidence for all the many claims of inefficiency that abound. At the very least, these claims ought to be subjected to the type of rigorous testing used above. One way to do this testing is to use the X-statistic, as we did above. This gives a way of comparing performances in terms of risk-adjusted profit.

It is not trivial to integrate technical analysis into a system of managing exchange risk. It is one more thing to think about, and its interactions with other considerations such as hedging can be quite complex. In effect, technical analysis becomes many more things to think about. One selling point of the efficient markets hypothesis is the way in which it reduces the complexities of management. The improved profits of rivals who integrate such analysis provide competition to force managers to overcome inertia. If inertia and conservatism keep money managers from flocking to these opportunities, however, managers in nonfinancial firms are likely to be substantially slower. This argues that the opportunities may persist.

Notes

1. See Sweeney (1990f) for an estimate of the costs, beyond brokerage fees, of running a technical trading system on U.S. equities and of the volume of trades required to make the system profitable.

2. This argument, that shifting risk premia can lead to poor measurement of performance when the observer knows only average risk, is similar to Dybvig and Ross (1986) and Adnati and Ross (1987). Sweeney (1990c) shows that their arguments generally do not apply for the X-statistic. For example, Dybvig and Ross assume that the return on the portfolio considered equals $x + s$, where x and s are orthogonal. The informed investor knows the realization of s in advance, the uninformed observer does not. For the informed investor, there is constant risk equal to the variance of x. Expected return changes over time and is s_t.

As Dybvig and Ross show, the investor may end up below an ex ante security market line. Sweeney (1990c) shows, however, that the X-statistic for the informed investor has a positive expected value if the investor shows declining absolute risk aversion, and has a nonzero expected value in any but a pathological case.

3. Exactly analogous problems arise if the evaluator uses the Sharpe measure. Similar to the Dybvig and Ross model described in note 2 to this chapter, there may be shifts in expected return over time. If these are balanced by changes in portfolio variance, there may be no profit opportunities. The point is that the evaluator would have to know about the shifts in variance in order to say that the extra high returns are simply rewards to extra high risk.

4. See note 3 for a discussion of the case where overall risk is part of the criterion.

12

Implications for Public Policymakers

Chapter 11 gives a review of the measured profits to technical speculation found in Chapters 5–10; the profits are economically and statistically significant. A major issue is whether these measured profits are economic profits. It is possible that the profits might be explained as due to some sort of data problem, though in Chapter 11 we explained why we think this in not very likely. More likely, the measured profits actually exist but might be explained as due to time-varying risk premia. The evidence on time-varying risk premia as an explanation is inconclusive; much more work is needed to be confident one way or another. But while these issues are debated, policymakers must act. Chapter 11 considered the implications for private policymakers; given that current evaluation techniques make no effective use of the possibility of time-varying risk premia, there are strong incentives for private policymakers to act to take advantage of these measured profits. To the extent that these profits are economic profits, these actions will of course tend to make the market more efficient. In this chapter we discuss appropriate public policy actions in light of this book's results.

The inefficiencies detected are across many foreign currencies, including some of the most important. As Chapter 5 noted, for each of the four technical approaches (Alexander filter, double moving average, single moving average and mixed rule), we found substantial, significant whole-period profits on a currency-by-currency basis for the Belgian franc, Deutsche mark, French franc, Italian lire, Japanese yen, and Netherlands guilder. We also found significant profits under one rule for the British pound and Norwegian kroner. Further, the first subperiod showed significant profits for the Austrian schilling, Danish krone and Spanish peseta. Clearly, these results cannot be ignored as applying only to minor currencies with thin markets.

It is not at all clear what an appropriate public policy response is to this book's evidence that foreign exchange markets show signs of inefficiency. It may well be that the best response is no response.

The political market does not constrain public policymakers to give a response in the same way the economic market works to force action on private policymakers. Government officials, if made aware of the evidence reported above, could well deny its relevance and would run a good chance of making the denial stick. The results we report clearly run counter to mainstream views among economists; public policymakers have with ease resisted for years policy views that have virtually unanimous support among economists—an example is international trade policy, where relatively few reputable academic economists would support the current melange of restrictions or the new restrictions that are periodically added or proposed.

It may well be that inappropriate government action is more of a danger than is lack of a public policy response. This book's evidence is not a prima facie case for government intervention in exchange markets; it is not true that government should undertake to correct all cases of market failure or inefficiency. Even if a public policymaker believes that the measured profits of earlier chapters can actually be earned and cannot be explained by time-varying systematic risk premia, s/he should still ask how the inefficiency could be removed, how much it would cost to do so, whether the benefits would be worth the cost, whether programs might be perverted to goals that are not beneficial, and whether good intentions might end in government failure that compounded market failure.

The efficient markets view stresses how private speculation in the face of profits such as we found will drive the profits to minimal levels that do not justify more speculative activity. Because the profits still appear to be there after more than a decade, a key issue is why they persist. The literature commonly offers three possibilities: destabilizing speculation of various types, insufficient stabilizing speculation, and government intervention itself. We discuss these possible explanations in turn.

The market may be dominated by destabilizing private speculation. This is the strongest case for a public policy response—with destabilizing private speculation, the government can step in to offset private mistakes. Many practitioners and other market observers argue that exchange markets are dominated by bandwagons, fads, and trends that can be laid to destabilizing speculation; other observers argue that the markets are efficient much of the time but are subject every now and then to bubbles, another type of destabilizing speculation.[1] It should be noted that this book provides no direct evidence to support the charge of destabilizing speculation, whether of the ongoing bandwagon type or the more episodic bubbles type; the results above, however, are at least some evidence that is consistent with destabilizing. The Alexander filter, double moving average, and single moving average rules all rely on being able to detect ongoing trends in prices. The fact that rises in the price of a currency are followed by further rises and falls in price followed by further falls with enough regularity to make profits is consistent with the bandwagon and trend effects that some observers attribute to destabilizing speculation. It should be noted that the rules' success is also consistent with other explanations, for example, the time-varying risk premia discussed in Chapter 11 or the insufficient stabilizing speculation discussed below. Further, even if one views the profits as due to destabilizing speculation, there is a danger that government action might itself be misguided and end up making things worse. That is to say, government attempts to stabilize may be destabilizing.[2]

One type of destabilizing speculation that has received much attention is speculative bubbles. Woo (1984) has developed evidence on speculative bubbles; see also Meese (1986), Evans(1986), and Frankel and Froot (1986a,b). Frankel (1985) and Krugman (1985) have both argued that there is evidence of exchange rate bubbles in the 1980s. This book made no attempt to test whether the profits it finds are due to bubbles. The existence of profits is, however, no indication by itself that there are bubbles. At best this book's results provide only very modest and tentative support for a bubbles view. Many of those who discuss bubbles view them as lasting possibly for several months or longer and as occurring only sporadically, with the markets otherwise efficient between bubble episodes (Frankel and Froot 1986a). Chapter 5's results generally find buy and sell signals that are much more frequent than if the bubbles lasted several months. Smaller triggers than those found optimal here are also profitable and provide even more frequent buy and sell signals; see Sweeney (1986a) and Mori and Murray (1990) for evidence on Alexander filters with small trigger values. Further, the work in Chapter 10 on the stability of profits does not seem consistent with the view that there are substantial periods without bubbles. In addition, many of those who believe bubbles are a serious problem view the dollar in 1984 and 1985 as a prime example (Frankel 1985, Krugman 1985). But earlier chapters showed that technical rules made profits not only in this period but also in earlier subperiods; indeed the profits in the four-year subperiod ending in early 1986 are noticeably smaller than in the preceding four-year subperiod. At the very least, then, it seems that sporadic bubbles cannot be the only story and perhaps are not the main story.

Instead of destabilizing speculation, there may be insufficient stabilizing private speculation (see Willett and Wihlborg 1990). In this view, there may be managers acting to take advantage of the profit potential in the patterns discussed in earlier chapters, but they may have such limited funds that they do not dominate the foreign exchange markets and thus smooth out the patterns that offer profits. The evidence in Chapters 5-10 is as consistent with the existence of insufficient stabilizing speculation as it is with destabilizing speculation.

Some view speculative activity, often heavy activity, as the sine qua non of efficient markets (see Sweeney 1985). In this view, nonspeculative shifts in demand and supply cause patterns in price over time. These patterns might well look like the patterns that technical analysis detects. Speculators detect these patterns and take open positions on the basis of the patterns in order to make profits. An unintended by-product of this speculation is the elimination of all patterns save those where transactions and opportunity costs make further speculation not worthwhile. If there is insufficient stabilizing speculation, patterns offering profits would still remain, however. Observationally, these remaining patterns could be the same as might be observed in the presence of destabilizing speculation; the existence of technical profits is consistent with either type of speculative failure.

One frequently cited piece of evidence for insufficient stabilizing speculation is the small open positions that banks and other financial institutions take in foreign exchange markets even on an overnight basis, let alone on a longer-term basis; Willett and Wihlborg (1990) distinguish between the facts that foreign exchange markets seem very thick in terms of gross turnover but much thinner in terms of net speculative positions. This is important because the detailed results in Chapter 5 show that average times between purchases and sales might be from, say, 16 to 35 trading days (though longer for some currencies in some periods and shorter for others in other periods); speculators take positions that as a by-product smooth cycles, these positions would have to be as long as perhaps several trading weeks in some cases.

The very small overnight exposure taken by banks and other financial institutions is often blamed on government regulation or on financial institutions' fears of regulators' actions if the financial institutions were to take larger open positions. In this case, the appropriate remedy would seem to be for government to stop hindering the market rather than for government to intervene in exchange markets. One might argue, however, that because federally guaranteed deposit insurance sets up inappropriate general incentives for risk management by banks and leads to too much risk, second-best considerations suggest limiting foreign exchange exposure. Of course, the optimum is to reform the deposit insurance system and then let banks take the foreign exchange positions they desire as dictated by risk-return considerations. A second-best might be to set up firewalls that prevent the deposit insurance from also in effect guaranteeing an institution's speculative activities in the foreign exchange market. It is difficult, however, to set up effective firewalls that are not also very inefficient at the same time. Further, there is some evidence that regulators view some banks as "too big to fail." In such cases, firewalls and other devices to separate some bank activities from insured deposits will simply be ignored when the bank is in danger of going under, and in effect, all of the bank's activities are insured.

In discussions of insufficient stabilizing speculation, the focus is on U.S. banks and it is seldom mentioned that at least some foreign banks are under regulation that gives them much greater flexibility, including flexibility in taking open positions. Hence, these foreign banks might offset any insufficient speculation due to U.S. regulation.

Third, government intervention may itself cause the profits. There is, for example, evidence suggesting at least some intervention is consciously designed to lean against the wind (Dornbusch 1980, Genberg 1981, Branson 1983). If governments lean against the wind when equilibrium exchange rates change, this may cause patterns in exchange rate movements that we can detect in the data, because the intervention is designed to slow down the exchange rate's adjustment instead of letting it adjust instantaneously as would happen in an efficient market. Note that it is quite possible that large enough private capital flows react to leaning against the wind and completely offset its effects. In particular, government intervention that is sterilized (that is, offset by opposite transactions in domestic bond markets) has no effect on the equilibrium exchange rate in many models; sufficiently large capital flows might move the exchange rate to essentially its equilibrium level (as perceived by market participants) no matter what the level of intervention. Thus, leaning against the wind or some other kinds of intervention are not sufficient to cause detectable profit opportunities but must also be accompanied by speculative schedules that are less than perfectly elastic or by a deficiency of stabilizing speculation. Efficiency carries no implication that speculative schedules are perfectly elastic. Further, a less than perfectly elastic speculative schedule is not the same thing as insufficient stabilizing speculation as long as "insufficient" is defined relative to what informed wealth-maximizing managers would do in the absence of misguided regulation.

It is unclear, both on theoretical and empirical grounds, whether sterilized intervention affects exchange rates. Some observers argue that sterilized intervention can have systematic effects in foreign exchange markets because the intervention conveys information about governments' policy intentions.[3] This would set up profit opportunities detectable in the data, however, only if speculative schedules are not perfectly elastic. Similarly, although it is generally agreed that unsterilized intervention affects the equilibrium exchange rate just as an open market operation does by changing the money stock, such intervention should cause profit opportunities detectable in the data only to the extent that the speculative schedules are not perfectly elastic. Thus, government intervention by itself is not a sufficient condition for the profit opportunities documented in earlier chapters.

The empirical evidence is mixed and controversial on whether government intervention helps to destabilize foreign exchange markets (Federal Reserve Bulletin 1983; Argy 1982).[4] One strand looks at whether government intervention is profitmaking or not (Taylor 1982). It is difficult to answer this question because of lack of data. With day-by-day data on a government's holdings of foreign assets, we could use X-statistics to test for the profitability of intervention, but such data are not generally publicly available. Davutyan and Pippenger (1989) use Canadian Exchange Stabilization Fund data from the 1950s and an approach based on X-statistics and attribute much of the speculative profits to government intervention. Of course, this is no proof that intervention is responsible for the measured profits we find in the 1970s and 1980s.

In Chapter 11 we raised another possible explanation based on market failure, an explanation seldom raised in this context. The work reported in this book required using up resources with substantial opportunity costs. It may be that market participants are unwilling to make this kind of investment because they believe that they will not be able to appropriate for themselves the rewards we seem to find in order to recoup the costs of their investment. There are two possible reasons why investors might be skeptical about recouping their costs. First, implementing these rules may move the market so much that the profits are very small. Second, observers may catch on to a successful technical system and by freeriding destroy the system's profits. Because these markets are large and thick, freeriding seems the likelier worry, with markets being moved largely by the effects of freeriding. The freeriding story involves market failure, because the current investor in knowledge is unable to reap the future (presumed) social benefits of acquiring it and hence spends too little private and social resources on this knowledge. If this is the problem, there is a prediction and a policy prescription. After publication of this book, we would expect under this view to find many people freeriding on the information given here at the low price of the book plus the cost of mastering its contents. The prediction would then be a distinct fall-off in the future in the measured profits we have found for the past. Further, this decrease in profitability should occur relatively shortly after publication. As for policy under this freeriding view, the market will be reaping the gains of academic research. Surely this is a case for larger subsidies for academic research; at a minimum, the reader should buy the book, not just reproduce a copy from the library.

It is important to note that many popular proposals for government exchange market policy are aimed at issues far different from inefficiency in day-to-day movements in spot exchange rates. Instead, much policy attention focuses on longer-term issues such as the large rise in the dollar from 1980 to early 1985 and its substantial fall after March 1985. Another longer-term issue is government policy to offset excessive deviations of the exchange rate from its purchasing power parity level.

As they stand, our results have virtually no direct implications one way or the other for these proposals and the problems they are designed to get at. Nevertheless, our results may seem to be related in two ways. First, evidence that something may be amiss in day-to-day exchange rate movements may illegitimately be construed as evidence that there are problems over the longer term at which many proposals aim. Second, many authors dismiss these longer-term, activist proposals under the general argument that exchange markets are efficient, as are all other financial markets, and hence there really is no problem. This dismissal is now substantially less tenable, we think.

This does not, however, mean that the proposals being dismissed necessarily have merit. Rather, it means that they must be studied on their own and that the problems they assert exist must be accorded more possibility of actually existing than if all financial markets are efficient.

There is much research currently under way on bubbles, purchasing power parity, and other related topics. We can expect progress over time on all these issues. The single most important help to progress might be for central banks to make available to researchers their internal data on the timing and magnitude of their exchange market interventions. These data would be extremely useful in narrowing the range of possible explanations of the profits documented in earlier chapters and in studying the interactions of the suggested explanations.

There can be little doubt that technical trading techniques allow for substantial, fairly consistent, statistically significant measured profits in major foreign exchange markets.

Two major intellectual problems arise from these results. First, are these measured profits due to time-varying systematic risk premia? Documenting a yes answer in a convincing way appears to be a huge and difficult task. Attempts to date in the spot and forward exchange markets, using standard finance models, have not been at all successful. Further, remember that what is wanted is not just documentation that there are time-varying systematic risk premia in the spot exchange markets, but that they explain all but an insignificant amount of the profits that can be earned by following the technical rules and the portfolio approaches explored above.

Second, if time-varying systematic risk premia cannot explain these measured profits, financial economists must face the task of explaining how it is that economically and statistically significant speculative profits can persist in well-known markets with very many transactors. This task may be the beginning of a drastic reformulation of the theory of finance.

Notes

1. It is possible to construct models of so-called rational bubbles. It is then arguable whether such bubbles are due to destabilizing speculation. When an

exchange rate is close to the peak of a bubble, however, it is surely giving mistaken signal about its long-run value in a way that would not happen in the usual efficient markets view.

2. It is possible to construct examples where the underlying market displays cycles that speculation makes worse. Various types of government intervention may, but need not, make the cycles larger.

3. Another possible way government intervention can affect the exchange rate is by changing the stocks of outside assets denominated in different currencies, which in turn affects the risk premium in the exchange market. Past studies, however, have found no evidence supporting this hypothesis. See, for example, Frankel (1982) and Rogoff (1984).

4. For a summary of the ten studies by the staff of the U.S. Federal Reserve System and the report of the working group on exchange market intervention, see Henderson and Sampson (1983).

BIBLIOGRAPHY

Adler, Michael, and Bernard Dumas. "International Portfolio Choice and Corporation Finance: A Synthesis." *Journal of Finance* 38 (June 1983): 925-984.

Admati, Adnat, and Stephen A. Ross. "Measuring Investment Performance in a Rational Expectations Equilibrium Model." *Journal of Business* 58 (1985): 1-26.

Alexander, Sydney S. "Price Movements in Speculative Markets: Trends or Random Walks." *Industrial Management Review* 2 (May 1961): 7-26.

Alexander, Sydney S. "Price Movements in Speculative Markets: Trends or Random Walks, Number 2." *Industrial Management Review* 5 (Spring 1964): 25-46.

Argy, Victor. "Exchange–Rate Management and Practice." In *Princeton Studies in International Finance* 50. Princeton, N.J.: Princeton University, Department of Economics, 1982.

Beebower, Gilbert, and William Priest. "The Tricks of the Trade." *Journal of Portfolio Management* 6 (Winter 1980): 36-42.

Berkowitz, Stephen A., Dennis E. Logue, and Eugene A. Noser, Jr. "The Total Costs of Transactions on the NYSE." *Journal of Finance* 43 (March 1988): 97–112

Bishop, George W., Jr. *Charles H. Dow and the Dow Theory*. New York: Appleton-Century-Crofts, 1960.

Bjerring, James H., Josef Lakonishok, and Theo Vermaelen. "Stock Market Prices and Financial Analysts' Recommendations." *Journal of Finance* 38 (March 1983): 187-204.

Black, Fischer. "Capital Markets Equilibrium with Restricted Borrowing." *Journal of Business* (July 1972), 444-455.

Bookstaber, Richard. *The Complete Investment Book*. Greenview, Ill.: Scott, Foresman and Co., 1985.

Branson, William. "A Model of Exchange Determination with Policy Reactions: Evidence from Monthly Data." Working Paper No. 1135. New York: National Bureau of Economic Research, June 1983.

Brealey, Richard A. *An Introduction to Risk and Return from Common Stocks*. Cambridge: MIT Press, 1983.

263

Breeden, Douglas. "An Intertemporal Asset Pricing Model with Stochastic Consumption and Investment Opportunities." *Journal of Financial Economics* 7 (September 1979): 265-296.

Bremer, Marc A., and Richard J. Sweeney. "Special FX: Beating the Foreign Exchange Market." *Journal of Corporation Finance* (Spring 1988): 25-32.

Burt, John, Fred R. Kaen, and G. Geoffrey Booth. "Foreign Exchange Market Efficiency Under Flexible Exchange Rates." *Journal of Finance* 32 (September 1977): 1325-1330.

Calderon-Rossell, Jorge R., and Moshe Ben-Horim. "The Behavior of Foreign Exchange Rates." *Journal of International Business Studies* 13 (Fall 1982): 99-111.

Chen, Nai–fu, Richard Roll, and Stephen A. Ross. "Economic Forces and the Stock Market." *Journal of Business* (July 1985), 383-403.

Chestnut, George A., Jr. *Stock Market Analysis: Facts and Principles.* Larchmont, N.Y.: American Investor Corporation, 1965.

Cornell, W. Bradford, and J. Kimball Dietrich. "The Efficiency of Markets for Foreign Exchange." *Review of Economics and Statistics* 60 (February 1978): 111-120.

Cootner, Paul. "Stock Prices: Random vs Systematic Changes." *Industrial Management Review* 3 (Spring 1962): 24-45.

Cross, Frank. "The Behavior of Stock Prices on Fridays and Mondays." *Financial Analyst Journal* 29 (November-December 1973): 67-69.

Cummins, Philip, Dennis E. Logue, Richard J. Sweeney, and Thomas D. Willett. "Efficiency in the Canadian/U.S. Exchange Markets, 1970–1974." Working paper. Washington, D.C.: Department of the Treasury, 1976.

Davutyan, Nuran, and John Pippenger. "Excess Returns and Official Intervention: Canada 1952–1960." *Economic Inquiry* 27 (July 1989): 489-500.

Domomwitz, Ian, and Craig Hakkio. "Conditional Variance and the Risk Premium in the Foreign Exchange Market." *Journal of International Economics* 19 (1985): 47-66.

Dooley, Micheal P., and Jeffrey R. Shafer. "Analysis of Short-Run Exchange Rate Behavior: March 1973 to September 1975." *International Finance Discussion Papers No. 76.* Washington, D.C.: Federal Reserve System, February 1976.

Dooley, Michael P., and Jeffrey R. Shafer. "Analysis of Short Run Exchange Rate Behavior: March 1973 to November 1981." In *Exchange Rate and Trade Instability*, eds. David Bigman and Teizo Taya, 43-69. Cambridge, Mass.: Ballinger Co., 1983.

Dornbusch, Rudiger. "Exchange Rate Economics: Where Do We Stand?" Brookings Papers on Economic Activity, No. 1. (1980): 143–206.

Dryden, Myles M. "A Source of Bias in Filter Tests of Share Prices." *Journal of Business* 42 (July 1969): 321-325.

Dusak, Katherine. "Futures Trading and Investors Return: An Investigation of Commodity Market Risk Premiums." *Journal of Political Economy* 81 (December 1973): 1387-1406.

Dybvig, Phillip H., and Stephen A. Ross. "Performance Measurement Using Differential Information and a Security Market Line." *Journal of Finance* 40 (June 1985): 383-400

Edward, Robert D., and John Magee. *Technical Analysis of Stock Trends.* Springfield, Mass.: John Magee, 1958.

Evans, George W. "A Test for Speculative Bubbles and the Sterling-Dollar Exchange Rate: 1981–84." *American Economic Review* 76 (September 1986): 621-636.

Fama, Eugene F. "Mandelbrot and the Stable Paretian Hypothesis." *Journal of Business* 36 (October 1963): 420-429.

Fama, Eugene F. "The Behavior of Stock Market Prices." *Journal of Business* 38 (January 1965): 34-105.

Fama, Eugene F. "Efficient Capital Markets: A Review of Theory and Empirical Work." *Journal of Finance* 25 (May 1970): 383-417.

Fama, Eugene F. "Forward and Spot Exchange Rates." *Journal of Monetary Economics* 14 (December 1984): 319-338.

Fama, Eugene F., and Marshal E. Blume. "Filter Rules and Stock-Market Trading." *Journal of Business* 39 (January 1966): 226-241.

Fama, Eugene F., and Richard Roll. "Some Properties of Symmetric Stable Distributions." *Journal of the American Statistical Association* 63 (September 1968): 818-836.

Fama, Eugene F., and Richard Roll. "Parameter Estimates for Symmetric Stable Distributions." *Journal of the American Statistical Association* 66 (June 1971): 331-338.

Federal Reserve Bulletin. "Intervention in Foreign Exchange Markets: A Summary of Ten Staff Studies." November 1983, 830-36.

Frankel, Jeffrey A. "In Search of the Exchange Risk Premium: A Six Currency Test Assuming Mean-Variance Optimization." *Journal of International Money and Finance* 1 (December 1982): 255-274.

Frankel, Jeffrey A. "The Implication of Mean-Variance Optimization for Four Questions in International Finance." *Journal of International Money and Finance Supplement* 5 (March 1986): S53-S75.

Frankel, Jeffrey A. "The Dazzling Dollar." Brookings Papers on Economic Activity, No. 1 (1985), 199-217.

Frankel, Jeffrey A., and Kenneth A. Froot. *The Dollar as an Irrational Speculative Bubble: A Tale of Fundamentalists and Chartists,* vol. 1 of *Marcus Wallenburg Papers on International Finance* (1986a), 27-55.

Frankel, Jeffrey A., and Kenneth A. Froot. "Using Survey Data to Test Standard Propositions Regarding Exchange Rate Expectations." *American Economic Review* 77 (March 1986b): 133-153.

Frenkel, Jacob A., and Richard M. Levich. "Transactions Costs and Interest Arbitrage: Tranquil versus Turbulent Periods." *Journal of Political Economy* 85 (December, 1977): 1209-1227.

French, Kenneth R. "Stock Returns and the Weekend Effect." *Journal of Financial Economics* 8 (March 1980): 55-69.

Genberg, Hans. "Effects of Central Bank Intervention in the Foreign Exchange Market." International Monetary Fund *Staff Papers* 28 (September 1981): 451-476.

Gibbons, Michael R., and Patrick Hess. "Day of the Week Effects and Asset Returns." *Journal of Business* 54 (October 1981): 579-595.

Giddy, Ian H., and Gunter Dufey. "The Random Behavior of Flexible Exchange Rates." *Journal of International Business Studies* 6 (Spring, 1975): 1-32.

Godfrey, M. D., C. W. J. Granger, and O. Morgenstern. "Random-Walk Hypothesis of Stock Market Behavior." Kyklos 17 (1964): 1-30.

Goodman, Stephen H. "Who's Better Than the Toss of a Coin." *Euromoney,* September 1980: 80-89.

Goodman, Stephen H. "Technical Analysis Still Beats Econometrics." *Euromoney,* August 1981: 48-59.

Granger, C. W. J., and O. Morgenstern. "Spectral Analysis of New York Stock Market Prices." *Kyklos* 16 (1963): 1-26.

Hansen, Lars P., and Robert J. Hodrick. "Risk Averse Speculation in the Forward Exchange Market: An Econometric Analysis of Linear Models." In *Exchange Rates and International Macroeconomics*, ed. Jacob A. Frenkel. Chicago: University of Chicago Press, 1983.

Henderson, Dale W., and Stephanie Sampson. "Intervention in Foreign Exchange Markets: A Summary of Ten Staff Studies." *Federal Reserve Bulletin* 69 (November 1983): 830-836.

Hodrick, Robert J., and Sanjay Srivastava. "An Investigation of Risk and Return in Forward Foreign Exchange." *Journal of International Money and Finance* 3 (April 1984): 5-29.

Hodrick, Robert J., and Sanjay Srivastava. "The Covariation of Risk Premiums and Expected Future Spot Exchange Rates." *Journal of International Money and Finance Supplement* 5 (March 1986): S5-S21.

Jensen, Michael C., and George A. Benington. "Random Walks and Technical Theories: Some Additional Evidence." *Journal of Finance* 25 (May 1970): 469-482.

Keane, Simon M. "The Efficient Market Hypothesis on Trial." *Financial Analyst Journal* 42 (March-April 1986): 58-63.

Keim, Donald. "Size Related Anomalies and Stock Market Seasonality: Further Empirical Evidence." *Journal of Financial Economics* 12 (June 1983): 13-32.

Kendall, Maurice G. "The Analysis of Economic Time-Series, Part I: Prices." *Journal of the Royal Statistical Society* 96 (Part I, 1953): 11-25.

Krugman, Paul R. "Is the Strong Dollar Sustainable?" in *The U.S. Dollar—Recent Developments, Outlook, and Policy Options*. Kansas City, Mo.: Federal Reserve Bank of Kansas City, 1985, 103–132.

Latane, Henry A., and Donald L. Tuttle. *Security Analysis and Portfolio Management*. New York: Ronald Press Co., 1970.

Levich, Richard M. "On the Efficiency of Markets for Foreign Exchange." In *International Economic Policy: Theory and Evidence*, eds. Rudiger Dornbusch and Jacob Frenkel, 246-267. Baltimore: Johns Hopkins University Press, 1979a.

Levich, Richard M. *The International Money Market: An Assessment of Forecasting Techniques and Market Efficiency*. Greenwich, Conn.: JAI Press Inc., 1979b.

Levich, Richard M. "Comment." In *The International Monetary System: A Time of Turbulence*, eds. Jacob S. Dreyer, Gottfried Harberler, and Thomas D. Willett, 65-109. Washington D.C.: American Enterprise Institute for Public Policy Research, 1982.

Levy, Robert A. "The Principle of Portfolio Upgrading." *The Industrial Management Review* 17 (Fall 1967a): 82-96.

Levy, Robert A. "Relative Strength as a Criterion for Investment Selection." *Journal of Finance* 22 (November 1967b): 595-610.

Levy, Robert A. "Random Walks: Reality or Myth." *Financial Analyst Journal* 23 (November-December 1967c): 69-85.

Logue, Dennis E., and Richard J. Sweeney. "White Noise in Imperfect Markets: The Case of the Franc/Dollar Exchange Rate." *Journal of Finance* 32 (June 1977): 761-768.

Logue, Dennis E., Richard J. Sweeney, and Thomas D. Willett. "Speculative Behavior of Foreign Exchange Rates During the Current Float." *Journal of Business Research* 6 (May 1978): 159-174.

Mandelbrot, Benoit. "The Variation of Certain Speculative Prices." *Journal of Business* 36 (October 1963): 394-419.

Mandelbrot, Benoit. "Forecasts of Future Prices, Unbiased Markets, and Martingale Models." *Journal of Business* 39 (January 1966): 242-255.

Mandelbrot, Benoit., and Taylor, Howard M. "On the Distribution of Stock Price Differences." *Operations Research* 15 (November-December 1967): 1057-1062.

Mark, Nelson. "On Time-Varying Risk Premia in the Foreign Exchange Market: An Econometric Analysis." *Journal of Monetary Economics* 16 (1985): 3-18.

Markowitz, Harry M. "Portfolio Selection." *Journal of Finance* 12 (March 1952): 77-91.

Markowitz, Harry M. *Portfolio Selection, Efficient Diversification of Investments.* New York: John Wiley and Sons, 1959.

McCormick, Frank. "Transaction Costs in the Foreign Exchange Markets Under Fixed and Floating Exchange Rates." Riverside, Calif.: University of California, June 26, 1975. Photocopied.

McCormick, Frank. "Covered Interest Arbitrage: Unexploited Profits? Comment." *Journal of Political Economy* 87 (April 1979): 411-422.

McFarland, James W., R. Richardson Pettit, and Sam K. Sung. "The Distribution of Foreign Exchange Price Changes: Trading Day Effects and Risk Measurement." *Journal of Finance* 37 (June 1982): 693-715.

Meese, Richard. "Testing for Bubbles in Exchange Markets: The Case of Sparkling Rates." *Journal of Political Economy* (April 1986): 345-73.

Merton, Robert. "An Intertemporal Capital Asset Pricing Model." *Econometrica* 41 (September 1973): 867-887.

Mood, Alexander M. "On the Asymptotic Efficiency of Certain Nonparametric Two Sample Tests." *Annual of Mathematics and Statistics* 25 (1954): 514-522.

Mori, Christopher A., and Michael P. Murray. "Still Beating the Foreign Exchange Market." Working paper. Lewiston, Me.: Bates College, 1990. Photocopied.

Poole, William. "Speculative Prices as Random Walks: An Analysis of Ten Time-Series of Flexible Exchange Rates." *Southern Economic Journal* 33 (April 1967): 468-478.

Praetz, P. "Rates of Return of Filter Tests." *Journal of Finance* 31 (March 1976): 71-75.

Praetz, P. "A General Test of a Filter Effect." *Journal of Financial and Quantitative Analysis* 14 (June 1979): 385-394.

Pratt, John W., and Jean D. Gibbons. *Concepts of Nonparametric Theory*. New York: Springer-Verlag, 1981.

Reinganum, Marc R. "Abnormal Returns in Small Firm Portfolios." *Financial Analyst Journal* 37 (March-April 1981): 52-57.

Roberts, Harry V. "Stock Market `Patterns' and Financial Analysis: Methodological Suggestions." *Journal of Finance* 14 (March 1959): 1-10.

Rogalski, Richard J. "New Findings Regarding Day-of-the-Week Returns over Trading and Non-trading Periods: A Note." *Journal of Finance* 26 (December 1984): 1603-1614.

Rogalski, Richard J, and Joseph D. Vinso. "Empirical Properties of Foreign Exchange Rates." *Journal of International Business Studies* 9 (Fall, 1978): 69-79.

Rogoff, Kenneth. "On the Effects of Sterilized Intervention: An Analysis of Weekly Data." *Journal of Monetary Economics* 3 (September 1984): 133-150.

Roll, Richard. *The Behavior of Interest Rates: An Appliction of the Efficient Market Model to U.S. Treasury Bills.* New York: Basic Books, 1970.

Roll, Richard, and Stephen A. Ross. "An Empirical Investigation of the Arbitrage Pricing Theory." *Journal of Finance* 35 (December 1980): 1073-1104.

Ross, Stephen A. "The Arbitrage Theory of Capital Asset Pricing." *Journal of Economic Theory* 13 (December 1976): 341-360.

Sharpe, William F. "A Simplified Model for Portfolio Analysis." *Management Science* 9 (January 1963): 277-293.

Sweeney, Richard J. "A Statistical Filter Rule Test, With an Application to the Dollar-DM Exchange Rate." Claremont, Calif.: Claremont Men's College and Claremont Graduate School, April 1981. Photocopied.

Sweeney, Richard J. "Intervention Strategy: Implications of Purchasing Power Parity and Tests of Spot Exchange-Market Efficiency." In *The International Monetary System: A Time of Turbulence,* eds. Jacob S. Dreyer, Gottfried Harberler, and Thomas D. Willett, 65-109. Washington, D.C.: American Enterprise Institute for Public Policy Research, 1982a.

Sweeney, Richard J. "Speculation, Trading Rule Profits, Interest Rate Differentials, and Risk." Claremont, Calif.: Claremont Men's College and Claremont Graduate School, 1982b. Photocopied.

Sweeney, Richard J. "Efficient Information Processing by Markets: Seven Years of Evidence from Foreign Exchange Markets." In *Exchange Rates, Trade, and the U.S. Economy,* eds. Sven W. Arndt, Richard J. Sweeney and Thomas D. Willett. Cambridge Mass.: Ballinger Publishing Co., 1985.

Sweeney, Richard J. "Beating the Foreign Exchange Market." *Journal of Finance* 41 (March 1986a): 163-182.

Sweeney, Richard J. "A New Test of Portfolio Performance." Claremont, Calif.: Claremont McKenna College and Claremont Graduate School, July 24, 1986b. Photocopied.

Sweeney, Richard J. "A Technical Approach for Beating the Foreign Exchange Market." Investment Study. Lomita, Calif.: A. B. Laffer Associates, 1987a.

Sweeney, Richard J. "Testing Performance Using Funds' Returns." Claremont, Calif.: Claremont McKenna College and Claremont Graduate School, June 28, 1987b. Photocopied.

Sweeney, Richard J. "Some New Filter Rule Tests: Methods and Results." *Journal of Financial and Quantitative Analysis* (September 1988): 285–300.

Sweeney, Richard J. "Time-Varying Risk Premia in Spot Foreign Exchange Markets." Washington, D.C.: School of Business Administration, Georgetown University, 1990a. Photocopied.

Sweeney, Richard J. "Time-Varying Risk Premia in Equities Markets." Washington, D.C.: School of Business Administration, Georgetown University, 1990b. Photocopied.

Sweeney, Richard J. "Testing Portfolio Performance with Observable Asset Weights." Washington, D.C.: School of Business Adminstration, Georgetown University, 1990c. Photocopied.

Sweeney, Richard J. "Risk Premia in Forward Exchange Rates: Systematic or Unsystematic?" *Journal of International Trade* 5 (Fall 1990d): 25-52.

Sweeney, Richard J. "Technical Speculation in Foreign Exchange Markets: An Interim Report." *Recent Developments in Banking and Finance* 4, forthcoming 1990e.

Sweeney, Richard J. "Evidence on Short-Term Trading Strategies." *Journal of Portfolio Management* 17 (Fall 1990f): 20-26.

Sweeney, Richard J. and Edward J. Q. Lee. "Profits in Forward Market Speculation." *Advances in Financial Planning and Forecasting* 4, Part A (1990): 55-79.

Sweeney, Richard J., and Arthur D. Warga. "The Pricing of Interest–Rate Risk: The Evidence from Equities Markets." *Journal of Finance* 41 (June 1986): 393-410.

Taya, Teizo. "Variability of Exchange Rates and the Efficiency of the Foreign Exchange Markets." In *The Functioning of Floating Exchange Rates: Theory, Evidence, and Policy Implications*, eds. David Bigman and Teizo Taya, 141-167. Cambridge, Mass.: Ballinger Publishing Co., 1980.

Taylor, D. "Official Intervention in the Foreign Exchange Market or, Bet against the Central Bank." *Journal of Political Economy* (April 1982): 356-368.

Taylor, Stephen. *Modelling Financial Time Series*. Chichester, U.K.: John Wiley & Sons, 1986.

Teichmoller, John. "A Note on the Distribution of Stock Price Changes." *Journal of the American Statistical Association* 66 (June 1971): 282-285.

Tinic, Seha M., and Richard R. West. "Risk and Return." *Journal of Financial Economics* 13 (December 1984): 561-574.

Westerfield, Janice Moulton. "An Examination of Foreign Exchange Risk Under Fixed and Floating Rate Regimes." *Journal of International Economics* 7 (May 1977): 181-200.

Wilder, J. W., Jr. *New Concepts in Technical Trading Systems.* Greensboro, N.C.: Trend Research, 1978.

Willett, Thomas D., and Clas Wihlborg. "International Capital Flows, the Dollar, and U.S. Financial Policies." In *Monetary Policy for a Volatile Global Economy,* eds. William S. Haraf and Thomas D. Willett. Washington, D.C.: The AEI Press, 1990.

Wolfe, Philip. "The Simplex Method for Quadratic Programming." *Econometrica* 27 (July 1959): 382-398.

Woo, Wing T. "Speculative Bubbles in the Foreign Exchange Markets." Washington, D.C.: Brookings Discussion Paper in International Economics, 1984.

Working, Holbrook. "Note on the Correlation of First Differences of Averages in a Random Chain." *Econometrica* 28 (1960): 916-918.

ABOUT THE BOOK AND AUTHORS

The consensus among financial economists is that financial markets are efficient and, thus, that it is impossible to make consistent, risk-adjusted profits in these markets using simple, mechanical, buy-and-sell rules. In other words, technical analysis is not supposed to consistently beat financial markets. In this important and disturbing book, however, Professors Surajaras and Sweeney establish that following carefully chosen rules can produce substantial and consistent measured profits over time.

This well-documented result, which holds up under risk-adjustment and allowance for transaction costs, has serious consequences both for the academic understanding of these markets and for the practical behavior of those who operate within them. Because of the immense size and scope of foreign exchange markets, the traditional academic wisdom that markets in general are efficient is also called into question.

Technically impressive and lucidly argued, this surprising book will change the way academics and professionals think about exchange rates and their markets. It is essential reading for anyone interested in foreign exchange.

Patchara Surajaras is a research associate at the Center for Economic Policy, Claremont Graduate School, and is vice president of equity research at Asia Securities Trading Co., Ltd., in Thailand. **Richard J. Sweeney** is Sullivan/Dean Professor of International Business and Finance at the School of Business Administration, Georgetown University.

INDEX